Mom-

Hope yo[illegible]
this book by what
I think is your fav-
orite author.

Merry Christmas 1973

love,
Curt.

TRAVELS THROUGH JEWISH AMERICA

TRAVELS THROUGH JEWISH AMERICA

BY HARRY GOLDEN
WITH RICHARD GOLDHURST

DOUBLEDAY & COMPANY, INC.
GARDEN CITY, NEW YORK
1973

Acknowledgment is gratefully made for permission to reprint the following material:

Lines from "Thirteen Ways of Looking at a Blackbird" from THE COLLECTED POEMS OF WALLACE STEVENS, Copyright © 1923 and renewed 1951 by Wallace Stevens. Reprinted by permission of Alfred A. Knopf, Inc.

Lines from "Love Calls Us to the Things of This World" from THINGS OF THIS WORLD by Richard Wilbur, Copyright © 1956 by Richard Wilbur. Reprinted by permission of Harcourt Brace Jovanovich, Inc.

"Unicops Go Crackers Over Matzah Mobile" was first published in *Ha'am*, Vol. 1, Number 2, May 1972. Reprinted by permission of the ASUCLA Communications Board.

An excerpt "On the Urban Crisis" from BRING FORTH THE MIGHTY MEN by Howard Singer, Copyright © 1969 by Howard Singer. With permission of the publisher, Funk & Wagnalls Publishing Company, Inc.

WITH THANKS FOR
Dr. Yale David Koskoff, Pittsburgh
Harry Golden, Jr., *Chicago Sun-Times*
James Lee, Los Angeles
Lee Wallas, St. Louis

AND WITH GRATITUDE FOR
Murry Shapiro, Hartford Jewish Community Center
Irving Kessler, Hartford Jewish Federation
many of whose ideas and thinking gave direction to this book.

CONTENTS

TRAVELS THROUGH JEWISH AMERICA

INTRODUCTION

TODAY I AM AN ETHNIC GROUP

I have written a great deal about the Lower East Side of New York City between the years 1905 and 1917, the years which saw a massive migration to America of Jews from Eastern Europe. I knew a lot about the immigrant Jew, his family, his beliefs, his hardships, his joys because I was part of that migration. In 1904, my father, Leib Goldhirsch, left his family in Mikulintsy, a village in eastern Galicia, then part of the Austro-Hungarian Empire, and with my oldest brother, Jacob, immigrated to the New World, where he hoped there would be more opportunities for his children.

Landsleit was the spur. Landsleit is the reason most immigrants got anywhere. Landsleit is the collection of friends, relatives, neighbors, who had arrived at someplace earlier. In New York, my father got a job teaching Hebrew in a Talmud Torah and my brother got a license and a pushcart and started peddling. Between them they saved enough money to pay the passage for my mother, my two older sisters, and me.

Wearing a babushka, my mother carried me down the gangplank of the *Graf Waldersee,* Clara and Matilda tugging at her skirts. The *Graf Waldersee* of the North German Lloyd Line left Hamburg on April 1, 1905, and beat the *Mayflower* to America. It took only eleven days for the *Waldersee* to get to New York compared to three months for the *Mayflower* to get to Plymouth Rock. When the United States declared war in 1917, the *Graf Waldersee* was in New York Harbor, but before we could intern the ship, the lousy Germans scuttled it.

Though my mother wore a big red tag which spelled our name, for their own convenience and probably through their own ignorance the immigration officials changed it from Goldhirsch to Goldhurst.

Thirty-seven years later, I changed the name again—to Golden—

when I started publishing the *Carolina Israelite* in Charlotte, North Carolina. I was not, however, putting the past behind me. For the next twenty-six years, I tried to re-create that past in the pages of my personal journal. Many of these stories, excerpted from the *Israelite* and published in several books, often shamelessly sentimental and nostalgic, amused and charmed a wide readership. They also instructed that readership because it is hard to believe that the Jews of that time and the Jews of this time lived on the same planet.

On the Lower East Side of sixty years ago, the life of the ordinary Jewish immigrant was demonstrably different from the life of his Christian neighbors. I can remember the massive army of garment workers out on strike marching up Houston Street, their ensigns' placards with the slogans in Yiddish.

The streets of the Lower East Side were filled with pushcarts and peddlers. There were even eyeglass peddlers with mirrors mounted on their carts so the customers could judge if the frames flattered them. I had a classmate named Harry Schwartz whose father peddled "broken" chocolates. These were big chunks of chocolate which he bought from a confectioner as "rejects," chocolates that could not be packed. Mr. Schwartz sold these irregular chunks for a penny apiece. I was visiting my friend Harry one evening when his father came home. He washed, said his evening prayers, and sat down at the dinner table, but before we began to eat he called his wife and in a lowered voice told her the story. A customer buying two pieces of broken chocolate dipped into his pocket for change and handed it to Mr. Schwartz and walked away. Mr. Schwartz opened his hand and there in his palm were two dimes instead of two pennies.

Once a week my mother sat at the table with a silk handkerchief over her head in her one good dress with the fleurs-de-lis print and knew supreme joy as she watched her family eat the Sabbath meal. In thousands of other tenements other mothers knew the same joy. The Lower East Side was still. The Sabbath is the key to the Jewish religion. When the Temple was destroyed by the Romans, the Jews took their temples with them into their homes.

My mother ushered in the Sabbath as all Jewish women ushered it in, by kindling special lights to do honor to this day. She spread her hands over the candles and recited the blessing, "Praised be Thou, O Lord, our God, King of the Universe, who has sanctified us by Thy commandments and commanded us to kindle the Sabbath lights."

Historically anyone born of a Jewish mother is a Jew whether the father is Jewish or not. The mother is the Jew because it is she who maintains the Sabbath so the men can worship. God told Moses, "There is a magnificent gift in my treasure chamber and its name is Sabbath and I shall give it to Israel." The Sabbath is probably the secret of the Jew's survival. My mother, in her one good dress and her silk kerchief, was Queen of the Sabbath.

I see no such differences between Jew and Christian today. In fact, the life of a suburban rabbi does not differ much from the life of the Congregationalist minister. But I do not think Jews are the worse for the disappearance of the old ways. Once upon a time we lived on one planet and now we live on others.

The difference between Jewish life then and now is that then there was a Copernican Center. The Copernican Center was the immigrant. The Jews who came to the United States before and a little after the Civil War were virtually unorganized as Jews. But the arrival of 2.3 million immigrants galvanized energies and efforts which eventually made Jews more than a community in America, made them, in fact, an entity. The Eastern European Jews who left their small hamlets called *shtetls* and the city ghettos were fleeing proscription, terror, and legal disabilities. But they were also seeking to survive as shtetl Jews, for Eastern European Jewry grew from 1.5 million in 1800 to 6.8 million a century later. The shtetls could no longer accommodate them.

Much has been made of this migration and its historical consequences which were crucial for world Jewry. Half the Jews in Eastern Europe left for America and another, smaller group left for Turkish Palestine. Their descendants would eventually found the State of Israel. Shtetl Jews appreciably affected American history. Jewish immigrant workers were the first to win the right of collective bargaining in a strike settlement; other immigrant Jews developed the movie industry; two Jews discovered a vaccine for polio.

But the migration was also one of the profound movements in Western religion. It re-creates in our time the parable of Joseph. His brothers banished Joseph and sold him into slavery. But it was this banishment which proved his brothers' salvation, for Joseph spared them when he was Pharaoh's first minister. And they ate of the fat of the land. And Joseph lived in Egypt a hundred and ten years.

The destruction of the Temple by the Romans and the exile of the Jews was the catalytic event of Jewish theology. But Hitler's Holocaust drained it of its mythic inspiration. The exile, the diaspora, has become Joseph's Egypt.

In the European diaspora, Jews were called a nation and in the English-speaking diaspora a community. Now we are called an ethnic group, although in my travels I met few Jews who thought they were ethnics. Ethnicity is one of those words the middle class has begun to conjure with. Probably as much thought and invention will go into the continuing popularization of "ethnicity" in the seventies as went into popularizing "charisma" in the sixties. Franklin D. Roosevelt won four times without using "charisma" once.

If we are ethnics, then Jews are the only ethnic group with their own religion. It is not Catholicism that makes the Chicanos ethnics nor Protestantism that makes blacks ethnics. Judaism is what makes people Jews. While the Chicanos can agree on what makes them Chicanos, the Jews have yet to agree among themselves what makes them Jews.

The rabbis—and not all of them—are the only ones who proclaim ethnicity. And they proclaim it for a political reason. They want to see the continued expansion and proliferation of their schools. There have always been Talmud Torahs and in many communities there are now extracurricular Hebrew high schools and in some an all-day Jewish school which prepares students just as Choate or Kent or Groton prepares students. The rabbis argue that since we have ethnic characteristics, we can only preserve them in our own schools. The growth of these schools was always inhibited because the Reform rabbis opposed them. Now some Reform rabbis champion them not because they have become ethnically conscious but because their congregants are worried about court-ordered public school busing. Orthodox rabbis and Catholic monseignors often agree about federal assistance for parochial school.

But federal assistance is not going to happen, President Nixon to the contrary. Leo Pfeffer, the general counsel of the American Jewish Congress, an authority on constitutional law, told me matter-of-factly, "This is not the way the courts are moving."

On behalf of the American Jewish Congress, Pfeffer has brought many suits as plaintiff and served as an *amicus curiae* in many more which challenged the constitutionality of appropriating federal or state monies for parochial school education as well as the right of school boards to prescribe even nondenominational prayers for the class-room. "Any case," he said, "which insists on a strict interpretation of the separation between church and state wins. The courts unanimously say no to religion. The Catholics who want to preserve a widespread parochial school complex will have to consolidate their holdings. The all-day Jewish school will be a luxury for rich Jews."

This is not to insist that there were not once ethnic differences between Jews. There were differences between Sephardic Jews who came from the Mediterranean countries and wore gold caftans at the Seder and the German immigrants who sang in the shul. And there was a difference between the peddler turned merchant prince and the immigrant from the shtetl who stuffed straw in his boots in November and took the boots off when the spring thaw arrived in April.

I remember explaining the need to obliterate these differences to my father. I showed him the tomato juice and the napkin and said, "The tomato juice gives us vitamins and the napkin makes us Americans."

He took the explanation in and said, "And the necktie around the throat down in Wall Street every day makes you a wise guy."

Some of our differences are preserved in the distinction between Orthodox, Conservative, and Reform Jews.

There were three sects of Jews in Roman Judaea—the Pharisees, the Sadducees, and the Essenes. Pharisaic Judaism survived. It survived with a theology and a monumental body of laws. Gloss after gloss and interpretation after interpretation has been added to both. The Talmud is the collection of Jewish civil and religious law which is written in scriptures; the Halakah is Jewish civil and religious law which is based on oral tradition. Orthodox Jewry is the direct descendant of the Pharisees.

The Orthodox believe the Torah, the five books of Moses—Genesis, Exodus, Leviticus, Numbers, and Deuteronomy—reveal an absolute truth. They are not the work of Moses, but the word of God. The Halakah prescribes the rituals for realizing God's presence and anger every minute of the day. An Orthodox Jew will spit three times in the morning lest in his prayers he mention "God" with a dirty mouth. The dietary laws, kashrut, confer sacred significance on food. The Orthodox wife will shave her head on her wedding day lest her beauty ever distract her husband from worship.

Conservative Jews believe that the traditional forms and precepts of Judaism are a valid guide for obeying God's commandments. Changes in practice are made only with great reluctance, but changes are made. Conservative Jews, for example, do not recite the prayers which describe animal sacrifice. They are liturgically innovative as long as innovations do not affect their devotion to the Hebrew language, the observance of kashrut, and the holiness of the Sabbath.

Reform Jews believe that the idea of God is a central religious truth and that the Bible is a record of the consecration of the Jewish people. Scientific discoveries must not be understood as antagonistic to the Jewish religion. Moral laws are binding but not all moral laws are consonant with modern civilization. The Halakah does not confer saintliness on man. Jews are not a nation or a people but a religious community whose destiny is not in the Homeland. Man's soul is immortal but there is no bodily resurrection. Religion is an aid in solving ethical problems.

The Orthodox call their house of worship a synagogue; the Reform call it a temple; the Conservative either. These differences once provoked acrimonious argument among Jews. In 1884, to cite one instance, one faction of Beth Elohim in Charleston, South Carolina, the second oldest synagogue in the South, sued another in court. The majority of the congregation had voted to install an organ in the synagogue. The Orthodox minority withdrew and charged before Judge O. M. Butler of the South Carolina Court of Appeals that the organ was a desecration of the Jewish ritual.

Butler ruled against them. He expressed sympathy with the Orthodox but he stated that for the litigants to ask the court to resolve the dispute was to invite a definition of judicial orthodoxy, implicitly prohibited by the Constitution of the United States.

Some of the acrimony persists, but on a subdued scale. It has dissipated principally because the children of the Orthodox married the children of the Reform and the children of the Reform married the children of the Conservative. And there are a great many Jews who are none of these but are simply milling around.

There are between 5.5 and 6 million Jews in the United States, "Less," as the theologian Milton Himmelfarb puts it, "than the smallest error in the Chinese census." This figure is a projection from the statistics collected by the Bureau of the Census for its survey, "Religion Reported by the Civilian Population of the United States: March, 1957." This report, intended to furnish data on the economic and social characteristics of Protestants, Catholics, and Jews, was almost immediately suppressed at the insistence of religious organizations and groups. Notable among these groups and organizations were the Jewish social-action agencies, who feared the news about Jewish incomes, education levels, and mobility would feed anti-Semitism.

The Council of Jewish Federation and Welfare Agencies has more recently come to its senses and has commissioned a National Jewish Population Survey. The Jews need to know how many homes for the Jewish aged they will have to build, how long and to what extent they can count on continuing financial support for Israel, and for how long the Jewish population can remain static. Dr. Fred Massarick of UCLA and the Greater Los Angeles Jewish Federation has begun to assess the samplings from communities everywhere. Smaller Jewish communities in the past twenty years have conducted accurate head counts. But smaller communities are never typical.

There always seem to be more Jews than there are. The one "Jew store" which existed in many Southern towns always convinced rural Southerners that there was a multitudinous network of Jews operating stores wherever there was commerce. There always seem to be more Jews than there are because in the United States Jews congregate in the big metropolitan areas. Jews constitute 10 percent of the Hartford population, but they do not constitute 10 percent of the Helena or Sioux Falls population. American Jews love the city, which was not universally true of their European residency.

Seventy percent of the Jewish population in America live in what the professionals in the Federation and philanthropic agencies and action committees call the Big Sixteen. These sixteen communities are:

New York	2,600,000
Los Angeles	500,000
Philadelphia	333,000
Chicago	269,000
Boston	176,000
Miami	130,000
Connecticut (Hartford, New Haven, Bridgeport)	103,000
Baltimore	100,000
Essex County, New Jersey	100,000
Greater Washington, D.C.	100,000
Cleveland	82,000
Detroit	82,000
Bergen County, New Jersey	80,000
San Francisco	73,000
Texas (Dallas, Houston, Fort Worth)	63,000
St. Louis	54,000

There are 28,000 Jews in Cincinnati and 23,000 in Milwaukee. There are middle-sized or minuscule communities in 400 other American towns and cities from Rosenberg, Texas, to Beersheba Springs, Tennessee.

This is not to say there are not Jews in the outposts. There are. There are 315 Jews in Fargo, North Dakota, which has a population of 55,000. Fargo has a Jewish mayor named Herschel Laskowitz, probably one of the few Jews elected to office not dependent upon the Jewish vote. For the most part, these Jews are the children and grandchildren of immigrants who went west to homestead. Fargo boasts the only rabbi in the state. The 200 Jews who live in Minot, Bismarck, Jamestown, Wahpeton, and Dickenson must import a rabbi from either Winnipeg or the Minneapolis-St. Paul area to celebrate the High Holy Days.

But I suspect you will find no Jews outside a manageable radius of a temple, synagogue, or community center. They will live within a perimeter where they have contact with other Jews. My dearest friend in Charlotte, Dave Wallas, who for thirty years has traversed all of the back roads in Virginia, the Carolinas, and Georgia selling soft goods, tells me the "Jew store" of the small Southern town is a thing of the past. The Jews have been moving to the larger cities. Sometimes, of course, the store remains. There is, says Dave, still a Jew store in St. Matthews, South Carolina, and it is still owned by a Jew, but it is run by a Christian manager, a graduate of the Textile School at North Carolina State University.

The population table represents one salient fact about the American Jewish community: the Jews in New York City are different from the Jews outside of New York City. The Jews in Greater New York represent roughly 46 percent of the total number of Jews in the country. New York is the one city Jews transformed into a Jewish city. They are the warp and the woof of its fabric. There is an organization of Jewish policemen in New York called the Shomrim (Watchmen) and an organization of Jewish firemen called the Naer Tormid. There is a Jewish Postal Workers Welfare League and an Association of Jewish Court Attachés.

There are, of course, Jews elsewhere who are policemen—a Ben Goldstein was the chief of police in Hartford—but there is no place else a Jewish *complement* of policemen. There are more Jewish teachers in New York City than there are in Israel. There are shopkeepers in New York who make a living selling only mezuzahs and menorahs.

For several blocks on the Lower East Side of New York they compete with each other. Jews are the muscles and the bones of the city. In other cities they are only part of the nerve centers.

Jews own roughly 80 percent of New York City's businesses. Small businesses are anything from a garment loft which cuts ten miles of cloth a year to a candy store near a public school selling four thousand pretzels over two semesters.

This means that the problems of the cities, which are magnified in New York—crime, the confrontation between blacks and whites, poverty, and welfare, which is now competitive with employment—directly affect Jews. In New York City alone are Jews in significant numbers among the disaffected.

It is hard for a suburban Jew in the Midwest or in the Bay Area of San Francisco to understand let alone sympathize with the Jewish Defense League of Meir Kahane. The Jewish Defense League is the Jewish Bush League. But there is an obverse to the coin. Meir Kahane is speaking on behalf of poor Jews and lower-middle-class Jews, city folks who will never know the affluence to take them out of the terrorized neighborhood which was once respectable. In these neighborhoods and at their work Jews are victimized and discriminated against by those as disaffected as they.

It is therefore impossible to say that the mind of the American Jewish community is at rest with itself. I have taken pains on at least two occasions during my travels to note that there may be as many as 500,000 Jewish poor. The fact has immediacy for me. When I first came to Charlotte I was the only poor Jew in town. I lived in drab bungalows whose siding often sprang for want of nails and there were occasions when I couldn't meet the rent for my room in a semi-transient hotel whose curtains were stiff from a decade's dirt. When I wore tan and brown summer shoes in December, Gentiles thought me eccentric.

They were right. I was trying to make a living by selling Pure Midas Mineral Spring Water to folks who drank Coca-Cola for breakfast.

I am not poor any longer and neither are the Jews who for the most part are the descendants of the Eastern European immigrants. Many, many of them are millionaires and millions of them are in the middle- and upper-middle-income groups. The shtetl Jews and the ghetto Jews of Eastern Europe did not nor did their children much lend themselves to an "Our Crowd" as did the German Jews, of whom Stephen Birmingham, though not a Jew, has written so tell-ingly. The Holocaust convinced all Jews that they may have a com-mon future no matter who or where they are. Under this threat survival becomes a democratic process. *Our Crowd* and *The Grandees* are in some respects an exhumation of a past Jewish experience rather than a description of a continuing class process.

The Jewish fund-raising organizations and the social-action agen-cies, originally the creation of the rich, have conspired between them to draw all American Jews together in one class. There are Jewish millionaires who are dropouts from Judaism just as there are ragged students who become Jesus freaks. They are only nominal Jews.

This book is, therefore, an adventure with the middle class, with that segment which identifies itself as Jewish. It is the end result of meeting with dozens and dozens of Jews in ten different cities each of which has a representative Jewish community. A community is a group of people who band together for their own protection so that the men can reap the harvest. In that sense the Jews are an ever-tightening community.

Jews want to thrive and they want to thrive as Jews. Perhaps the rootlessness of urban and suburban life in America forces this quest for identity. In a nation in which the average family moves once every five years, identity needs to be more than geographic, identity needs roots into the past. In this case the Jew is lucky. His identity pursues him rather than he it.

To limn the outlines of a community, one must visit the places where the folks convene, talk to the teachers from whom they learn and to the leaders they follow, meet the families they nurture, and judge the work they do.

Accordingly, Part I of this book concentrates on the Jewish houses of worship and on the Jewish network of organizations; Part II on the changes of political opinion evolving not so slowly in these perilous decades; Parts III and IV continue these themes; Part V describes the old and the young and the family; Part VI, the professions.

Another reporter on the same assignment might find himself in a completely different community.

If you get lost, apologies. Perhaps you were not as familiar with the flight plan as you thought.

PART I: THE ENTITY

CLEVELAND: Rabbis and Fund Raisers

NATIONALITY CITY

New York and Connecticut Yankees decided Cleveland was a good place for a dirty city. Once they built it and made their money, they got out and took their money with them.

The first Connecticut Yankee to leave was Moses Cleaveland.

In 1622, Charles II of England ceded vast Western lands to Connecticut. After the Revolutionary War, Connecticut turned these territories over to the federal government to facilitate the admission of new states. But it saved one 3.5-million-acre tract in northeastern Ohio by the sale of which it hoped to provide itself with a school fund. This tract, called the Western Reserve, was held by the Connecticut Land Company which dispatched Moses Cleaveland in 1796 to survey the Reserve and lay out a capital city. Cleaveland staked out a town where Benjamin Franklin had guessed one ought to be, where the Cuyahoga River (an Indian word meaning "crooked") runs into Lake Erie. Bestowing his name upon it, Cleaveland returned to Connecticut.

Word reached him a year later that the first child had been born in his namesake city. Cleaveland wished the new citizen well and expressed the hope that Cleaveland would one day be as populous as his native West Putney. Very little has been heard of West Putney since, and less of Cleaveland. In 1822, one of the newspapers dropped the "a" out of Cleaveland to shorten its masthead.

A lot of people who pass through Cleveland are never heard of again. The modern Jewish "back-to-the-farm" movement was founded in Cleveland in 1947 when three hundred Jews set out for Geneva, Ohio, to till the soil. The Bureau of Missing Persons is still hunting for some of them.

There are, however, a great many people who did leave their mark.

William Howard Brett, the librarian who introduced the open-shelf system, came from Cleveland; and James Garfield, the second martyred President was born in Orange, a hamlet on the Cuyahoga. Also, Archibald Williard, whose painting "Spirit of '76" all know; Edward Wyllis Scripps, the founder of Cleveland's "Penny Press"; Albert Michelson, who won the Nobel Prize for Physics in 1907 for his invention of the interferometer; and Commodore Oliver Hazard Perry.

Jo Sinclair and Herbert Gold, the novelists, come from Cleveland. But it is not a city of intellectual ferment. Though it has four universities—Case Western Reserve, Cleveland State, Baldwin-Wallace, and John Carroll—and Cuyahoga Community College, the teachers and the professors have little impact on the community. Case Western Reserve has excellent schools of law and medicine, but its undergraduate admissions policy is not competitive; Cleveland State, formerly Fenn College, has just become part of the Ohio State University system, and Baldwin-Wallace runs on monies received from the patent on a salad-oil preparation.

Cleveland seized upon its future when the Erie Canal opened in 1822. In the same year, the state connected Lake Erie with the Ohio River. It was Cleveland's good fortune to find itself midway between the coal fields of Pennsylvania and the iron ore of the Mesabi Range.

Steel, paint, oil, auto bodies, chemicals, hides, Great Lakes shipping, once railroading, and, of course, banking make Cleveland one of the major industrial cities in America. These are, however, conglomerate industries whose nameless and multitudinous owners neither participate in nor much care about the city's welfare. A Cleveland industrialist was named one spring to head one of the welfare drives—a position of trust and confidence, he told the press, he was glad to accept. The next day he announced he was moving his factory to Akron.

In 1972, unemployment was the most serious problem in Cleveland but it was still at 4.9 percent while elsewhere it hovered at 6 percent. In good times, unemployment in Cleveland is virtually at point zero.

Seven hundred and fifty thousand, eight hundred and seventy-nine citizens live here, down from 900,000 in 1950. Cleveland began to lose population when space-age technology, electronics, and science-based industries started to absorb workers from heavy industry.

Many nationalities live in Cleveland—the workers are the blacks, Slovaks, Poles, Irish, Italians, Litvaks, American Indians (of which Cleveland has a sizable population), and Appalachian whites, the unskilled rural worker fleeing from an abandoned West Virginia coal mine or played-out Kentucky acreage. The city has America's largest settlement of Slovenes and it is a leading center of Hungarian life. In the past ten years, its mayors have been consecutively British, Slovenian, Irish, Italian, black (Carl Stokes was the first Negro elected mayor of a major city), and its present mayor, Ralph Perk, is a Czech.

"Eleven Slovenian Girls to Make Their Bows at Cotillion Ball" is not an unusual head for the society page of the *Press* or *Plain Dealer,* and one of the fillers will read: "German songs will mark the annual Mother's Day celebration, sponsored by the German Central Women's Organization." This population of 750-odd thousand is evenly divided between Protestants and Catholics (the diocesan parochial school system is the second largest system in the state).

There is little outward difference among these nationality neighborhoods probably because all of them are crowded with Pork-n-bun, MacDonald's, Mahalia Jackson Chicken, Red Barn Instant Food, King Cole, Beef Corral, and Peter Pan Do-nuts dispensaries. The predigested hamburger, chicken leg, or pastry has an appeal which obliterates ethnic differences.

Over 1 million middle-classniks live in a galaxy of suburbs surrounding Cleveland to the east and southeast: East Cleveland, University Heights, Cleveland Heights, South Euclid, Beachwood, Mayfield, Lakewood (the one western suburb), and Shaker Heights—the last one of the original settlements of the American Shakers whose members tremulously danced in public at the manifestation of spiritual power. Shakers called the area the Valley of God's Pleasure.

Cleveland is the only big city in the United States without a school busing problem. There is a simple reason for this: no one in Cleveland has ever brought a suit against the Board of Education. This is not to say the city's racial crisis is any more or any less extreme than it is in other places but in one of its neighborhoods, Ludlow, the population is divided between blacks and whites.

Forty years ago, Cleveland had black high school principals and black police chiefs. Integration as we know it had proceeded in Cleveland before the United States Supreme Court made the term a legal concept. One result of this is civility, which the visitor finds in policemen, park attendants, bus and taxi drivers, and City Hall employees. Another is a genuine black middle class, who, like the rest of the middle class, have moved into the suburbs. These middle-classniks even bypassed one suburb, Cleveland Heights, in favor of another,

Shaker Heights. Shaker Heights at the time had more Jews and the blacks said they felt "safer" with Jews than with anyone else. It is also true that once Jews make a successful encroachment into a neighborhood, a lot of the fight goes out of the pristine elite.

Downtown Cleveland, the center city, is all black. The big department stores, Halle's and May's, do more business with blacks now than with whites. There are the hotels for the conventioneers and two movie houses no one goes to. If Cleveland ever had a gaudy night life, it is an adventure of the past.

The city has excellent surface transportation. Every five minutes buses fan out through the city to the suburbs. Since 1918, Cleveland has also had a Rapid Transit System, high-speed trolleys proceeding on open tracks east and west. For seventy-five cents, a traveler can take the Rapid from the Sheraton to the Cleveland Hopkins Airport. But this mode of transportation was planned with the expectation that passengers would want to go downtown, a trip nobody in the suburbs wants to take any more.

Once Cleveland was a beautiful city. In 1922, before she married me, Genevieve Gallagher took a two-dollar Pennsylvania Railroad excursion to Cleveland from Cresson, Pennsylvania. Usually the train left its terminal at 6 P.M., deposited its tourists at their destination by dawn, and left for home that same evening. The Pennsy included Cleveland as a matter of course. It was as interesting a city as New York, Philadelphia, or Washington, D.C. It was a place to see with a lakefront, museums, fine restaurants, and particularly Euclid Avenue, lined with the homes of the rich, impressive and startling.

Today, Euclid Avenue probably looks its best during the Christmas season, when the forbidding angularity of its office buildings is relieved by strings of Christmas lights and the somber atmosphere of its stores enlivened by the frenzy of the shoppers.

Cleveland has been called the Best Location in the Nation and the Best-kept Secret in the United States. It has more boosters per capita than live in Sinclair Lewis's Zenith. Their only complaint is the weather (the wind off Lake Erie makes winter hazardous), but the boosters cannot boast of the city's beauty.

It has no architectural grandeur. Its skyline is nondescript. The boosters swell with pride over the Terminal Tower, built by the Von Schweringen brothers, whose father advised them to seek success by speaking truth, working hard, and building railroads. The Terminal Tower, Clevelanders say, is a building a Russian would love. Indeed, when the Russian delegation passed through Cleveland on its way to Iowa in 1956, the commissars were thunderstruck. Other Clevelanders have described the Terminal Tower as a twenty-three-story office building topped off with a wedding cake. All are too modest. The Terminal Tower resembles a skyscraper in the form of a three-quarters-opened triptych on whose roof the architect has cleverly set Grant's Tomb.

There are other sights. In spring, when I was last there, the dandelions at Cleveland Hopkins made the airfield look as though it were gripped by a yellow frost. Every bar had an electronic dart game you could play for fifty cents.

The lakefront is three blocks north from the Civil War Memorial, where statues of infantry, cavalry, and artillerymen stand guard for the Terminal Tower. Wharves and piers, swinging cranes, hooting whistles, docked cargo ships, are convincing proofs of the enormity of the industrial complex that is Cleveland. Passing over a wide esplanade that affords a long horizon of the lake, I saw below a disassembled steel mill, three thousand tons neatly assembled for loading on Dock 28-West. The Buckeye Booster, the only one on the Great Lakes, a 150-ton-capacity crane, tirelessly lifted shining ladles, flooring equipment, and cranes from the dock and swung its cargo gently over the hold of the *Progresso,* bound for St. Nicholas, Argentina. The mill had been cast for Somisa Steel by the Morgan Engineering Company.

Near Dock 28-West is Cleveland's Convention Center, a mammoth hall which that week in May was filled with mining machinery for the inspection of the Congress of Mining Engineers. There were the giant gougers used for strip mining, wheels taller than a man, and drills with bits big enough to sink a battleship at one boring.

At 1 A.M. in the morning of the twelfth, an official from the United States Bureau of Mines reached Zigmund Snyder, the production manager who staged the display. Fiery disaster had trapped men in the Sunshine Silver Mine in Kellogg, Idaho. At Convention Hall was a safety braking device, the only one in the country, newly developed to keep the cables on mine elevators from tangling. The work crews at Kellogg needed it.

Snyder awakened teamsters Joe T. Lawler and Joe Magovich, riggers who belonged to the Truck Drivers Local, 407. They sped to Convention Hall in Magovich's truck and with acetylene torches cut the eight-hundred-pound device from its cage. They hauled it to the airport, where other recently aroused teamsters loaded it on a North-west Orient flight leaving at 6 A.M. With it went Robert Jones, the engineer who helped design it.

Cleveland is a town which can do big things.

WAHOO, TRIBE IN FIRST!

The last time the Cleveland Indians were in first place, Lyndon Johnson was in the White House. The last time the Indians had won five in a row, Richard Nixon was in his first term as vice-president.

This May evening portended great things, therefore, because the Tribe and its new manager, Bob Aspromonte, were on a winning streak and in first by one game.

Alas. By the third inning, they were up and throwing in the Cleveland bullpen.

Municipal Stadium on the lakefront is a fine ball park. When an Indian hits a home run, firecrackers go off from the top of the center-field scoreboard and keep going off.

It was a long wait before I could buy my ticket. The line moved slowly. Yet only 10,000 came out for the game. The Cleveland fans are less than ardent. At the ticket booth they were asking what did the man have behind first or third? The Met or the Yankee fan asks for a seat in section 19 or section 33 because he has been to the ball park often enough to know where he wants to sit.

The sparsity surprised me because Cleveland has a special transportation system direct from the suburbs to the stadium. I asked the gent beside me why the folks didn't come out, and he said you could only come out when the team was winning. If you came out to the park when the team was losing you would probably come alone and the chances of getting mugged in downtown Cleveland were better than average.

Well, there are rationales upon rationales for boob-tube rooting. I had been walking around the area for several evenings while the team was on the road, and the risk of my being mugged never dawned on me.

When it comes to buying bourbon, Cleveland is a Tel Aviv. A thirsty man can buy his bourbon only at the state-controlled liquor stores. There is only one such downtown. As a matter of fact, that little oasis was only two blocks from this very Municipal Stadium, whose neighborhood threatened risk and terror for the baseball enthusiast. The neighborhood, however, didn't menace those who simply wanted to indulge a good man's weakness, of whom I might say from personal experience that there are a good many in Cleveland.

LEAVING

Cleveland high schools haven't graduated a Jew since the beginning of the nineteen-sixties. One of the last of these students was thirty-three-year-old insurance man Stanley Weiss, from California, who had returned to visit his parents. Weiss wears a mustache and affects an attaché case, but no somber accouterments dim the city-boy wit.

"We used to say Glenville High was half Jewish and half black and the white Catholics could meet in the telephone booth. At the end of the day, we played Russian roulette with the streets. Which one would get us home safe? The streets off Euclid went through colored neighborhoods which the gangs called 'turfs.' You took your life in your hands trespassing on someone's turf.

"Sometimes we sent out a decoy. While the gang chased him, the rest of us got home. Sometimes *I* was the decoy. I was on the track team, the only white on the Glenville track team. I ran the mile, never breaking five minutes. But I used to go through those streets like Roger Bannister."

I asked what was good time for a high school miler and Weiss, laughing, said, "Four-twenty, the good ones. I was on the track team for the exercise. School was just as rough on the colored kids. Their fathers were postal workers or teachers or die operators. They weren't ready for the jungle any more than we were. The fear of the turf was what we had in common. And we got along pretty good. One year we staged a succah in the classroom and the colored boys told us it was 'real gone.' My friend was Garry Thomas, one of the artists who worked on the murals in the Football Hall of Fame at Canton."

One has to believe Mr. Weiss. Earl Williams, a black who directs Cleveland's community relations programs, says that, of all the groups in Cleveland, the Jews were the most sympathetic to the black cause. That sympathy is waning. The leadership was sympathetic, but Jewish leadership isn't always in communication with the constituency. "On this problem," said Williams wearily, "now the leadership is in communication and leadership is withdrawing."

Still, Shaker Heights has a voluntary busing program for its white and black students. But then Shaker Heights is populated in part by whites who didn't run at the approach of the Jews and Jews who didn't run at the approach of blacks—the exemplar rather than the norm.

Of the 82,000 Jews who live in the Cleveland area, perhaps 2000 live in the city. They live on Shaker Square, which runs into Shaker Heights. The children in the Cleveland neighborhood go to the Shaker Heights schools. The Jews are almost without exception older, retired people, living in inexpensive city-owned developments. The men's clubs of the temples operate a car pool to bring these old folks out to Sabbath services.

When Stanley Weiss came home from his freshman year at college, his father, a small-business man, had moved to a new apartment development in Mayfield Heights. It was a bitter decision for Weiss, Sr. The Cleveland synagogue was now a black Baptist church.

One of the few businesses to prosper as the blacks began to occupy the old Jewish neighborhood were the delicatessens. "Outside of a Jewish neighborhood," said Weiss, "you can meet a lot of people who never heard of rye bread. The delicatessen was an exotic treasure trove to blacks. Pumpernickel, bagels, lox, chicken liver, pastrami—friends of my father's used to boast they couldn't afford to leave."

What happened in Cleveland, of course, is what happened to urban Jewish communities everywhere, with this exception: it happened in Cleveland first. Eugene Lipman and Albert Vorspan published *A Tale of Ten Cities* (Union of American Hebrew Congregations) in 1962, describing Cleveland then as a "City Without Jews."

The Jewish suburban settlement is a crescent curving from north to east. The five most populous of these towns are Cleveland Heights, where 15,300 Jews constitute 25 percent of the population; Shaker Heights, where 14,700 Jews are 40 percent; University Heights, 14,200, comprising 83 percent; South Euclid, where 10,200 are 34 percent; and Beachwood, where 7800 are 80 percent. The last has a recently elected Jewish mayor.

The Jews have done no more than the Protestants did before them or the Catholics did along with them.

Ten years ago, the Catholic bishop declared, "The Catholic diocese is not following the shift to the suburbs, it is ahead of it. It owns twenty-five properties in suburban areas ready for future expansion."

The suburbs were originally founded and populated by Protestants.

Protestants still dominate the administrative machinery, the tax review boards, the Board of Education, the planning and zoning committees. The difference is that neither the Catholic nor the Protestant workingman left Cleveland. Nor the Hungarian nor Slovak laborer. *All* of the Jews left.

Sentiment against their migration always precedes them. When Jews appear before the zoning boards for their variances to build temples or synagogues the argument raised is that during their residence in Cleveland they have lived in five different neighborhoods, each of which was white when they came and black when they left. What guarantee do older residents have in Shaker Heights or Beachwood that the Jew will not one day abandon this neighborhood, and by the abandonment turn the neighborhood black, with all the attendant problems of a drop in realty values, skyrocketing welfare costs, and frightening, crime-filled streets?

Already there is a small Jewish outmigration from Cleveland Heights and Shaker Heights. But again, the Jews are following rich Protestants and Catholics who moved on ahead of them. The argument is specious, but it contains one kernel of truth: Jews are not among urbanites who pioneer in building a new neighborhood. They prefer to buy a home already built on a street already developed. They prefer the enclave and they will seek it in preference to the newer street where newcomers have not yet determined the quality or character of the neighborhood.

It may come down to a compromise. If the Gentile lets the Jew build his temple or synagogue the Jew will promise to give up the delicatessen so that no one will follow him.

THE NEW ELITE

The genius of the American Jew is not in his ability to organize, for anyone can organize; nor is it in the effectiveness of his organization, for Alcoholics Anonymous is far more ingeniously effective and cheaper than any Jewish organization. The genius of the Jew is in his willingness to federate his organizations so that a network of them perpetuate the identity of the Jewish community.

Marshall Sklare writes in *American Jews* (Random House, 1971) that "one assumption of the Jewish family system is that all Jews share a common ancestry. The Jew is thought to be connected with all other Jews and the Jewish community is often viewed as a kind of extended family. . . . Why then does an organized Jewish community exist? Why are new Jewish agencies established at a time when dependence upon them ebbs? The answer resides in the fact that the community persists because identity persists. Community serves the need of identity, and while serving it also stimulates a feeling of identity."

In 1880, the Russian Jews began immigrating to America, an immigration perhaps as crucial in the history of world Jewry as the exodus from Egypt or the founding of the State of Israel. The Russian immigrants, however, were poorly prepared for the cities of the New World. They disembarked at Ellis Island unskilled, uneducated, and poor. A matrix of already existing American institutions helped them assimilate. Two examples are the free public school and the local Tammany Hall Club, which provided many of them with peddlers' licenses.

German Jews who had preceded the Russians by forty years established a second matrix of social organizations to facilitate assimilation. The Educational Alliance, a settlement house on the Lower East Side, became a template for other settlement houses and the De Milt Dispensary on Twenty-third Street provided free eye examinations and prescriptions for immigrant children.

The Russian immigrants themselves set up still more agencies—*vereins,* fraternities which provided widows with insurance, as well as the Hebrew Immigrant Aid Society, which facilitated the immigration of relatives left behind.

As the immigrants flooded in—over 2 million all told and as many as 400,000 a year—these charitable agencies proliferated. And as they proliferated, they began to compete fiercely for the charitable dollars of which, unfortunately, there are only so many. Priorities went awry.

First in Boston in 1892, then in Cincinnati in 1896, then in Cleveland in 1903, the rich Jews began to federate these charities and social organizations. All were responding to the massive influx of Russian immigrants, some of whom had made their way to Cleveland in large numbers by 1900.

Jewish philanthropy came under the direction of one board of Jewish leaders, who determined the amount of money needed to support all the agencies. One fund drive raised it. The concept of federation is one of the significant contributions of Jews to American philanthropy, the forerunner of the Community Chest and the United Fund.

In 1972 there were 230 federated Jewish communities. These Jewish Federations undertake the support of causes as varied as building a new community center or the settlement of twelve Polish Jews (who didn't like their accommodations and staged a sit-in at Federation offices).

Perhaps the premier Jewish Federation of the country is in Cleveland.

For thirteen local agencies and its commitment to the United Jewish Appeal, which claims sixty cents on the dollar for Israel, the Cleveland Federation raised $14.1 million in 1972.

This preeminence is due to the resources of the Cleveland Jewish community. Sixty-four percent of the Jews in Cleveland own their own home, 82 percent of them are native born, 49 percent are engaged in professional services or wholesale and retail trades, 11 percent in education, and 10 percent in manufacturing. Twenty thousand Jews belong to the Federation by virtue of a gift totaling $10 or more.

But the money comes from the big givers, who call themselves the *balabatim* (important men). These men raise the money from one another by face-to-face encounters, by private meetings where solicitation is made, and by annually increasing their gift by 10 percent over last year's. Nor does a heavy air of sacrifice attend their energies. Instead, the drive produces an esprit, a contagious enthusiasm. The balabatim plunge into the Federation drive with the frenzy of men throwing sandbags against the flooding Mississippi.

These balabatim are not all rich, though many are. Invariably, they have guaranteed their livelihoods by a profession which is self-perpetuating in their absence—for fund-raising demands enormous quantities of time.

"Bringing individuals together for fund-raising purposes," writes Sklare again, "inevitably results in heightening their sense of community. And the success of the Federations serves further to reinforce the sense of community."

The balabatim are invested with a sense of purpose as well as a sense of their own worthiness and Jewishness. There are those who argue that the balabatim consider themselves more worthy and more Jewish than others, but every religion in history has subtly insisted the man who is rich is better than the man who is poor and the man who works with his head better than the man who works with his hands.

The Federation is a secular religion, as vigorous a religion as the one which depends upon the Talmud. It is a religion based upon the efficient rather than the final cause, as Aristotle would have it. It has created, as all religions must, an elite, a Jewish elite, identifiable as an elite even to Christian neighbors, who certainly know what $14.1 million means. In the spring of 1972, when the goal of $14.1 was not forthcoming by $1 million, twenty of the balabatim met and among themselves made up this difference. This is the "Our Crowd" of the nineteen-seventies.

Nor are the balabatim of Cleveland content with Cleveland. Nine of them now serve as presidents or high officials of national and international Jewish organizations. Their energy is indefatigable. Arthur Lelyveld was for six years the president of the American Jewish Congress, and Ezra Shapiro has succeeded to the directorship of the Keren Hayesod in Jerusalem, the Israeli organization which raises funds from Jews in the rest of the world.

The critical resource of the Federation, however, is the professional skill of its staff, who are trained community or communal workers. In Cleveland the staff is commanded by Henry Zucker, the executive vice-president, Sidney Vincent, the executive director. I also met one of their colleagues, Judah Rubinstein, a research associate. Zucker, the oldest, is gray-haired, calm, and gentle and could pass easily for the successful and intelligent businessman. Vincent is slight, dark, volatile, as excited about Jews and Judaism as a rabbinical student. And Rubinstein, the youngest, with prematurely white hair and horn-rimmed specs, is the college professor. These are not men to whom the balabatim pay salaries simply to keep the schedules straight and the lines of communication between them open. An efficient executive director in some cities can command $50,000 a year. He commands it for his brains, imagination, and expertise.

For one thing, the executive director and his staff must guarantee that whatever cause to which the Jewish community lends itself will be successful. Success fills men with prestige. Failure discourages them. And there are some causes to which the Jewish community *must* lend itself—the cause of Soviet Jewry, for example. Whether it is wiser to try to fill an auditorium before whom a Catholic bishop, a Jewish expert, a Protestant minister, a politician, and a black leader can express sympathy for this cause or to recruit college and high school students for a State House demonstration depends on how well the Federation staff understands and can assess the probable response of the community.

These professionals must be adept at achieving a Jewish consensus which is not 51 percent but 80 percent. They must be quick and skillful at quelling incipient internal dissension or serious fissures will develop. They must ensure as well that the Federation constantly develops, not only in monies collected and members added but in program and causes. Programs must grow not only in variety but in sophistication.

American Jews were once at pains to secularize their religion, to integrate themselves within the American scheme of values. Immigrant Jews did not wish to accede to the traditional authority of the rabbi and lay officials of the temple or synagogue. They invented the office of the executive director to manage their communal organizations, the lay official administrating and implementing the decisions of other laymen, the most inspired invention in the history of good deeds.

The quality of professional leadership is of singular importance, say, in the continued existence and development of Israel. During the Six-day War, the Jews in South Africa, Holland, Antwerp, France, England, and Australia raised almost as much money in two weeks for the Israeli cause as the Jews in America did. After the war and in the ensuing years, the contributions of world Jewry depreciated while the American contributions every year increased.

American Jews asked, "Since we are all in the same boat, need we pull all the oars?" The difference between American Jews and world Jewry was not in resources but in professional leadership. The American Jewish community is latticed by professional workers. None in Europe. Consequently, through the Jewish Agency for Israel, Jews have begun a training program to provide these community leaders for the rest of the Jewish world.

The Jewish Federation of Cleveland is housed in a modern building of its own on Euclid Avenue. The downtown location makes it equidistant from the suburbs and puts it within taxiing distance of the active constituency during the work week.

My father, Leib Goldhurst, was president of a verein, whose members all came from Mikulintsy. Its purpose was to facilitate the immigration of relatives from the old country. The Cleveland Jewish Federation would knock his eye out. The Cleveland Federation serves a buffet lunch every day it has a meeting—a kosher buffet lunch!

The Federation does more than collect and disburse monies. Out of twenty-one employees in Cleveland, only two work full time at organizing the fund-raising campaign. The Cleveland Federation is also a data-processing plant for other, Jewish communities in Ohio and in Atlanta and Worcester. It is the source for all demographic information for the Jewish census now in preparation. It maintains a kashrut board whose rabbis supervise the meat markets. An agency of the Federation runs classes for the conversion of Christians affianced to Jews.

Though rabbis often complain that the Federation has subtracted the *mitzvah* (the daily kindness) from Judaism, it is equally true that the Federation often accepts responsibilities because the rabbis collectively will not.

Messers Zucker, Vincent, and Rubinstein do not work in a hierarchy, one the boss and the other two assistants with differing powers. It is obvious in talking to them that they are a trinity of skills, an isosceles triangle of brains. They cannot, of course, by themselves create an elite. But they can see where one needs creation. Just as they have realized that the rabbinate is often dilatory in accommodating change, so, too, do they realize that the national organizations are often irrelevant to many Jewish problems. It makes more sense and is more effective, for example, for Clevelanders to explain Israel to Cleveland newspapers, media, universities, and the Christian fellowships than it does for professionals out of New York. An Israeli Task Force composed of Cleveland rabbis and Jewish laymen counters Arab propaganda, disseminates background information and research for all who request it, and works with college groups.

As the rabbis are the critical intelligence of the Jewish community, the Federation staff is the animating intelligence. The executive director and his staff are expected to provide the rationale which spurs the effort of the Jewish community toward goals. And they do. The number of balabatim who repeat, "The Federation is the address of the Jewish community," a phrase original with Zucker, is numberless.

A larger reason for the almost total cohesion and facility of the Cleveland Jews is probably that Cleveland is the optimum community. Among its 82,000 Jews many run or manage major industries. Were the size of the community larger, perhaps they would not be as influential. Were the community smaller, membership in the elite would not be as prestigious. As a matter of fact, suggested Judah Rubinstein, the Jewish community in America is probably the most viable of all subcultures because it probably numbers 5.8 million. More and the members would fragment and diffuse; less and it would lack economic clout.

THE OLDER DISCIPLINES

A tradition of strong, visionary, and intelligent rabbinic leadership also explains the cohesion of the Cleveland Jewish community.

The Cleveland rabbi who achieved national prominence was Abba Hillel Silver of The Temple. A Reform rabbi, tall, imposing, with silver hair and a supreme oratorical gift, Silver was one of the first Jewish leaders to espouse liberal causes, to champion organized labor and social-welfare legislation. What distinguished his fifty-one-year rabbinate in Cleveland, however, was that in that half century he had led the German Jews into a love of Zionism.

Born in 1893, Silver came to The Temple from Wheeling, West Virginia, before the United States entered World War I, at a time when the German Jews in America were still in ascendancy. These Jews were hostile to Zionism because they thought the existence of a Jewish state would compromise their integrity as American citizens.

Silver argued, "The upbuilding of a Jewish national home in Palestine is one great, urgent, and historically inescapable task of Jewry. The upbuilding of Jewish religious life in America and elsewhere throughout the world is another. One is no substitute for the other. One is not opposed to the other."

In this cause, for many years an unpopular cause and for many years a cause treated with indifference, Rabbi Silver was joined by Barnet Brickner, the rabbi of the Euclid Temple. These two made Cleveland a center of political Zionism.

In the forties, Silver became the chairman of the American Zionist Emergency Council, which began mobilizing public opinion in the United States for the establishment of an independent Jewish state after the war. The Council persuaded both Republicans and Democrats to include such a plank in the party platforms of 1944.

By the time Brickner died in 1958 and Silver died in 1963, it was impossible to imagine the Middle East without Israel.

Silver's successor to the pulpit at The Temple is his son, Jeremy Daniel, only the fourth rabbi in 120 years. It is worth noting that many Jewish institutions in town are staffed and directed by native

Clevelanders. Sidney Vincent is a hometown boy and so is Henry Zucker and so are another dozen rabbis and lay leaders. This continuity perhaps explains why the outmigration did not result in diffusion of the old Cleveland Jewish community.

The Temple is the last Jewish house of worship left in Cleveland. It is located at University Circle in Silver Park, surrounded by a black neighborhood. The congregation did not abandon this temple principally because its architecture makes it supreme among Jewish religious edifices, and its setting, in this beautifully tended park, is protected by several contiguous institutions—museums, college buildings, and a concert hall.

The bus that carried me stopped at Euclid Avenue and 105th Street. Across the street, blacks waited for the eastbound bus. From an undetermined location, a loudspeaker broadcast rock music to inattentive pedestrians and passersby below. Beside a parking lot a vendor dispensed hot dogs and ice cream cones. A three-block walk took me to Silver Park and The Temple. And everywhere in this center city, I saw buildings which had been burned out, their flame-licked windows boarded.

Jeremy Daniel Silver, as tall as his father, broad-shouldered, and beardless, said the congregation decided to stay put because it thought that one day Jews might move back to Cleveland. In the meantime, The Temple maintains a branch in Beachwood with a school, counseling services, and meeting hall. The older congregants, he said, simply cannot come to Cleveland by bus.

While the neighborhood through which I had just walked was peaceful and pleasant enough, Rabbi Silver said that one evening four years ago he had opened his study door to an imperative rap and found a white-helmeted police officer carrying a shotgun. A gas mask was slung over his shoulder and he informed Rabbi Silver politely and apologetically that the police had to commandeer The Temple's parking lot for a command post.

"There were armored cars in the lot and the police set up their communications net there. This neighborhood is called Hough, and it is Cleveland's Watts. The riot started with a shootout in a bar and it ended like the San Francisco earthquake."

The younger Silver is, of course, a noted Zionist as well as a theologian of growing reputation. When I remarked that he looked like neither a rabbi nor a theologian but more like a Cleveland Browns tight end, he rubbed his face and asked, "What does a rabbi look like? I married a young couple last week, and of the whole wedding party, the one man without a beard was the rabbi."

The Jews in Cleveland, he told me, had been ahead of all other groups in providing for black housing, employment, and school integration. But their efforts did not survive the confrontation as the black population kept growing and as it needed more and more help from the suburbs in schooling, services, and space. "When it comes to the goring of the Jewish ox," Rabbi Silver said, "there is no reason to expect Jews to be better than anyone else."

The rabbi at Fairmount Temple is Arthur Lelyveld, the activist on behalf of liberal causes. Rabbi Lelyveld, who resembles Arthur Godfrey, recently completed six years as president of the American Jewish Congress. He was among the liberals who, long before the March on Washington, argued for equity for blacks from his pulpit and in the national Jewish magazines. In 1964, Lelyveld was among the white clergymen who went to Birmingham, where he was badly beaten up for his advocacy.

One must admire his courage, not in risking a beating—there are people who visited the South who never thought they were risking a beating and got one—but in insisting that liberalism survive.

It is neither fashionable nor respectable in many circles to insist that liberalism still has meaning and that the liberal attitude can guide the political and ethical response.

Lelyveld is refreshing. He is not apologetic. Once the bullies are upon you, you must bear the beating, like it or no. But the liberal must brave the epithets "fuzzy," "bleeding heart," "sentimentalist," and "idealist," and these are often as hard as fists.

But I do not think Lelyveld is a liberal because he is an idealist any more than Abba Hillel Silver was a Zionist because *he* was an idealist. Lelyveld is a liberal and Silver was a Zionist because they are and were Jews.

"What the argument for a 'divorce' (from liberalism) . . . reduces to," writes Lelyveld, "is a demand that Jews plan their political and civic activities solely on the basis of a calculation as to what is 'good for the Jews'—shades of the second-class citizenship of pre-Zionist days! One exponent of this view flatly calls for the endorsement of candidates of 'any political persuasion' so long as they are pro-Jewish and pro-Israel. Another says, 'The most important question, therefore, is: what type of society will be best for the survival of the Jewish community?' Do not struggle for the rights of others, we are warned, because they will neither love you nor repay you and, in the end, they may even turn against you. . . .

"The mandates of our heritage would be self-defeating if they required us to cooperate with forces that would destroy us, but they certainly do not require us to put our own welfare above the central task of *tikkun olam,* the perfecting of our world."

Rabbi Armond Cohen of the Park Synagogue in Cleveland Heights will probably not agree. "Every year," said Cohen, "Lelyveld and I have a public debate. Every year, someone asks, 'How are you two going to vote?' Every year, I say, 'Republican,' to thunderous silence, and Lelyveld says, 'Democratic,' to thunderous applause."

I found Cohen an original thinker. He does not like all-black schools because they will produce dissident citizens. Nor is he happy about the power of the Jewish Federation, believing the tumult and excitement of fund raising are reserved only for the well-to-do. While he was on the subject, he also added that the national Jewish organizations did not represent their constituencies.

Do not, however, think the man ill tempered or crotchety. He is humorous and equable. Rabbi Cohen occupies the pulpit of the largest Conservative congregation in the Midwest and, at 106 years, one of the oldest. He is only its sixth rabbi, a post he has held since his ordination, and he, too, is a native Clevelander.

As long as he was on the subject, I asked Rabbi Cohen what programs he advocated for our number one problem, whatever it might be.

"Our number one problem is mixed marriages between Jews and Christians. You would be surprised at how thorny some of these problems are," he said.

He leaned forward. "There's a family in my congregation of substantial means and responsible position. The daughter became engaged to a boy from an Orthodox family, which is nothing unusual. But when the two sets of parents get together, a secret pops up from their small talk. The mother of the Conservative girl is not Jewish.

"It seems the father was a flier in World War II who fell in love with an English nurse whom he married in a civil ceremony in London. They came to Cleveland when the war was over and settled into a normal suburban Jewish life without telling anyone.

"But to the Orthodox Jews this is a serious, serious secret. Only a child born of a Jewish mother is Jewish and an Orthodox rabbi will not marry a Jew to a non-Jew.

"When they came to me, I said that there was a way to solve this problem quickly. All the daughter had to do was convert and since she had led a Jewish life, it could be a technical conversion, the *mikvah* [ritual bath].

"As long as we were at it, the mother said she might as well convert, too, and so did the other daughter. But that, my friend, is not the end of the story. The Orthodox rabbi who was to perform the ceremony called me before the wedding. He had a grievous problem. The groom-to-be, he told me, was an *adopted* child. I told him it was a secret we should take to our graves. And so they were married and hopefully will live happily ever after and some of us can stop converting good Jews to Judaism."

"BEEN HARD SINCE ROOSEVELT"

"In the beginning, all the Jews were Republicans. Cleveland was Republican. The Jews became Republicans because 'Czar' Bernstein went into the old Woodland neighborhood and converted the immigrants. And while Czar was converting the greenhorns, Morris Maschke was making the party into an adjunct of the rich and the powerful."

My informant was Saul Stillman, chairman of the Republican Central Committee of Cuyahoga County. We were in his office on the ground floor of a Lakeside Avenue office building. Everywhere there were piles of census reports, voting lists, and registration tabulations. Tacked on the wall were maps of Cleveland voting precincts and above them photographs of ex-Governor James Rhodes and President Richard Nixon.

Stillman is short, gray-haired, and since he has been an active politician since the mid-thirties perhaps one could say his eyes are the clear alert eyes of a man who has weathered the cigars of a great many smoke-filled back rooms.

"Czar Bernstein was a talker," Stillman went on. "A good talker. A good talker in Yiddish, German, Litvak, and English. I'm a good talker. I like to talk. I like to persuade people. And the Jews love talkers. They have what I call an 'oratorical fetish.' They loved Carl

Stokes for that reason. He was a talker. Went from City Hall into
television. The first time he ran, the Jewish cause and the black cause
were one and the same. There were full-page ads in the press signed
by rabbis urging his election. That was five years ago. The second
time around the Jews supported him, but there were no full-page
ads. After that, they were disenchanted. They thought he was just
a talker. He hadn't made Cleveland into Paradise. He wasn't a good
enough talker to convince the suburbanites that Cleveland needs
an income tax. Which Cleveland still doesn't have. Without a city
income tax, a mayor is all warts."

Ninety percent of the Jews in Cleveland are Democrats. Franklin
D. Roosevelt changed them. They have remained Democrats. "He
was a talker," said Stillman. "It's been hard in this job since Roosevelt."

While they are Democrats, however, they are not Tammany Hall
Democrats. There is big Jewish money in and around Cleveland,
and Stillman rattled off the names of Stone, Rattner, Josephs, Cole
of National Key, and Miller of Columbia Metal. "When Nixon needed
money in Ohio in '68," he said, "we convinced some of these Jews
there was no reason not to have a friend in the other camp. They
contributed. Not like they contributed to Democratic candidates, but
they contributed."

For many years, the Jews in Ohio were not active office seekers.
Their importance politically was that 90 percent of them were registered voters and 90 percent of those who were registered voted and
of them 90 percent voted the same way. The Jews in politics aimed
for the judgeships. But this is changing and Stillman thought it was
changing not because of any lessening of Jewish influence but because of a heightening.

A black man interrupted us. He was a Republican district leader
with money for several reservations for the Republican National
Convention. Name by name, Stillman asked about the health and
happiness of the other party workers as he made the entry in a ledger.

"Howard Metzenbaum, a Jewish lawyer, ran for the Senate in '70
and came within 100,000 votes of beating Robert Taft, Jr. Anyone
who comes within 100,000 votes of beating a Taft in this state is a
comer. That there will be more Jewish candidates for office is an
inevitable course of events, especially in a city where Jews are as
organized as they are in Cleveland. That's what politics is, understanding how to move the organization."

GURNISHT

During the week May 10–14, the American Jewish Congress held its convention in the Sheraton Hotel in Cleveland. Cleveland was the choice because Arthur Lelyveld was stepping down as the American Jewish Congress president and the delegates wanted to honor him in his hometown.

In his opening remarks to the delegates, Lelyveld reminded them that the Congress was the first of the Jewish organizations to condemn publicly the American excursion into Vietnam.

Then Rabbi Lelyveld introduced the convention's principal speaker. It was Yigal Allon, the Deputy Prime Minister of Israel, who swept into the hall at that very instant. His entrance was dictated not by a sense of his own drama but by security. A cohort of Israeli and Secret Service agents escorted him.

Allon assumed the lectern. The audience was requested to remain seated. Only the agents remained standing, eyes scanning the backs of attentive heads.

While there may have been some sympathy for Allon's speech, there was very little for its length, which was just over an hour and fifteen minutes. He devoted a good half hour to an explanation of the Israeli educational system, which closely resembles our own with the exception that the junior high school is called the "intermediate" school—big news for some of the folks who have weathered the course of many a PTA meeting.

The Deputy Prime Minister next described the fate of Soviet Jewry, then plunged into his peroration. Israel is secure, he said, because of American credibility. If America wasn't in Vietnam, the Russians would be in the Middle East. The Israelis think our commitment to Southeast Asia is sublime. They often wonder why American Jews don't see this.

Some of the dozing newspapermen woke up.

As my father would say, *"Gurnisht,"* by which he meant *"Gurnisht helfan"* (Nothing helps [Jews]).

Later, Richard Cohen, dapper, bon vivant director of the American Jewish Congress's public relations, confided that he had never been one to spot trouble before it developed. But he thought he saw a cloud on the far horizon and that one day the American Jews were going to have to tell the Israeli Jews they were not the Home Office.

The next morning as the convention proceeded, Meir Kahane of the New York Jewish Defense League, the militant yarmulka-wearing karate experts, tried to invade the assembly. There were a lot of Jews in one hotel and Kahane seized upon this opportunity to tell all of them to emigrate to Israel before American anti-Semitism did them in. Since he neither was an elected delegate nor had any delegate asked him to speak, his way was barred.

Kahane, dark-haired, slim, eyes blazing, collar open, is a man from Belfast. Everything except the trenchcoat. He stood in the Sheraton lobby arguing with those who guarded the doors while several of his disciples in beards and dirty sweaters waved cardboard torn from cartons on which they had crayoned, "Kahane speaks."

"It is fallacious to believe that Jew killers are only a godless, pervert, lunatic fringe," began Kahane.

Now there are a great many people who could kick their way into the convention of the Congress without awakening the house dick. But Kahane on the rampage summoned newsmen from Akron and other points. Before he had finished, there were three crews rolling television cameras on dollies across the Sheraton lobby. Before poised cameras, Kahane took off, while Lelyveld waited to rebut him impatiently.

But then just because there's a ball park on the lake doesn't mean you are in a big-league town.

HARTFORD: Shul-schlepping in the Suburbs

BLACKBIRDS

Wallace Stevens may well have been describing his hometown in "Thirteen Ways of Looking at a Blackbird":

> I was of three minds
> Like a tree
> In which there are three blackbirds.

A stately man, who tapped his cane vigorously as he walked to work every day, Stevens put aside the metrical schemes for *Harmonium* and the *Auroras of Sutumn* when he settled behind his desk as the vice-president of the Hartford Accident and Indemnity Company.

The city has a tight New England quality. Connecticut produced the original Yankees. They were the first peddlers and gained notoriety by selling wooden nutmegs. Nutmeg was the big trip of the seventeenth century. It was unfortunately, easily counterfeited. In its natural state, nutmeg resembles wood, and the Connecticut Yankees were quick to take advantage of this similarity.

The first Jew in Hartford was David the Peddler, who was arrested in 1659 and charged with selling nutmeg to the mistress of the house when "ye head of the family was absent." The court socked him twenty Colonial shillings, too.

While some of the pragmatists were getting rich on wooden nutmeg, Thomas Hooker, the Congregationalist minister who founded the state, and others framed one of the first constitutions ever written. The "Fundamental Orders" was the original American document to outline the principles of political democracy. It was the basic law of Connecticut from 1639 until 1662, when the Connecticut Charter superseded it. The charter proclaimed the primacy of the community over that of the individual and also opted for independence. William III of England didn't like this last and in 1667 he dispatched Sir Edmund Andros, governor general of New England, to tear up the charter. Rather than surrender it, the colonists spirited it from the Town House and hid it downriver in a huge white oak which dominated a hilltop, a landmark to travelers along the waterway and the Boston Post Road.

During the winter of 1856, the Charter Oak came down. Botanists from Yale University estimated its age at over a thousand years. One of the Hartford historical societies trimmed the fallen tree of branches and roots and, with the aid of winches and crowbars, hoisted the trunk atop a wooden sled. They hauled the tree to the home of a Farmington cabinetmaker. Out of this bole, the cabinetmaker chiseled the ornately carved chair from which the lieutenant governor presides over the Connecticut Senate.

Secession as a political alternative was first broached in Hartford in the Convention of 1814, when many of the Yankees convened to deplore the war with England. By the time they got around to seceding, Andrew Jackson had come home from New Orleans a war hero.

For two centuries the city was dominated by a Yankee elite. Then it became a port of entry for foreign workers. Of its 300,000 metropolitan population, 30,000 are Jews, one in ten, which makes it probably the largest per capita Jewish concentration outside of New York City.

The skyline is dominated by the tower of the Travelers' Life Insurance building, as straight in its stirrup as the tower at Chartres, which inspired Henry Adams. To the Travelers' left is the gold dome of the state capitol building. Above, as you leave 91 North, is the blue, flame-shaped dome of the Hartford Coke Company.

Hartford is the life insurance center of the United States. There are almost seventy major insurance companies in this city, along with many smaller ones. Among the former is Hartford Fire whose directors at ITT caused such a tragic misunderstanding between the Justice Department and San Diego as to the site of the 1972 Republican National Convention. Hartford Fire is housed in a white, columned structure, an eclectic attempt to re-create the Parthenon and the Decatur, Illinois, Police Station. On narrow Farmington Avenue is the Aetna Life Insurance Company. Its six thousand workers inhabit a gigantic, vine-covered building, a city landmark which also boasts a gold dome and rather resembles the college in which MGM executives once supposed Andy Hardy would matriculate. In these buildings and in countless others there are men who daily must imagine ways to invest millions of dollars every minute.

Insurance and banking money have liberated the architects. Connecticut General blazed new horizons fifteen years ago when it located its offices in a newly made park in suburban Bloomfield, the utility of the free-form home office punctuated by Noguchi statuary discreetly placed in a large garden for the edification of the insurance clerks on their lunch hours.

The Jews thought they were daring when they retained Walter Gropius of Architects Collaborative to design a new community center, which included not only a raked-seat auditorium but a sand-blasted frieze from Genesis in Hebrew. Gropius is old-hat these days. The new Unitarian Meeting House looks like a chocolate cake cut into slices by eight concrete cleavers. And the Phoenix Life Insurance building in Constitution Plaza is called "the fish." Built in the shape of an acute green ellipsis, it looks front and back like the bow of the *Titanic*. It is perhaps the only office building in the world with only two walls.

Hartford boasts about Constitution Plaza, the first urban-renewal project constructed with private money. Every self-respecting city built one of these in the fifties and sixties to save downtown and every self-respecting city will lay out a Rapid Transit System in the seventies to save downtown. Downtown is a delinquent boy no amount of gifts will reform.

Do not mistake Hartford for thine alabaster city. For the rest it is an identifiable New England town, most of its buildings and houses post-and-beam construction, the sidings brick or clapboard, shutters, cupolas, dormers, and gables adding variety and interest. Its many neighborhoods are filled with the old double- and triple-deckers which accommodate two or three families, one on each floor. Each apartment offers the street a porch. The narrow driveways which proceed to backyard garages barely accommodate an auto and the garbage cans. The backyards are crisscrossed with clothes-lines, which reel from the decks to the garage portals and back. The poet Richard Wilbur, who teaches at nearby Wesleyan in Middletown, must have seen these when he wrote in *Things of This World:*

> Outside the open window
> The morning air is all awash with angels.

It is a city for poets, lexicographers, and novelists. Noah Webster was born in West Hartford two centuries ago and Mark Twain went broke here after publishing Ulysses S. Grant's *Memoirs.* Twain's spacious home is now a city shrine on Farmington Avenue. It was from here that Twain went to lunch once a week at the Heublein Hotel with James Dudley Warner, the editor of the *Hartford Courant,* the paper with the longest history of publication in America. At one of these luncheons, Warner is supposed to have remarked, "Everyone talks about the weather but no one does anything about it."

The University of Hartford with both a prestigious School of Music and a School of Art, the University of Connecticut's School of Law and School of Social Work, St. Joseph's College, the Greater Hartford Community College, and Trinity make the city something of a college town. These campuses, a generous allotment of larger parks, and the good luck for the Dutch elm disease to have spared its trees make Hartford a green, spacious place.

There are a dozen storefront libraries on Hartford's main streets, always a sign the neighborhood is changing. Storefront libraries do not have a children's section.

The Atheneum Museum has probably the world's finest collection of Baroque art.

Hartford is a stop for every philharmonic orchestra. Bushnell Auditorium accommodates 3000.

Prices are as high in Hartford as they are in New York, but salaries are generally lower.

In 1944, the main tent of the Ringling Brothers, Barnum & Bailey caught fire, claiming the lives of 168 women and children. Out of this tragedy emerged a mystery, that of the identity of a little girl never claimed. She is buried in a grave marked "Miss 1594," the number of the mortuary slab she occupied. The florists of Hartford decorate her grave into perpetuity.

Hartford is also infamous as a city that has had four major racial disturbances in the past five years.

The first of these occurred in the north end when a troublemaker harassed a black pharmacy. When the police handcuffed the trouble-maker, bystanders grew restless. State Representative Leonard Frazier, a black, bailed the boy out, but it was too late to reason with the crowd. Molotov cocktails set fires and mobs threatened the occupants of passing autos. Subsequently, the mayor, the police, community leaders, and young blacks agreed to keep swimming pools open, initiate on-the-job training programs, do something about prices in white-owned slum stores, and ask the police for more restraint.

A year later, the assassination of Martin Luther King set off another riot in which warehouses were fired and firemen sniped at. Albany Avenue, which curves from a point on Main Street almost to the city line, was burned out. Passing along it now, one sees the deserted stores boarded up, blackened apartment houses, and the saloons caged forlornly with protective steel.

The Comanchero motorcycle gang set off still another in August 1969 near the Palm Cafe in the Puerto Rican neighborhood.

And in 1970, in the South Green, a riot erupted after a fight broke out between rival black and Puerto Rican gangs. "They are throwing everything at us except the garbage cans," reported a policeman to his superiors. Rioting lasted three days before tear gas and shotguns quelled the looting.

The city is wiser now. It does not think open swimming pools are the answer. Black leadership in Hartford, though responsible, is not influential. The young militants are often contemptuous of it. Unemployment steadily mounts. United Aircraft, the largest employer in the state, weekly lays off workers. Things go poorly for Fuller Brush. New England industry has been packing up and moving south for the last half century.

The problem that stays at home is housing.

In Hartford, the city has the poor and the suburbs have the space. The suburbs are not talking trade.

Hartford is every city. Yet on its own it has fathered the Hartford Process, a pioneering effort to make the social services of the nineteen-eighties more immediate and helpful for the needy. Where in the past, welfare, social, and medical agencies have received funds to bring their services to clients, the Hartford Process pools all state, federal, welfare, and municipal monies in one agency, the neighborhood Community Life Association, which then pays each of these other bureaus and agencies as their services are purchased for clients.

The city needs no think-tank creation when the pocketbook of its white middle class is affected. In the early summer of 1971, the legislature passed a state income tax. The legislators were distracted in this venture first by the howling of the constituency and second by the ticking capitol clock, whose hour hand they had to keep moving backward to remain legally in session. The hurriedly passed state income tax did little credit to their actuarial acuity. The bill became law that Saturday noon.

Governor Thomas Meskill had an important funeral to attend Saturday, which spared him the agonizing decision of whether to veto the bill or let it become law without his signature.

One thousand citizens showed up on the State House lawn on the afternoon of July 8. Booming, "Ve-to! Ve-to!" they paraded in shirtsleeves and sweaty faces.

"Governor," read one placard, "I voted for you. Now you vote for me."

"Impeach the rummies," read another.

"Stamp out inflation. Give your paycheck to Connecticut," read a third.

The prize for banner day went to "We've been sandbagged by a slippery bunch of rascals."

The governor was far, far away, his head bowed in meditative prayer. But as Wallace Stevens puts it in stanza X:

> He rode over Connecticut
> In a glass coach.
> Once a fear pierced him,
> In that he mistook
> The shadows of his equipage
> For blackbirds.

On Monday, Meskill reconvened the legislature and then the politicians took the state out of the income-tax business.

ON THE RESERVATION

The difference between the Jews in Cleveland and the Jews in Hartford is that the Jews in Cleveland moved always east and the Jews in Hartford moved always west.

By 1960, all of the Jews in Hartford, with the exception of a small complement of elderly poor, had left the city for West Hartford, a suburb of 69,000 citizens, the eighth largest city in the state, where all the streets are named after the Indians—Iroquois, Seneca, Mohawk, King Phillip. Residents call West Hartford the "Jewish Reservation." Twenty thousand Jews live there in split-level tepees.

As early as 1777 there was a Jews' Street in Hartford where brokers dealt in tea and spices and merchants ran the "cheap stores," the colonial euphemism for flea markets.

German Jews started to come in the eighteen-forties. By 1847, they chartered the first Hartford congregation, Beth Israel. In 1856, they bought the First Baptist Church, refurbished it, and named the synagogue Touro Hall in honor of Judah Touro of New Orleans, who had given each of the fourteen synagogues then in America a gift of $5000. Beth Israel rented the downstairs of Touro Hall for public meetings and other space to stores.

"In the depression of 1872 and 1873," writes Rabbi Morris Silverman in *Hartford Jews: 1659-1970* (Connecticut Historical Society, 1971), "the hard-pressed Congregation Beth Israel had to borrow $1000 from the First National Bank; and Touro Hall's lessees, the owners of the Dollar Store, could not pay the rent of $1500. . . . Beth Israel members paid dues ranging from $30 to $100 (a considerable sum at the time)."

In 1880, the Russian Jews began arriving. Furriers came from Pinsk and cabinetmakers, skilled at reproducing antique furniture, from Lithuania. From Poland, Russia, the Ukraine, Hungary, Rumania, and Galicia came enough immigrant peddlers to form the Hartford Hebrew Peddlers Association (which changed its name in the next generation to the Hebrew Merchants Association) and enough painters, carpenters, flooring men, masons, bakers, and laborers to form the Hartford Workmen's Circle.

Where there were 1500 Jews in Hartford in 1880, there were 18,000 in 1920. Their original community was in the east end of the city, where Constitution Plaza stands now, by the Connecticut River near the Charter Oak Bridge. By 1910, some of them had already started an exodus to the northwest, to the Blue Hills area. To all intents and purposes the move was completed by 1935 when Beth Israel left its home on Charter Oak Avenue for a new one on Farmington.

After World War II, a second Jewish exodus pushed farther west over Prospect Avenue into the burgeoning suburban developments of West Hartford. By the mid-nineteen-fifties, the move from Blue Hills had reached epidemic proportions.

Still it continues. There are not only Jewish families but new synagogues in the smaller suburbs of Bloomfield, Glastonbury, Newington, Manchester, Rocky Hill, Windsor, and South Windsor, which has a Jewish mayor. And there is every expectation on the part of the Hartford Chamber of Commerce of reverse immigration, that Jews will move back to the city into the luxury apartments planned for the childless and older couples.

There are many reasons advanced to explain Jewish mobility. Chief among these reasons is that the black man chases them. But the black man chases all middle-classniks. The young Jewish families who settle in the small hamlets of the Farmington Valley in Avon, Simsbury, Granby, Canton, and Farmington are not fleeing the black man, they are fleeing the inflated realty values of West Hartford.

Perhaps Jewish mobility is a genetic inheritance. For centuries the *goyim* owned the house and the street and the Jew owned nothing but the ordered table with the *zayde* at its head. The Jew cared deeply about the table and nothing for the house and the street. This rootlessness became ingrained. But the statistics from West Hartford hardware men belie this. The Jews, they say, spend more money on lawn mowers and crabgrass killer than all other subcultures put together.

Or maybe it is the psychological disposition of the Jews to say of the old neighborhood or the old house or the old furniture, "It's not nice enough." Thorstein Veblen, however, did not need to mention Jews once to elucidate conspicuous consumption in *The Theory of the Leisure Class*.

Mobility is a characteristic of the twentieth-century American Jew but not of itself a Jewish characteristic. This is not to insist that Jewish mobility does not by this time have characteristics all its own. It does. The mobility depends upon the rung of the middle class to which the local Jews have mounted.

The last Jewish school principal has retired in Hartford. Out of 2595 teachers in Hartford and West Hartford public schools, only 248 are Jewish. There are three Jews quartered in the State Police Barracks. There are not many Jewish postal workers nor are there many Jewish taxi drivers. If there are 100 cabs in the city, there are a lot (while in New York City 2000 of the city's 11,000 medallion cabs are driven by Jews).

Twenty-one percent of all the doctors in Greater Hartford are Jews; 33 percent of the lawyers; 41 percent of the dentists; and 50 percent of the pharmacists. Eleven out of forty-four Circuit Court judges are Jews.

Thus the Hartford Jewish community is affluent, with values common to the affluent. And the lines of communication are short.

A Jew in Hartford's suburbs cannot opt for anonymity. Sooner or later another Jew will ask him to contribute to the Federation Drive or to join a new synagogue or to enroll his children in the Community Center summer day camp or another Jew will plead, "For God's sake we need the tenth man today like we never needed him before."

He need do none of these but over and over he will be counted as a Jew by other Jews. The Christians may count him covertly, but the Jews will count him openly and will keep on counting him because though he may be one in ten still he is not a multitude.

In counting him, of course, the community determines his commitment. Sooner or later, this subtle or not so subtle tabulation enforces an identity. Without that identity the suburban Jews will find little social commerce in Jewish or non-Jewish societies.

The count often proceeds from unlikely sources. The Tumble Brook Country Club in Bloomfield, whose initiation fee would enable many a man to buy two Cadillacs, has lent itself and its questionable influence to Jewish causes, not causes in the sense of weddings or Bar Mitzvahs or testimonial dinners but causes such as those espoused by the National Council of Jewish Women, Federation Committees, and Jewish day-care organizations, for whom the club willingly provides a meeting place. When potential initiates come before its Membership Committee, the Tumble Brook chairman will often ask the Federation for the candidate's "giving record." This "giving record" is not a *sine qua non*—with the right kind of golf score and a toothy, pretty wife, the "giving record" can be downstate in Yalesville, for all the committee cares—still, Tumble Brook is a tabulator in the ever-continuing census.

Affluence and the census explain two of the obvious characteristics of Jewish mobility: when the Jews move, they all move at once and they all want to move to the same place.

For Jews want the enclave. They cluster. In fact, they often cluster more determinedly than blacks, sometimes to their distress. The King Phillip Elementary School in West Hartford is more than 80 percent

Jewish, not exactly the introduction to the open society for the children liberal fathers want. But the enclave in the King Phillip area is now impenetrable. Rabbi Howard Singer of Temple Emmanuel remembered as a boy that his was the only apartment on the block without a Christmas tree. Last year along Mohegan Drive there wasn't a home with Christmas lights.

What the Jews prefer is the enclave that is 50 percent Jewish. It is hard, however, to establish a cut-off point with Christian or Jewish real estate agents who find it easier to sell Jews houses in Jewish enclaves. Classified real estate advertising in newspapers proves the point. Many ads will read, "Near Temple Beth El" or "Near Jewish CC."

There are, to be sure, pioneering families who venture into the new neighborhood alone. But two or three families inevitably attract another dozen and this dozen allies itself with another dozen and still another to form a new temple or to become the advance guard beckoning the battalions in the rear to schlep the old shul out to the woods. Temples and synagogues leapfrog into the suburbs.

Fifth Avenue in New York is no longer an Irish or for that matter a Catholic neighborhood, but St. Patrick's remains the cardinal's cathedral. St. John the Divine on Amsterdam Avenue is a lone lighthouse in a sea of Puerto Rican storefront churches, but St. John's is still the Episcopal bishop's pulpit.

There were Jewish congregations near St. John the Divine, but when these Jewish communities disintegrated and broke up, the congregations disbanded because everyone moved in a different direction. Temple Emmanuel in West Hartford, one of the largest Conservative congregations in America, is now in its third home since 1919, having moved from Windsor Street in Hartford to Woodland in 1927 and from Woodland to Mohegan Drive in 1965.

The Hartford suburbs number twenty-two Jewish congregations, fifteen of which had been schlepped from the city. Shul-schlepping, however, is not a facile exercise, even for Jews.

Emmanuel, for example, was built in sections (like most new temples). The classrooms and the rabbi's study were constructed first; then the auditorium which served for temple affairs and for worship; then finally, the sanctuary was added. While the temple has a membership of nine hundred families, many are old and many are middle-aged and many are the sons, grandsons, and even great-grandsons of the congregation's founders, who first came together in worship in the old North Methodist Episcopal Church. Impatient with praying on folding chairs, the rabbi facing them on a small stage, the present congregation plunged ahead with the new and gorgeous sanctuary while the old temple on Woodland was still for sale.

Schlepping a shul means schlepping two mortgages. Temple Emmanuel had to raise its dues, which could not help but discourage new, younger, and less affluent members. Its classrooms are half empty. Its other facilities are often idle.

Tiferes Israel moved into Bloomfield and created a community-relations problem with poor planning. The parking lot was not large enough to accommodate the cars of the congregants. Neighbors complained when they found their streets jammed with parked cars and their driveways clogged with still more. Drainage was inadequate. Problems pyramided.

Conservative Tikvoh Chadoshoh was organized in 1942 by refugees from Hitler's Europe. The congregation built a temple on Cornwall Street after the war, which it sold in 1969 to the Faith Seventh-day Adventist Church and moved to Still Road in Bloomfield, where it promptly borrowed money to build another.

Now the rabbi of Tikvoh Chadoshoh is an older man and the congregants are older, too. It is a shrinking rather than an expanding congregation.

A concerned member of the Jewish community casually asked the banker why his bank had let this congregation assume a mortgage its members had no chance of living long enough to pay off.

The banker replied he had no worries about his money. The banks knew that the Jewish community would never let any congregation default on its obligations. Tikvoh Chadoshoh might well disband because of death and old age, but the Jewish Federation would certainly clean up any outstanding debts it left behind. Tikvoh Chadoshoh was a good risk.

To which the Jew replied that the sentiment was truly beautiful, it did credit to the Jewish heritage and tradition, but why should the existence of a responsible Jewish community give bankers the right to declare a free fire zone of irresponsible borrowing and lending?

The sensible answer for Tikvoh Chadoshoh was to have merged with another of the smaller congregations moving out. The reason it did not merge and some of the other smaller temples did not was that a merger between two shuls means deciding between two rabbis. Every rabbi has his own *geshaft* (business) which he is not anxious to dismantle no matter how sensible or realistic the dismantling may be. Rabbis have proved veritable Demostheneses in persuading congregants to throw up new shuls. Not an Isocrates among them.

Hannah Stein, the executive director of the National Council of Jewish Women, remarked in all seriousness that she thought Jews, and Christians, too, ought to spend some of their money to devise portable structures and foundations which they can carry with them when they move instead of spending millions on new edifices which too soon become inaccessible.

O PIONEERS!

While the laymen in Hartford worry about Jewish identity and values, the rabbis are writing novels (Howard Singer), demonstrating on behalf of black civil rights (Stanley Kessler), and pioneering in interfaith housing for the elderly (Abraham Feldman).

Rabbi Singer of Temple Emmanuel is tall, mustachioed, and far from lighthearted. He is the author of three novels, *The Devil and Harry Raftin, With Mind and Heart,* and *Wake Me When It's Over,* and a polemic on violence and the Jewish character, *Bring Forth the Mighty Men* (Funk & Wagnalls, 1969). Rabbi Singer minces no words:

On the Urban Crisis
One would think Jewish philanthropies would cast a sympathetic glance at the plight of the Jew in the integrated areas of our big cities. These people are not members of the affluent society. This is still the world of Bernard Malamud's fiction, of the neighborhood mama-papa grocery store and the tiny corner stationery. These are the Jews who are being beaten into the ground by black-Jewish tensions, and they need help. They are not getting any from the WASP establishment, but then I never really expected that. What horrifies me is that they are not getting it from the Jewish establishment either. The Federation of Jewish Philanthropies in New York has not made efforts to ransom Jewish businessmen from the ghettos. The government agencies set up to encourage the development of black capitalism will not lend a hand to the burned-out Jewish merchant who can no longer get insurance, and needs help to relocate in a white neighborhood. No attention has been

paid to the fact that the Hassidic community in Williamsburg, Brooklyn, is the third largest poverty area in New York City. The WASPs worry about the blacks but the Jewish establishment does not worry about the Jews. One problem is that the Jews who control the Jewish organizations cannot get any headlines out of helping their own people. There is no prestige in it, no cachet. The only way to sell such a program to wealthy liberal Jews who allocate the funds is to convince them that relocating poor Jews would help to improve relations with the blacks.

Said Rabbi Singer, "Mobility is the curse of Jewish life." Whatever the relationships between Jew and Gentile in Hartford are today, they were different thirty, forty, and fifty years ago when there was a complement of Jewish merchants in town who owned hardware, luggage, shoe, and clothing stores. Mobility has destroyed such enterprise. Small merchants find their livelihood now in the department stores on a franchise or concession basis. Only the big department stores can offer the variety to attract the disparate suburban trade.

Mobility also destroys the epicenter of Jewish life, the combination of temple and family. It makes the young vulnerable to fads. One day they are pro-civil rights, the next anti-Vietnam, and the next pro-ecology. The extreme left, a political vogue, is overpopulated by young Jews. "Abbie Hoffman and Mark Rudd," Rabbi Singer said, "are not coincidences."

Rabbi Stanley Kessler of Conservative Beth El on Albany Avenue, dark, sanguine, and lean as a cowboy, is also a writer. On his trips to Russia, South America, Europe, and Selma, Alabama, he is one of the correspondents for the *Hartford Courant*.

The rabbi is an activist with lines of communication into the black community despite the intransigence of the militants. In fact, one of the black Baptist churches sent off a petition in behalf of Soviet Jewry to President Nixon because of Kessler's activism in their behalf.

When the rabbi went to Selma in 1965, some of his congregation tried to dissuade him. Their suggestion that he stay home was couched strongly enough that Kessler wondered if Beth El would ask him to stay on.

Throughout this bitter history, the pressure of Jewish congregations more often than not has persuaded rabbis to desist. Some Jews are racists and some Jews do not want to upset the applecart.

Beth El's Jews did not dissuade Kessler. In fact, Beth El gave him life tenure. It is obvious that the suggestion of some was not the sentiment of all.

When Kessler discussed Hartford, he said, "The Jewish community here is untouched by race. Its problems are with the Jewish commitment of the young."*

Abraham Feldman, rabbi emeritus of Beth Israel, is still a vigorous community figure though in his seventies. All that betrays his age are eyes magnified by thick spectacles. Feldman, a Litvak and a Zionist, came to this Reform temple populated by parochial Germans in 1925. When it came to a Jewish homeland, the German Jews liked the tall grass and they shuddered at Feldman's Yiddishisms.

But he became Hartford's "goyishe Jew," the Jew whom the Christians approached when they wanted access to the Jewish community.

Christians have philanthropies, too, and they know that not only are Jews capable but they understand philanthropy. Christians have political causes. And many Christians like Jews.

For many years Hartford Catholics and Jews worked in tandem on certain issues. The Jews helped the Catholics lobby for stringent adoption laws and the Catholics helped the Jews lobby against humane slaughtering bills. Protestants and Jews work easily on the problem of world hunger and Protestants often lend themselves to Jewish ecumenism.

Feldman became the goyishe Jew simply by making himself available. He was the Jewish chaplain for the Connecticut National Guard and the rabbi for the Institute of Living, a world-famous mental-therapy center in Hartford. "Pastoral duties" never claimed him from controversial causes. Feldman was also the rabbi priests and ministers sought to help them put together an interfaith housing project for the elderly poor of Hartford.

The altruism of the clergy was rewarded with a project not only completed with efficiency and dispatch but which is now self-

---

* What always strikes me as odd about these worry sessions is the unwillingness of the adults to admit that religion often bores the young. There is, after all, a lot in most religion which bores adults. We know from historical research that the biblical Jews had trouble collecting the daily minyan. Murry Shapiro of the Hartford Jewish Community Center, a superb raconteur, tells an appropriate story. A young boy from New York City was registered in one of the Center's summer programs by his uncle. During the registration interview, Shapiro asked the youngster what school he attended. "Yeshiva," said the boy. The following summer, the boy registered again. To the question what school he attended, he said, "P.S. 107." "How come you don't attend yeshiva any more?" asked Shapiro. "Because I stink in Chumash," said the boy.

supporting. Elderly Catholic, Protestant, and Jewish couples live in amity and comfort.

Once the project was announced, the Jewish Federation asked Feldman if he needed its energies and organization. Feldman said, "These are priests and ministers who have churches. They understand a rabbi and a temple. The Federation will confuse them."

The Federation saw the sense of this. "Later," said Feldman, "the Federation undertook a similar project for the Jewish elderly. But they had a legal fight with the Jews on Bishop's Corner when they tried to locate the project on the reservation."

THE HONORS OF THE LAND

"The center of gravity," said Rabbi Howard Singer of Temple Emmanuel, "has shifted from the synagogue to the Federation." This articulation did not make the rabbi happy.

"The most prestigious post for a Jew in Hartford," said cigar-smoking Rabbi Harold Silver (a nephew of Abba Hillel), "was the presidency of Beth Israel. No one competes for it any more. The Federation has usurped the talent." The rabbi took a hearty puff. He looked as though he could live with the fact.

The rabbis were discussing "Jewish leaders," words dear to the Jewish vocabulary, the fulcrum term in the dialogue between the rabbis and the professionals.

Jewish leaders are a variety of men. Sometimes they are rich. Lou Rogow of Hartford is without peer as a Jewish leader because he contributes $1 million every year to the Federation drive. Not many cities of 30,000 have a leader of this caliber.

Sometimes the Jewish leader is a successful fund raiser. When Hartford planned a new community center a decade ago, the drive recruited a great many Jewish leaders never recruited before principally because this new center would house a deluxe health club. Once the steam opened the glands, some of these leaders resigned their commissions. Still, the remaining leaders raise almost $5 million every year.

One might think that the executive director of the Hartford Federation, Irving Kessler, is the prototypical director. But piety and thoughtfulness characterize Kessler rather than aggressiveness and urbanity. His wit is professorial and dry. He is, I suspect, the only successful mystic in Federation work.

Sometimes the Jewish leader is a pillar of the community, well known, admired. Lou Roth, an RCA distributor, was surety to Hartford banks that whatever money the Jewish community borrowed would be repaid. Bill Savitt, a jeweler, invented a phrase which has passed into Hartford's language. His advertising promised customers POMG—Peace Of Mind Guarantee. Savitt was probably the only merchant in the United States who took out full-page advertisements to welcome a new Korvette's to town.

The Jewish leader need not be rich; often he is not. Nor need he be particularly adept at fund raising: Everett Fink, a Hartford lawyer, interrupted himself to take a phone call, spoke two minutes, hung up, and said to me in cheerful amazement, "The Federation asked me to solicit only one man for his pledge *and he called me!*"

Jewish leadership depends not so much on commanding influence as it does on commanding *derekh eretz,* respect (literally, the honors of the land). A man commands derekh eretz when he can help resolve not only tensions within the Jewish community but tensions within the larger community of which it is part.

One of these leaders is Harry Kleinman, identifiably a Jew, president of a gamut of organizations from the B'nai B'rith to the Zionist Council; also, chairman for the last ten years of the West Hartford Democratic Town Committee.

During his tenure, West Hartford has elected its first Democratic mayor and councilmen, and at this writing Democrats control the Board of Education. While West Hartford is far from a Democratic stronghold, it is no longer a Republican fief.

A lawyer from Yale and the Harvard Law School, Kleinman rattles off his sentences like a Sten gun. "There are three reasons why West Hartford changed," he said. "Being a Democrat is no longer economically unwise, politically stupid, or socially unacceptable. The chief executive officer of the Connecticut National Bank is a Democrat. The junior executives in big business are Democrats. And labor is Democratic."

Until the fifties the Democratic Town Committee of West Hartford was an Irish political club composed of workingmen and ward heelers. The Republican Town Committee was composed of men who had all gone to the correct prep schools. Then the new people started to move in—college-educated Irish Catholics, Jews, Protestant brokers who had attended the Downtown Pensacola Teachers College, and veterans, groups which refused to be submerged by the prevailing mores.

About his success as the party chairman, Kleinman has the modesty born of confidence. He describes himself as an amateur (lawyers are always amateurs, like Russian hockey players). Evolution in politics consists of ringing doorbells, licking envelopes, and registering voters. Someone, however, has to direct this, organize it, and it was Harry.

"The Democratic Party," continued Kleinman, "is the party of the moderates. Polarization kills us. We have no cadre like the Republicans. We must always have the coalition."

The West Hartford Democrats are a coalition of workingmen and white-collar insurance-company employees, of Irishmen, Protestants, and Jews, of whom there are sixteen out of forty-three members on the Town Committee.

Make no mistake about the Jews, he warned. They are moderates, much more moderate than the others. Moderate on all issues. They may be called extremists because on a Board of Education budget, they will always opt for curriculum. But the extremists are the Republicans, who always opt for plant. The Republicans will put industrial carpeting in a new school because they think it saves money on maintenance. On a rainy day the school smells like the muskrats' burying ground. The sixteen Jews on the West Hartford Town Committee voted for a legalized-abortion plank in the state Democratic platform because they see legalized abortion as a religious issue.

Politics is important to the Jews of West Hartford. They do not have meaningful representation on the communitywide activities like the United Fund or the Red Cross or the Hartford Process, nor are many on the Board of the Atheneum Museum, nor the trustees of the universities and colleges. But in the Democratic and Republican political arenas (more Jews are Democrats but a great many are Republicans) they join with Gentiles on an absolutely equal footing.

Attribute this to the nature of Connecticut politics. Connecticut was a state with a political apparatus, a machine. Senator Abraham Ribicoff, a Jew, and John Bailey, the State and later National Democratic Party chairman, were John F. Kennedy's first supporters. But the state and city machines, Kleinman said, are now moribund. They can no longer deliver. The constituency took power away. Connecticut along with New Hampshire lent Eugene McCarthy's candidacy momentum in 1968 with delegate primaries in dozens of towns. Earlier,

antiwar Democrats ran congressional primaries and third-ticket candi-
dacies against incumbents who supported Lyndon Johnson. In 1970,
dissident Democrats backed antiwar Joe Duffy in a senatorial primary
and beat the machine (but Joe lost the election to Lowell Weicker).
Members of the Connecticut delegation helped draft the McGovern
rules for convention representation. The success of these efforts depended upon the grass-roots constituencies, the committed citizen
who read and understood the election and primary laws and applied
them in order to effect change. Minority and cultural as well as economic differences have been subsumed under ideological allegiance.

Not that Harry Kleinman is happy about West Hartford primaries.
He asked what was wrong with the smoke-filled back rooms which
had produced a Franklin D. Roosevelt, a Robert Wagner, and a Harry
Truman. I learned from another source that his own candidacy for
the West Hartford Town Committee had been dangerously challenged
by insurgents.

Jews have been known to cut a Democratic candidate in favor
of a Republican. But the moderates always cut, said Kleinman, for
their own interests. The Democratic Irish cut Emilio Daddario in favor of Thomas Meskill for governor because Meskill was an Irish
boy who had once studied for the priesthood. Republican Jews voted
for Ribicoff almost to a man. But Jews in politics rarely confuse form
and substance. He pointed to the primary election between Bella
Abzug and the late William Fitts Ryan in New York City. "Bella
lost because the Jews didn't vote for her. They knew the issue wasn't
over women's rights or Vietnam. Bella is one of the ultra-ultra liberals
who always want it all their own way. No compromise. No moderation. The ultra-ultras always count on the Jews. But the ultra-ultras
are wrong. Without the Eugene McCarthys and the Joe Duffys and
the George McGoverns, the ultra-ultras would get zilch. The Jews
do not buy Vietnam amnesty, increased welfare, or women's lib. The
Jews in Connecticut were not for McGovern, they were for Muskie."

He paused. He had the lawyer's tactic of punctuating his opinions
with rhetorical questions. He asked one now. "But you know what
Voltaire said?"

Since we had been discussing Bella Abzug and the women's liberation movement, I answered, "Voltaire said women are dumber than
men but their legs are nicer than men's."

"No!" said Harry crossly. "Voltaire said, 'I may not agree with what you say but I will fight to the death for your right to say it.'" I fully expected him to turn to an imaginary judge and complain, "Yer Honor, will you instruct the witness to cease utilizing his own knowledge."

Another of Hartford's Jewish leaders is Jerry Wagner, also a lawyer, who lives in nearby Bloomfield. A pipe smoker with rugged good looks, he sat beneath a framed Yale diploma. The Jewish lawyers I talked to in Hartford went to Yale or Harvard or the University of Connecticut Law School. These schools obviously are the first strands of the legal web up there.

Wagner is more immersed in Jewish affairs than any other layman. He is the chairman of a half dozen Federation Committees, an officer of the American Jewish Congress, a prime mover in the Hebrew High School, an organizer of the Solidarity Day program. He has undertaken the unexciting community tasks but in accomplishing these has established a reputation. No matter what the subject I broached in Hartford, men said, "You gotta talk to Jerry Wagner about this."

At the moment, he was involved in a project of his own. He was starting a census of Jewish students in Connecticut colleges. He told me there was a time when Jewish students went to six schools in the state, each of which had a Hillel chapter. Since the college explosion, these students go now to twenty colleges, some of them only two years old, schools which offer Jewish students little of extracurricula Jewish interest.

Wagner's concerns about students who already have a universe ranging from pot to mutiny to occupy them might be amusing except for the realization that this man is a citizen twenty-four hours a day.

An authority on housing, Wagner is the author of a paper outlining the trends in suburban zoning and their implications for the Jews (which he authored as a vice-chairman of the Council of Jewish Federations and Welfare Funds).

He makes these points: because of the scarcity and high cost of urban land, housing needs must be satisfied in the suburbs; additionally, the movement of industry to the suburbs has increased this pressure as the labor force in the cities becomes more remote and isolated from jobs. But the suburbs have insisted on large-lot zoning in a successful effort to realize the maximum in property taxes while keeping service costs to the minimum.

As for implications for the Jews, I shall let Wagner speak for himself:

> Unlike many other aspects of the so-called urban crisis, which is really a national crisis, the action is in the suburbs, where large numbers of Jews live, have their synagogues and community institutions. Because of both our ethical and social-action commitments, we cannot afford to remain out of the action. The corollary of this first proposition is that precisely because so many Jews live in the suburbs, a major job of interpretation to our suburban Jewish community lies before us, and must be given a high priority on our agenda.
>
> Second, I am afraid that there is little evidence to suggest that suburban Jews are very different from other suburbanites in their zeal to protect their property values and neighborhoods and thereby justify exclusionary zoning practices. . . .
>
> Our job is to develop the forces of moderation, and avoid the type of polarization which has developed on the issues of school desegregation and busing. . . .
>
> The basic point must be made that a local community will be far better off if it voluntarily opens its doors, pursuant to a locally conceived plan, rather than to be compelled to do so under pressure from the courts, or the state or federal government.

A third Jewish leader is Murry Shapiro, a professional, the executive director of the Hartford Jewish Community Center. Shapiro, a Brooklyn boy, is in his early fifties, short, combatative, intelligent, humorous—and fluent in Italian. "Not," he says, "because I am a linguist, but because I was a master sergeant guarding Italian POW's during the 1941–45 shootout."

Shapiro has been in Hartford for the last fifteen years, a time of significant changes.

"Fifteen years ago," he said, "we hung a poster on the bulletin board to celebrate Israeli Independence Day. Today the center holds seminars in *aliyah* (immigration).

"The difference in these last fifteen years is not in our identity but how we come by it. Fifteen years ago, the Christians fueled our sense of identity. We were Jews because the hostile world made us Jews and we wanted to prove to that world we were like everyone else. But the society is an open society and likely to remain so. We no longer have a low image of ourselves, nor do the Christians. The Yiddish accents of Allen's Alley are as passé as the Lux Radio Theater of the air. There's little Christian animosity and what there is doesn't help us to become Jews. And when we discuss family 'dysfunction,' which is social-work jargon, we find that drug addiction, a higher divorce rate, and the generation gap make Jewish families like other families."

The Jewish Community Center (sometimes the Young Men's Hebrew Association) flourishes in virtually every city in America, even in towns as small as Holyoke, Massachusetts. The center is the invention of the German Jews who established the first in Baltimore in 1854. These centers were suddenly and increasingly invigorated by the immigration of the Russians. Hundreds were established to help "Americanize" the immigrant, to teach him the language, culture, and mores of the New World.

Even among themselves, the Jews find no peace. Solomon Schechter, the great rabbinical scholar from London who came to America as the head of the Jewish Theological Seminary, resigned from the board of the Educational Alliance in 1902 charging that the immigrant did not need "Americanizing," he needed "Judaizing." The "unsectarian religion" of the community center, Schechter charged, would one day devour Jews just as ruthlessly as the prejudice of Christians.

Marshall Sklare writes, "The overriding fact is that the center should now be the prominent institution in the Jewish community. As Jews have become more secularized the center should have emerged as a logical option to the synagogue. Indeed it should have largely replaced the synagogue. But judged by any yardstick—the size of membership, the amount of resources, or institutional morale—the synagogue is far ahead of the center."

But temple membership does not mean much to Jews. Rabbis are quick to complain that Jews join the temple for their children. Nor does theology much interest Jews, even though they have produced theologians as profound as Richard Rubenstein, Emil Fackenheim, and Jacob Neusner from Hartford itself, whose father, Sam Neusner, published the *Jewish Ledger* for thirty years.

"Change is slow," said Rabbi Harold Silver, studying the twirling smoke from his fourth cigar, "and Jews are slower. But the center and the Federation promise Jews something the synagogue cannot. They are promising we can participate in an international community, not only with Israel but now with Soviet Jews and sooner or later with South American Jews and with European Jews. That is what our identity is about, the hope of a world community. The center fosters political identity and the temple fosters religious identity."

Murry Shapiro is a Jewish leader, because the center has become a vehicle for Jewish identity. Like the Tumble Brook Country Club, it serves more than a recreational purpose. It is the nondenominational meeting place for Reform, Conservative, and Orthodox Jews. It is a model of unity and a model with prospects.

My lawyer friend Ev Fink mused that Hartford was a small town. "It makes us who are Jews turn inward. In other towns, Pittsburgh or Cleveland, if you don't get certain business from the banks, why you can probably get it from the corporations or the developers or the state. Here, if you don't get certain business, you don't get it at all. You start to rely on fellow Jews. And this reliance creates a society. We need a Federation and a center and a hospital to convince us we're a society."

HOUSEGUESTS

Not long ago, the American Jewish Committee issued a report, picked up by the *New York Times,* that in Hartford there wasn't one Jewish vice-president in all of the insurance companies. One of the insurance companies took exception to this. They named their Jewish vice-president. To which the Committee replied that it was easy to miss a Jew who did not belong to a temple, was not a member of the Federation or any of the Jewish organizations or fellowships, and did not have Jewish friends.

But the gravamen of the Committee's charge, that the insurance industry discriminates against Jews, which is true, was lost in the welter of the dispute, "Who is a Jew?"

Jolly Everett Fink, president of the Hartford chapter of the American Jewish Committee, told me a similar story. It happened when he was implementing the Executive Suite program (in which Jewish men of substance try to persuade industry and business it is to their interest to hire and advance Jewish workers). Fink had approached the president of a utility company, of which there are few in Hartford, though all are powerful, and in which there are no Jews.

The utility company president said, "But we have a Jewish vice-president. Mr. Wolff is Jewish."

Fink stared bewildered. He had never heard of Mr. Wolff and, after all, a utility-company vice-president who is Jewish is *sui generis*.

The president explained that the man's employment was not token. The utility had competed with several others to obtain his services from Detroit.

"You never announced his coming in the newspapers," said Fink. "Don't you think it has some public-relations value?"

"Mr. Wolff asked us not to," said the president.

"Then it dawned on me," said Fink. "This guy was kosher, all right. He wanted to slip into town. He didn't want the Federation on his doorstep the next morning asking him for a five-thousand-dollar pledge."

The Executive Suite program produces an amazing wealth of anecdotes. In Cleveland, the Committee filled a big industrialist with a desire for social equity. This employer, who heretofore had hired no Jews, promised he could put on dozens of young Jewish women as secretaries, analysts, personnel staff, and public-relations advisers. Joy turned to despair when the Jewish girls said they wouldn't work where there were no Jewish boys.

There are 200 working-class Jewish families in Hartford who act out the same attitudes and manners of other working-class families, among which is an inability or unwillingness to relate to the community in any meaningful way. They are not the Boy Scout leaders or the blood bank donors (unless their employer leads them to the needle) nor the PTA Council members. Nor are these Jews among the members of a temple or synagogue. For the workingman, the bowling team is sufficient.

The Jewish professor or college teacher is also apt to leave the Jewish community. He joins another community, of course, the academic community, a tighter community, perhaps a more attractive one. Rabbis and communal workers say the majority of Jewish college teachers are probably circumcised, were probably married in a temple if they married a Jew, and may be buried in a Jewish cemetery.

It is hard to assess the character and sentiments of the escaped Jews because they are outside the network. Curiously, these Jews—and I am not describing here the Jew who is an amateur Gentile—often become the Jewish representatives to the Gentile community. Clifton Fadiman, who for years refused to let *Who's Who* list him as Jewish, was in the late thirties and the forties *the* Jewish intellectual. Bernard Baruch was the personification of Jewish influence in

Washington and Wall Street. Baruch was as unstereotyped as a Jew can get—he wore a floppy hat, sat on a park bench, and fed pigeons when he wasn't advising presidents. His wizardry on behalf of Jewish interests was much like that of the Wizard of Oz, who confessed to Dorothy in the end that he was a very good man but a very bad wizard.

These Jews are the houseguests of the community. They eat as much food as anyone in the family, take up as much space, and muss as many beds. But one has to wait until they leave before making family decisions.

One such Jew in Hartford is Sam Rome—Major Sam Rome—for thirty-three years the toughest cop in the Detective Bureau of the State Police. Rome was the police officer who caught the Boston Strangler, Albert Di Salvo, who raped and assaulted women in Connecticut as well as Massachusetts. Rome traced the rapist's journeys across the state and compared his method of operation with that of the Strangler. They were one and the same. Rome realized the Strangler was murdering his victims in Boston and Cambridge because they might recognize him, recognize him because he lived there. He spared his victims in Connecticut because he was away from home. Rome took two of these victimized women to Boston, where one of them fainted when the Boston cops showed her, among a dozen mug shots, a photograph of Albert Di Salvo.

Rome has been a controversial cop because he is tough and mean. He described a case which came across his desk one morning: a woman who lived with two men in a trailer camp had been murdered. Rome didn't bother with the case because he saw it was obvious that one of the two men did it. But that evening the investigating team reported they could establish a case against neither.

Rome went to the morgue, inspected the murdered woman, saw that she had been kicked to death, and then presented himself at the local precinct, where police held the two suspects. He sized up the men and said to the husband, "I've got to talk to you alone."

The suspect said that was a violation of his constitutional rights.

"What constitutional rights?" asked Rome shocked. "Your wife has been murdered. The State of Connecticut will spend $1 million to catch her killer. You have to help me. Your wife, man, is dead."

Once alone, Rome commanded, "Pull up your pants or I'll pull them up for you." There on the suspect's socks and on his skin was the splattered blood of the dead wife.

Retired now, blue-eyed, muscular Rome is the chief of Sanitast Security, a company that provides private police for industry and small business. Rome said, "Sanitast is growing. Everybody needs security these days."

When I discussed my meeting with him with other Jews, one of them asked, "Why would you come to a perfectly viable Jewish community like Hartford and spend your time with Sam Rome, who is an exotic?"

Rome had told me that for many years appointments to the State Police were part of the political system and that that political system favored the Irish. In 1937, the year the merit system went into effect, Rome was the first Jew ever appointed. He had finished eighth out of five thousand applicants. He made ninety dollars a month, one day off out of every thirty.

Overt anti-Semitism was popular in the nineteen-thirties, and Sam Rome had to live with it. "Unusual facility," he said matter-of-factly, "excites jealousy, and I had unusual facility. Cops call it 'gut sense.' Sometimes when my tour was over, I used to ask the captain if I could go home for the night like the other troopers. The anti-Semite always gave me permission but he always insisted I ride the motorcycle. Hell, I lived forty miles away. Getting to the barracks in the morning was a day's work."

Everyone in Hartford knows Sam Rome is a Jew. He rode a motorcycle back and forth to prove it.

PITTSBURGH: Club Walls

THE GATEWAY CITY

Fort Duquesne was the center of the French picket line. It commanded the confluence of the Monongahela and Allegheny Rivers, where they join in a Y to become the Ohio. If the French could hold New Orleans, Fort Duquesne, and Montreal, they denied the British everything to the west.

In 1755, Major General Edward Braddock with 700 Colonial militiamen and 1400 British regulars marched on Duquesne. The French and the Indians ambushed the expedition while it was crossing the Allegheny, inflicting 977 casualties. Washington, one of the Colonial officers who had warned Braddock about guerrilla tactics, survived the massacre to command two regiments under General John Forbes in 1758, when the British tried again. Forbes was smarter than Braddock. He moved on Duquesne with a force of 7000, establishing supply depots along the way. The French, after an initial skirmish, realized they were outnumbered, razed the Fort, and left.

Forbes wrote the British Prime Minister, William Pitt, "I have used the freedom of giving your name to Fort Duquesne, as I hope it was in some measure the being actuated by your spirit that now makes us the masters of the place." And the British remained masters for the next eighteen years, until George Washington took matters into his own hands.

After the Revolutionary War, Pittsburgh became the "Gateway City." The settlers moved over the Alleghenies along the road, which had once been the French supply line, and from Pittsburgh pushed into Ohio, Indiana, and on to the Mississippi.

When John Knox, the founder of the Presbyterian Church, threw himself to his knees and prayed, "O Lord, give me Scotland," God threw in Pittsburgh, too. One half of the Presbyterians in the United States live within a hundred-mile radius of the city.

Pittsburgh gave birth to the concept of a free and independent Czechoslovakia.

Jan Masaryk, the first president of the ill-fated republic, had married an American and came to the United States during World War I to talk to Woodrow Wilson.

On May 30, 1918, Masaryk attended a meeting of American Czechs and Slovaks in Pittsburgh. This convention drew up a plan for a union of these two peoples in which Slovaks would have a separate parliament, administration, and court system. Masaryk signed it. It was known as the Pittsburgh Treaty and guided the peacemakers at Versailles and Geneva.

In 1885, the Reform rabbis of America met in Pittsburgh. For half a century thereafter, the Pittsburgh Platform articulated the principles of Reform Jewry. The rabbis met under the auspices of Temple Rodef Shalom, which had been organized in a room over the Vigilante Fire Department. You could put five Vigilante Fire Departments in the present Rodef Shalom on Forbes Street.

Cotton was once important to Pittsburgh's economy and so was shipbuilding. In World War II, the Pittsburgh shipyards launched hundreds of Liberty vessels down their ways while its factories produced $19 billion worth of munitions.

It is the home of United States Steel, founded by Andrew Carnegie, for whose mills Henry Clay Frick once provided coke. Where Fort Duquesne guarded the river approaches, the Mellon Banking Building rises like a lone sentinel, high enough to compare with any skyscraper in New York or Chicago. Alcoa manufactures aluminum in Pittsburgh and H. J. Heinz started making catsup here. Pittsburgh Plate Glass, Westinghouse, Gulf—it is a city which boasts a corporate rather than a conglomerate image, productive rather than actuarial. With a population of 600,000, it describes itself as too small to be a big town and too big to be a small one.

Because it is the home of big business, it is also the home of big labor. The United States Steelworkers are headquartered here. From a plateau on one of the neighborhood mountains, one can look south across the Monongahela to the Homestead area, steel mills lining the riverfront like the walls of a medieval fortress, smoke pouring from their cylindrical chimneys. The wives of the steelworkers never complained about dirty curtains because grit and smog meant the mills were working. Clean curtains signaled unemployment. Science has since scoured the smoke. The mills no longer deposit Alleghenies of soot along the window sills.

Above the mills, houses climb haphazardly, crowding together, as Carl Sandburg put it, like hundreds of dice tossed against the side of a hill. When the workers went on strike in 1892, Frick hired three hundred Pinkerton agents to guard property and protect the lives of scabs. These agents arrived in Homestead on barges. As they disembarked, the strikers attacked. In one of the bloodiest battles of the labor wars, almost a hundred men lost their lives. The governor of Pennsylvania called out the National Guard, which broke the strike. Things have changed in Homestead. Television aerials porcupine from the dice. But the bars in Homestead are as busy on Saturday night as they ever were.

No matter how urbane or sophisticated, the visitor to Pittsburgh will have to admire the city's unexpected beauty. It is no mill town. Neither is it megalopolis.

Lewis Mumford once argued that the test of a beautiful city was whether the citizen could "see" himself within it. If he joined a parade, could he see the line of march turn ahead of him? Could he see the neighborhood in perspective or could he see only a grid? Did the geography add variety to the city?

From any one of the bridges which stitch the parts of Pittsburgh together, the pedestrian can see a dozen more up and down the river. Below, coal barges noiselessly push against the current. The Allegheny and Monongahela, which slice through the mountains, divide Pittsburgh into three parts, each of which is a self-contained unit. With a little stamina, the citizen could walk to any of the neighborhood's natural borders, and because he can, he feels less anonymous, more of an integer.

One goes downhill to work in the morning and uphill toward home at dusk, as farmers used to, for the bottom land was always the richest. The bottom land in Pittsburgh is the Golden Triangle, the business and shopping district, and from one of the viaducts which traverse this valley or from a vantage point in one of the steep parks, the Golden Triangle looks at night like an illuminated Erector Set construct placed carefully in the bottom of a big bowl.

SQUIRREL HILL

Many of the first Jews to come to Pittsburgh came with the Neu-landers—the Slavs, Czechs, Poles, and Hungarians recruited by agents in the eighteen-forties and -fifties to work in the mills and on the railroads. The agents recruited the Jews to run the company-owned stores.

Forty years later, the shtetl Jews came to Pittsburgh. They were peddlers, storekeepers, bakers, carpenters, and a great number of them found work in Pittsburgh's stogie industry. Cigar making always numbered many Jews. Samuel Gompers, who helped found the American Federation of Labor, was a cigar maker. There are reasons why the Jews chose employment in this rather than in the heavy industries of Pittsburgh. Jews worked in the foundries and mills only when they could pass as Hungarians or Rumanians. They lacked skills for other industries. Stripping and rolling the cigar, however, were not demanding tasks. They were easily mastered. Lastly, these newly immigrated Jews were Orthodox and wanted work in an industry which would allow them to observe the Sabbath and the Jewish holidays. German Jews owned the cigar factories. It was a natural place of employment.

Forty-five thousand Jews live in Pittsburgh today. They work in many of the professions, in small businesses, in education (it is said there are too many Jewish teachers and not enough Jewish principals), and in the scientific complexes of big industry. Almost all of these Jews live in the Squirrel Hill district, the city's Fourteenth Ward, which they populate fifty-fifty with Christians.

Pittsburgh is one of the last major cities whose residents have not left it. There has been no substantial outmigration to the suburbs. There are small towns surrounding Pittsburgh, but their dependence on the city is symbiotic, not parasitic. People who come from Pittsburgh live in Pittsburgh, within the city limits, their taxes supporting municipal services, schools, and parks. The very rich—the Mellons, the Heinzes, the Kauffmans, who made their money in Pittsburgh—did not leave. Nor did their money.

Place, and the sense of place, has a sustaining value to Italians, Poles, and Hungarians. Within the city, their neighborhoods often remain inviolate. They want to die in the house they were born in and sometimes they die in the house their father was born in.

Squirrel Hill has this sustaining value for the Jews for three reasons. The first of these is convenience.

Squirrel Hill is cut through the middle by Forbes Street and Forbes Street is the direct line downhill to the Golden Triangle. It is easy to get to work. Before Forbes dips to the valley floor, it bisects Oakland. The Oakland district, part of Squirrel Hill, houses the University of Pittsburgh, which, despite its Cathedral of Learning, has a reasonably spacious campus. Pitt's neighbor is the Carnegie-Mellon Institute, once Carnegie Tech, a prestigious engineering school. Not far away, toward downtown, is Catholic Duquesne University, and in Squirrel Hill itself are Chatham College, a swank girls' school, and Carlo College, another Catholic institution.

Lining Oakland's bluff are three hospitals, clinics, dispensaries, medical and graduate schools, one massive structure after the other. Here in Oakland, too, are the offices of the doctors.

There are also several Mellon and Carnegie Museums scattered here and there as well as a Civil War Memorial Auditorium.

Oakland's streets are filled with blind people, tapping their way with a white cane. The area houses a school for the blind and the newcomer later learns that nurses and teachers follow close behind. But it is disheartening at first to see so many blind passing among so many unconcerned.

If the Jewish community wanted to move, still the topography of Pittsburgh conspires to keep it in Squirrel Hill. To leave Pittsburgh means traveling through a tunnel. No builder who has ever pinned blueprints has thought it profitable or easy to throw up a development on the side of a precipice.

West Hartford is separated from Hartford and Cleveland Heights from Cleveland by an imaginary line. Passage from the city to the suburb is imperceptible to the autoist. But a tunnel is not a symbolic line; the countryside on one side of the tunnel is different from the countryside on the other and tunnels, as any autoist knows, are no way to facilitate heavy traffic.

The streets of Squirrel Hill are lined by hedges behind which trees, which could thrive in concrete bunkers, spread their shade. The homes do not proceed from the modest at one end of the street to the ostentatious at the other. The Frick, Kauffman, and Mellon estates still survive, but a rich man who wants a big house in Squirrel

Hill has to buy and tear down three small ones. So there are startling homes, cheek by jowl with smaller ones.

The third reason the Jews have stayed put is that the blacks in Pittsburgh have made no encroachment upon the white neighborhoods. The blacks live in three separate districts in Pittsburgh, one of them the Hill district, above Squirrel Hill, where once the Jews lived.

Pittsburgh was never a stopping-off point for the black migration from the South nor did steel ever recruit black workers as the motor industry did. When Pittsburgh's Human Relations Committee ordered desegregation with attendant busing, neither the Jews nor their Christian neighbors boycotted the schools. But so far, this integration has been minimal. The blacks in Pittsburgh are not militant and there are proportionately fewer of them than in many other cities.

There is some peripheral anti-Semitism. Mount Lebanon, a small town near Pittsburgh in which another 10,000 Jews live, is often called Mount Leibowitz, and some of the private schools, which are numerous, denote Jewish students with "OT," which the kids have discovered means "Old Testament." Few Jews have influential positions within the corporations, and consequently fewer Jews are on the boards of directors or among the trustees of the venerable and powerful institutions.

But the professional who operates Heinz Hall, the home of the symphony, is a Jew, and without Jewish support there would probably be no Pittsburgh Symphony Orchestra.

The governor of Pennsylvania, Milton Shapp, is Jewish, and the number of Jews who are federal or state judges is out of proportion to the Jewish population.

In Pittsburgh's Squirrel Hill, the Jews have an investment of 19 Orthodox, 9 Conservative, and 4 Reform temples. Not to mention 6 *yeshivot,* a Hebrew high school, a weekly newspaper, a community center, some small libraries, and the headquarters of the Jewish Federation, which last year raised $4.5 million.

Few of the Jews in Pittsburgh ever go on to the vice-presidency or the presidency of the national Jewish organizations. When they do, they serve reluctantly. These honors and responsibilities do not attract them. But perhaps there is another reason. There are greater internal differences between Jews in Pittsburgh than in comparable cities. These are not divisive differences but still they are differences. Jews live amid an intellectual milieu which fosters self-criticism.

They live in a stable community. They are familiar with one another. They may have ceased trying to impress their neighbors. There are Jews of position and influence, for example, who do not contribute to the Federation drives. They have lived within view of the very rich, and the very rich are often unconcerned about their money and what others think they ought to do with it.

One Jewish businessman told me that if I wanted to use his name he would tell me where he was when the Japs bombed Pearl Harbor and what he was doing when Kennedy was assassinated. If I didn't use his name he wanted to tell me that it was neither imaginative nor necessary for the American Jewish Committee to integrate the Duquesne Club, one of the famous men's dining clubs in the country. "The three Jews eventually invited for membership were already vice-presidents of the firms for which they worked, so neither the Duquesne Club nor the AJC was doing them any favors," he went on.

"The Duquesne Club has over two thousand members. There are always fifty openings reserved for the board members of Gulf whether they are good fellows or bad fellows, whether they will pay their dues or not. These memberships are one of the ways Pittsburgh has of thanking Gulf for setting up shop in the city. But the AJC did not move to integrate the Concordia Club, which has only three hundred members, all of whom are Jews, and which from time to time turns down applications of Jews who are corporation vice-presidents.

"You know what Jews do to Christians in this town?" he asked. "They threaten them. John O'Hara made a lot of money writing novels, some of them even good novels, about the Pennsylvania rich. There are men in Pittsburgh who spend as much time choosing a foursome for golf as they spend choosing stocks for their portfolio. They cast their dinner parties with the professionalism a Broadway producer casts his show.

"The Jews threaten them because the Jews are right below them on the ladder. And the Jews are frenzied about their fund raising. But they are allocating prestige, not power. The Mellon Foundation gave Montefiore Hospital $200,000. That's the kind of integration we should aim for. I am not sure whether we can support Israel or our agencies forever. Maybe we will have to ask someone else for this money someday. I am willing to make a deal with the Christians. For that $200,000 and their kindness, they can keep the Duquesne Club, which was theirs to begin with."

THE UNIDENTIFIED FLYING YARMULKA

Murray Avenue, in the middle of Squirrel Hill, plunges precipitously for three long city blocks. Its steep descent does not distinguish it in Pittsburgh, where some of the streets drop like an elevator shaft. What does distinguish Murray Avenue is that it is the center of an old-time Orthodox Jewish neighborhood. Its kosher shops and stores might have been transposed from New York's old Lower East Side or from modern Tel Aviv's Ben Yehuda Street.

The Orthodox housewife shops every day. When she needs six eggs, she buys six eggs, not a dozen, and they are a kosher six, which is to say there is not a spot within the shell. An egg candler has tested each of them. When she boils a chicken, it is a chicken she bought that morning. Nor was the chicken done in by an electric needle. There is a shop on Murray Avenue which deals in kosher fowl exclusively. In it, you can buy a jar of schmalz (chicken fat). Beef comes from a steer slaughtered while conscious with a single deft cut. The Orthodox housewife will buy vegetables from a stall where she can test them tactilely. Madison Avenue has yet to convince her that white bread wrapped in wax paper, doubly protected by a cellophane bag, will appreciably lengthen her life.

Murray Avenue offers her a variety of butchers, grocers, and bakers. A Murray Avenue toy store, which also boasts the last of the lending libraries, sells sacramental wine as well. The window of a vegetable store holds watermelons corded in the corner, beside them carrots, their tops a foliage, then cauliflower, then spinach, the effect as colorful as a first-grader's experiments with finger paints. Bananas hang upside down, clustered on their stalk wheeling slowly on a chain. In the back, near the cash register, I saw an old, old man sitting on a melon case, watching everything. He was the zayde, the grandfather, who opened the stall in 1922 and now spends his last days watching his son, probably a grandfather himself, run the store. The chances of subsequent family succession are running out. Another zayde, with a booming voice, presided over his delicatessen but I noticed his grandson, dishing up chopped chicken livers, wore a T-shirt emblazoned with Texas Tech. Few Texas Tech alumni are in the family delicatessen business unless the delicatessen has gone public.

Missing are the Yiddish accents. In one of the shops that sold religious objects, I talked with a middle-aged gent in black yarmulka and vest of gorgeous colors who was delicately polishing a Chanukah candelabrum. He wondered whether he ought to stick to the Jersey Turnpike and go over the George Washington Bridge into Connecticut or cut off at Harrisburg and go up and around into Trumbull to see his son, an engineer with Xerox. "Maybe the Turnpike," he concluded and shuddered, plunging into one Hebrewism as suddenly as Murray Avenue plunges: "How I hate the *malachim mova* [angels of death]," by which I presume he meant the trailer trucks.

Three pizzerias have made incursion into Murray Avenue and at the base of the hill is one of the state-controlled liquor stores. On a crayoned sign in the window beside the bourbon the lottery number of the week was posted and another printed sign advised lucky winners how to submit their stubs within. Many of the states I visited sponsor lotteries for special income. In Connecticut the winners turn their stubs in at the local Motor Vehicles Bureau, in Pittsburgh at the liquor stores. I await breathlessly the day when the several states federate their lotteries and every month we will have one instant Howard Hughes, which means more work for writers.

Midway down the hill is the Orthodox synagogue Shaare Torah. There are no reliable statistics on the affiliation of Jews to their temple. One of the most likely statistics about Pittsburgh is that 38 percent are Reform, 38 percent Conservative, and 14 percent Orthodox (the remaining percentage just Jews). There are always, however, more Orthodox synagogues than Reform or Conservative temples. That is because the Halakah insists the Orthodox Jew walk to the shul for the Sabbath service. The Orthodox synagogue is a neighborhood rather than a community place of worship. Consequently, it is smaller in size and has fewer congregants. There are, of course, Orthodox synagogues with parking lots. In Hartford, Rabbi Abraham Avigdor put a chain across the parking lot on Rosh Hashanah, to the distress of his congregants, who had to accept traffic tickets for parking in other people's driveways.

Shaare Torah's rabbi is Bernard Poupko. Rabbi Poupko is a man in his fifties, broad-shouldered and bearded with a face of such solemnity that one can only call it biblical. He was born in the Soviet Union, the son of Eliezer Poupko, the Valiezar Reb, whom Stalin sentenced to Siberia.

To Poupko, a Jew is a Jew whether his identity is manifested by daily presence at the shul for the morning minyan or by his use of the swimming pool at the YMHA. "The swimming pool," he proclaimed dogmatically, "is a link with the Jewish heritage as much as the *talis* [the shawl worn in prayer]."

Rabbi Poupko was one of nine rabbis who composed the delegation sent by the Rabbinical Council of America to the Soviet Union in 1956. Its mission was to persuade the Soviet Union to grant visas to American Jews who wanted to visit relatives in Russia. The mission sparked the drive to Save Soviet Jewry.

As Poupko and his fellow rabbis walked around Leningrad, shepherded by an Intourist guide, Jews came out of their shops and disembarked from buses to talk. The American rabbis wore yarmulkas and Russian Jews said they hadn't seen a yarmulka in ten years. When the Americans visited the Baron Ginsburgh Synagogue in Leningrad, the Intourist guide covered his head with his raincoat. "He was of the seed of Jacob, too," said Poupko, eyes glittering.

Jews whispered to the Americans that they could not persuade the Soviet Ministry of Cults and Religions to give them a cemetery and when Poupko tried to determine the whereabouts of his wife's family, he drew a blank from the authorities. Later, when the Americans asked to speak to the aged Abraham Panich, the chief rabbi of Kiev, Soviet hosts said they had no idea where he lived.

In America, Poupko took up the cause of the Soviet Jews by arguing in the rabbinical journals that their plight had to be separated from the politics of the cold war. He believed that by granting rights to its Jewish minority the Soviet Union in no way interfered with the social experiment of Communism.

The Six-day War aggravated the condition of Soviet Jews. Russia, which had supported the Arab cause, became openly anti-Zionist. Poupko's contacts within the Soviet Union informed him that the authorities were more and more repressive.

In 1969, Golda Meir lent the campaign to Save Soviet Jewry impetus. The Prime Minister of Israel had received a petition from eighteen families in the Georgian Republic which asked her to dispatch two enclosed letters to the United Nations Human Rights Commission. These Jews wanted to emigrate to Israel. Before the Knesset, Madame Meir said Israel demanded, as an elementary human right, that the Soviet Union allow all Jews who wished to settle in the Homeland to do so.

For the past three years, the drive to Free Soviet Jewry has steadily gained momentum. On the weekend I was in Pittsburgh, every synagogue, temple and Jewish organization was festooned with banners exhorting, "Free Soviet Jews!"

On the shelves of Rabbi Poupko's study are the traditional books. But there are also piles upon piles of *Pravda,* Soviet foreign-policy journals, newsletters, pamphlets. He dealt six Russian-language magazines from a stack as though they were playing cards and said, "Anti-Zionist. Anti-Semitic. Anti-Jew."

He sat behind a littered desk in a well-oiled swivel chair. As he talked, his whole body responded to his topic and he twirled from right to left and back again for punctuation and emphasis. With each twirl, his yarmulka flew off. Each time he retrieved it adroitly in midair, replaced it, and continued without interruption: "The Jews got up from the Valley of the Bones. Nine thousand Jews left Russia last year. Fourteen thousand will go to Israel this year. All who want to go will leave. It will be a miracle. After fifty years of repression, still they are Jews. We Jews need miracles."

He did a 180-degree swivel. "It is a miracle because the Jews can demand to leave without the threat of death. After Stalin, the Russians stopped killing people. The Jews are the only people in the Soviet Union with an option. Maybe 10 million Russians want to live in Pittsburgh. That is treason. But the Jews can ask to go to Israel because that is not a political but a religious decision."

When I asked why the Russians would let them go, Poupko swung again. "Russia has sixty divisions along its borders facing sixty Chinese divisions. The Communists want a détente with the West so they can deal with the Chinese. The Soviet Union is sensitive to public opinion in the West. Keeping the Jews may not be worth the Big Bear's trouble.

"Now you are going to ask me about the Egyptians," he said, holding up a finger to silence the question. "*Pravda* complains that Egypt sent more Jews to Israel than all the Communist countries put together. Which is true. Russia is making a subtle threat. If the Egyptians do not carefully regard Soviet interests in the Middle East, Russia will send its Jews to Israel.

"This, of course, is good for Israel. The Soviet Jews who come are university graduates, Jews with skills and expertise. They are not shtetl immigrants fit only for brutal work. True, they leave everything behind, but still they come with their brains.

"And the enterprise is good for American Jews, too. We are an ethnic group. Ethnic identity is legitimate, respectable, and desirable. Auschwitz taught us we are never safe and the Soviet Jews give us a chance to work for the cause of Jewish survival."

This time the spinning yarmulka was laid to rest on the desk. Poupko is a persuasive man and a yarmulka juggler beyond repute. But I am not ready to cede him the last word. I am not sure Jews need moral redemption from the Holocaust. Jehuda Bauer of Hebrew University in Jerusalem, the Jewish authority on the Holocaust, has described it as a mountain of such magnitude that history has yet to estimate its size. A Conservative rabbi elsewhere confided that he had no assurance that emigrating to Israel was the prevailing sentiment among Soviet Jews, of whom there are almost 3 million. Even if 1 million left, which would be astronomically high, that would still leave 2 million in Russia as hostages. Because ethnic identity may serve us here, he went on, is no reason to suppose it will serve Jews there. There must be hundreds of thousands of Jews in the Soviet Union who are Communists before they are anything else.

One of the truths about the mission to Save Soviet Jewry is that it is a crisis situation, and American Jews are cohesive in emergencies, which is why they have so many of them.

In many cities, the campaign to Save Soviet Jewry climaxed with Solidarity Day, on which petitions were dispatched to President Nixon to take with him to the Soviet Union. In Hartford, 1500 citizens massed on the capitol lawn to wish these petitions godspeed. The politicians, however, let these New Englanders down. Senator Abraham Ribicoff said he couldn't attend because of the recent death of his wife and Senator Lowell Weicker because he had pressing Senate business to attend to. But how could they guess 1500 constituents would turn out on the first warm afternoon in May?

In Cleveland, 3000 attended the Solidarity Day ceremonies. This was the Sunday before the presidential primary and the politicians there did not let the folks down. If nothing else, 3000 Clevelanders learned what Humphrey, McGovern, and McCarthy were going to do for the citizens of Ohio.

But in Pittsburgh, the home of the movement, only 300 heard Poupko in the rain. William Shaffer, the executive director of the Pittsburgh branch of the American Jewish Committee, said he doubted that the campaign inspired the mystical overtones for Jews that the foundation of Israel or the Six-day War inspired. "The young are enthusiastic about Soviet Jewry," he said, "because it puts them in the traditional role of the underdog. They are uncomfortable as part of the middle-class majority. But they do not realize how protracted a process saving Soviet Jewry will be."

Indeed, Solidarity Day coincided with the end of the Federation campaign in many cities. Whatever else it may be, no one can doubt that the cause of Soviet Jewry lent itself to a renewal of interfaith communication. The executive director of the Protestant Council of Churches availed himself of this opportunity to condemn the atheism of the Soviet Union and so did the Catholic bishop and all his auxiliary bishops. It is good politics and let us hope it will prove effective government.

Walking up the Murray Avenue hill toboggan slide, I realized that out of this small, virtually antique neighborhood, still had come a movement which had inspired intense loyalties and unleashed powerful energies. The United States government has offered refuge to some of the Soviet Jews, and Congressman Jonathan Bingham of New York has introduced a resolution appropriating $85 million for their rescue.

PRE- AND POST-HOLOCAUST RABBIS

Temple Rodef Shalom's rabbi is Walter Jacob, perhaps forty years old, tall, reserved, with the look about him of the passionate pilgrim. When he succeeded to this pulpit five years ago, Walter Jacob was taking the place of one of Pittsburgh's eminences, Rabbi Solomon Freehof, a scholar of impressive reputation here and abroad, a man interesting enough to command two columns in the new Jewish Encyclopedia. Freehof had immense stage presence. For years he filled the auditorium to overflowing on Saturday afternoons with Jews and Christians who came to hear his book reviews. He was an engaging critic with an incisive point of view, although most of the literature he dealt with had little to do with Judaism. He delivered his lectures without notes, which made his audience marvel. But he was in the same situation as Arturo Toscanini, who conducted without a score: both had eyesight so bad the one couldn't read the score and the other couldn't read notes.

Jacob is self-effacing, quiet, not at all flamboyant. The Rodef Shalom board wondered whether Jacob, who had been Freehof's assistant, would be a suitable replacement. The board decided upon the appointment because some of the members argued that at least

Jacob was passive. Subsequently, the board discovered he was not nearly so passive as they had hoped. Rabbi Jacob had no desire to become a notable in the general community, but his scholarship is as instructive as his predecessor's. Jacob is an authority on Christianity as Jews in the modern world have understood it. His book will soon be published. But the subject does not fill the auditorium with overflowing. Then, Jacob has never tried to.

Christianity as a significant area for Jewish theological speculation, he told me, has produced reputable scholars only in countries whose Christian population has assimilated Jews—in pre-Hitler Germany, England, and the United States.

The most interesting of all these theologians was Isaac Meyer Wise (1819–1900), the founder of American Reform Judaism, the first president of the Hebrew Union College in Cincinnati. Wise added little to the study of Jesus and Paul, his special fields; the novelty of his writings was that he was the first American rabbi to pursue such speculation. But he followed other Jewish theologians in pointing out Jewish elements in the life of Jesus and a Jewish basis for Christianity. Wise was sure that Judaism purified of its rabbinic elements would be the religion of the future. "He was an energetic man," says Jacob, with a barely perceptible smile. "He not only reformed Judaism, he wanted to reform Christianity as well."

Whereas Rabbi Jacob is tall and almost diffident, Dr. Herman Heilpern, rabbi emeritus of the Conservative Tree of Life Synagogue, is short and almost garrulous. Now seventy-three, Heilpern is adjunct professor of theology at Duquesne University. He holds forth in a specially insulated room in the Duquesne Library that houses the Heilpern Collection—three thousand volumes on medieval philosophy. These books represent the scholarship Heilpern put into his thirty-year-long research for his book *Rashi and the Christian Scholars* (University of Pittsburgh Press, 1963).

Rashi, who wrote in the eleventh century, takes his name from his initials, *R*abbi *Sh*elomo *I*zhaki. Jews honor wisdom by conferring a nickname on the wise man. Maimonides, the chief philosopher of the Renaissance, is known as the Rambam. Jews do not have a corner on this tradition. Plato translates as "Highbrow."

Rashi owed his intellect solely to Judaism and devoted his life to an explication of the Bible. He remains the supreme commentator whose explications are important to Jewish and Christian scholars alike. Dr. Heilpern's book illuminates the philosophic give and take between Jews and Christians as revealed in their medieval biblical commentaries.

Heilpern is the son of a rabbi. At ordination, he knew what it takes many another rabbi a lifetime to learn, that synagogue attendance never plays the same role in Judaism that church attendance plays in Christianity. He chose as a young man to immerse himself in the study of medieval Judaism because he foresaw that the end of immigration was going to force the American Jewish congregation to become spiritually self-reliant. The steady flow of Talmudists and learned rabbis from Eastern and Central Europe would end.

Despite the similarities among these three rabbis, a chasm separates them, a chasm produced by the Holocaust in Nazi Germany. Freehof and Heilpern are pre-Holocaust rabbis and Jacob post-Holocaust. The first two were always interested in fostering a certain familiarity with Christians, in instilling an admiration in Christians for Jews rather than Judaism. Jacob and the rabbis of his generation are more critical of Christianity and the secular Christian world.

The Holocaust made Jewish theology imperfect. No universe can have both God and a Holocaust. Judaism survived, however, and rabbis ordained after the Holocaust are intent in emphasizing that Judaism is a way that is different from the Christian way. As Jacob poignantly reminded me, Jewish theologians in France, Germany, Russia, and Poland always imperfectly understood Christianity because those Christian countries sooner or later gave them good reason to discontinue their studies.

BALD EAGLES

Montefiore Hospital, one building rising above another like steps, climbs the bluff and ends its procession not far from dun-colored Pitt Stadium.

Other hospitals also besiege the bluff on Forbes Street in Oakland. The gatekeeper for them is a life-sized statue of Stephen Collins Foster, the Pittsburgh boy who wrote "Old Black Joe" and "My Old Kentucky Home." Paternally Foster's statue pats a slave boy on the shoulder. On the spring morning that I passed them, someone had put a bouquet of fresh flowers in the bronze hand of each.

Montefiore, named after the British philanthropist Moses Montefiore, was the Jewish Hospital for decades. Now it is part of the Pittsburgh University Medical School.

"Why would Jews want to give away a $60 million hospital?" I asked.

"Because Jewish doctors like to be called professors," answered an informed source.

Until the turn of the century, hospitals were considered terminal stations on the way to the grave. The invention of anesthesia and antisepsis taught the rich the advantages of hospital rather than home care and convinced them they could buy health just as they could buy anything else.

Shortly thereafter the poor began to think they deserved health as much as their more fortunate brethren.

In 1901, seventeen Jewish women, calling themselves the Ladies Hospital Aid Society, pledged themselves to contribute ten cents a week to build a hospital. They also toured the Jewish neighborhood with their *dushkies* (little tin cups).

In her thesis filed at the Graduate School of Public Health, Lois Michaels, the wife of a Pittsburgh hematologist, attributes the growth of Jewish hospitals to the have-a-littles trying to provide for the have-nots. What spurred the financing was the realization by German Jews that the large influx of poor Eastern European immigrant Jews damaged their advantageous social position. Or, as Oscar Handlin once put it, "Charity, traditionally a religious virtue of Jews, became a categorical imperative."

Passing dushkies was no way to build a hospital. The village customs of the newer immigrant Jews were often ineffective. The older American Jews came to the rescue, but they never came in concert. Each family had its own idea of what a hospital should be and what it should do and usually an even more positive idea of after whom it should be named.

Jewish hospitals, as Mrs. Michaels notes, differ from others in that they are a function of the community, not of the church or the religious bodies. The one goal diverse Jewish groups have in common is providing help for their fellow Jews. Montefiore was established to provide care for sick Jews in a familiar environment. More important was the urge of the Jewish community to establish an institution not only where Jewish doctors could practice but where Jewish doctors and nurses could train as residents and students.

Montefiore opened in a converted mansion in 1908 at the very moment medical costs started rising precipitously (although they had been rising since Hippocrates submitted his first bill). Despite the receipt of $253,500 in 1918 from the state, the rich who could pick up the tab for a college, a museum, or an orphanage had begun to realize no matter how multitudinous they were nor how plentiful their resources, they could not afford to keep picking up the tab for a hospital.

When the Jews needed a new Montefiore, the fund raisers went to the entire community. The new hospital opened in 1929, in trouble from the start. The Crash not only made many of the pledges worthless so that Montefiore had to struggle on mortgage-bound and debt-ridden, but it changed the way people dealt with each other and the way they dealt with their institutions.

The doctors, who had always served on the board of the hospital, resigned lest they risk conflict-of-interest charges. This left the hospital in the hands of businessmen. The best interests of a hospital as an economic unit are not always consonant with the best interests of the patients or the staff.

During the Depression, ten hospitals closed in Pittsburgh. There were times when Montefiore couldn't pay its milk bills, times when its doctors were requested not to bill their patients for medical services until the patients had paid the hospital. Montefiore tried a variety of ways to cut costs. Its board suggested it dispense with the *mashgach* who supervised the preparation of kosher food in the kitchen. To this suggestion, the Orthodox rabbis responded with silent, uncomprehending, yet somehow savage rage.

The hospital survived with funds raised by the Jewish Federation, with grants from some of the foundations, with money received from the state for the care of the indigent. But hospitals really survive because patients subsidize them. The man recovering from a simple left inguinal hernia operation helps pay for the heart machine for the patient with a serious cardiac condition. The child undergoing a tonsillectomy helps pay for the social worker, important for counseling and for the therapist, important for convalescents. It is the patient who must live amid financial dislocations during illness. His medical-insurance plans pay costs of a hernia operation or tonsillectomy, not total charges. Sometimes his insurance compromises by paying the charges, but only 80 percent of them.

People do not relish being sick and they like paying for it even less. They like it not at all when they are not sick. Which is among the reasons why Jews have abandoned and continue to abandon their hospitals. Forty percent of the funds collected by a Jewish Federation for local use are allocated for the upkeep of the Jewish hospital, but this money constitutes but 3 percent of the hospital's expenditures. In a majority of these hospitals, Jews number only one third of the patients. Mount Sinai Hospital in Chicago is in the middle of a black community where barely 10 percent of its patients are Jewish. In a Boston survey conducted by the Combined Jewish Charities, only 17 percent of the Jewish community expressed a preference for a Jewish hospital. The Jewish environment, the kosher food, and the presence of the rabbinate are certainly available in Catholic, Presbyterian, and nonsectarian hospitals. And so are Jewish physicians. As for the training of Jewish doctors, would another Beth Israel in Cambridge, Massachusetts, make sense when a Jew named Epstein is the head of the Harvard Medical College? Non-Jewish hospitals raise funds on their own initiative. Perhaps there are better ways for Jews to spend their money than in supporting these medical complexes.

If nothing else, then, there were practical reasons for transferring Montefiore to the University of Pittsburgh. Still, when the transfer occurred, a court fight threatened. Irwin Goldberg, Montefiore's executive director, did not wish to discuss this internal quarrel. "A great many more difficulties attend hospitals," he said, "which we might more profitably talk about."

While Mr. Goldberg wears thick eyeglasses and affects the academic bow tie, he is as physically well put together as Joe Frazier—indeed, Goldberg was a Navy boxer—and when he wants to change the subject, the alert journalist changes it.

Hospitals, Goldberg went on, are a reflection of their communities, often with the same personality, and they change as their communities change. Hospitals are often caught between the expectations of the people they serve—who want immortality—and the realities of medical and financial expertise.

"Medical research in this economy, for example," he said, "is at a standstill. What funds research receives are always the same, which means they are always less because of inflation."

I explained to Mr. Goldberg that the book was about Jews and not about hospitals, and he said that Montefiore Hospital was a more responsive hospital now that it was guided by a board of trustees than when it was guided by congeries of Jewish families.

Mr. Goldberg is responsible for the preparation of more meals than are most hotel managers in Pittsburgh. The kitchen must prepare not only wholesome meals but kosher meals and meals for patients on special diets, about which patients and their families complain as often as they have nothing else to worry about. The laundry at Montefiore is larger than the laundries at nearby Aliquippa. Mr. Goldberg must find the wherewithal to pay the escalating salaries of its workers. When one of the Montefiore surgical units fired a black girl for not doing her job properly, the National Association for the Advancement of Colored People threatened a court suit if she were not rehired. Mr. Goldberg had to convince the doctors of the need to file efficiency reports on operating-room personnel in the future. It was his acumen which has guided the expansion of the hospital over the last decade. He convinced the board it was wiser to build the garage, for instance, before the new clinic, because the garage would produce income which would help finance the clinic.

But if Mr. Goldberg doesn't want to discuss a serious internal division, there are others who do.

"Jews argued that becoming part of the university was Montefiore's destiny," said Dr. Yale David Koskoff. "In 1929, they had the opportunity to build the hospital cheaply on flat land or more expensively on the bluff. They chose the bluff which is one way, I suppose, of defining destiny."

Koskoff is a sixty-two-year-old neurosurgeon who was Montefiore's first director of neurological research. He is the senior neurosurgeon in Pittsburgh. He has been an associate professor in psychiatry and neurosurgery at the medical school for many years. He has performed a famous surgical experiment. In 1947, with the permission of the court and at the criminal's insistence, Koskoff lobotomized a three-time loser named Millard Wright who was facing a life sentence. The purpose of the experiment was to determine if this lobotomy would relieve the severe depression and anxiety which drove Wright to crime. After a short prison sentence, Wright found employment, then got a better job, even married, but returned to burglary and committed suicide after he was caught. Koskoff described this melancholy failure in *The Dark Side of the House* (Dial Press, 1969). These facts were again recited, when I visited Pittsburgh, by a film critic in his review of Stanley Kubrick's *A Clockwork Orange,* which had just opened.

Koskoff lives on Hobart Avenue in a brick house on a corner

lot. It is an old house, a comfortable house, one which by its preservation reveals that every family who lived in it loved it. Koskoff moved in the day after the Japanese attacked Pearl Harbor. The living room was large enough to make a grand piano unobtrusive.

He has raised two families within: Ellen, a music teacher at the university, and Eric, an attorney, were children by his first wife, who died of diabetes mellitus; Karen, a sophomore at Goddard, and Benjy, finishing high school, the children by his second wife, Betka, who not only assists him as a nurse during delicate brain operations but serves as his office manager.

The upstairs study was lined with bookshelves. There was the complete work of Sigmund Freud and a tremendous sampling of books about Jews and Judaism. Betka confided that she reads these and only these. She finds them uniformly well written and she is always hungry for news about the Jews which went unsatisfied in her girlhood, spent as a Catholic in one of the Hungarian neighborhoods of Pittsburgh.

I surveyed Koskoff's comfort and he said, "I want you to remember that I was the first Jew in the Yale Physiology Department and the first Jew at the Lahey Clinic in Boston and the first Jew in neurosurgery at the university here."

"And you are worried about the possible extinction of the Jewish hospital?"

Koskoff laughed. "It is probably insane," he said, "to pass a law which will deprive a man of two or three years of his freedom for shooting a bald eagle from a Piper Cub. And it is insane unless you are quite serious about preserving bald eagles. The Jewish hospital is a bald eagle. There are few of them and they have a symbolic value past all worth."

At this moment, Koskoff himself looked like an eagle with his mane of white hair, the sharp eyes, the aquiline features. In his dark-blue suit, beneath a photograph of Freud, he looked as imposing as a bald eagle in his eyrie.

"When there is a dearth of doctors, the minorities get a break," he said. "There may not always be a dearth. Maybe the minorities won't be as lucky in the coming decades as they have in the past, if lucky is what you want to call it."

I asked about the photograph and the volumes of Freud.

Koskoff said he was a serious student of Freud's writings. "Freud," he said, "taught me everything I know about being Jewish."

"Which is what?"

"That being Jewish is a traumatic neurosis."

"One last question. Who will pick up the mortgage on Montefiore? The university?"

"Did you ever know anyone to relieve Jews of their burdens?" asked Koskoff.

TENDING THE CLUB

Koskoff, the eagle, took me to the ball game at Three Rivers Stadium. The world champion Pittsburgh Pirates were at home to the St. Louis Cardinals. The scoreboard, which is a city block long, works by a computer and lights up with pictures like the old Wrigley Spearmint sign on Times Square. It cost $1 million.

We sat beside the Pittsburgh dugout, on the first-base line, the guests of Dr. Joe Finegold, who has been the Pirates' physician for twenty-seven years. He is a short, compact man but he still looks fit enough to make the snappy, underarm hit-saving throw from third to first with ease. He is ruddy, probably because he sees every home game the Pirates play. He goes south with the club in the spring and in 1971, while the Pirates beat off the challenge of these same Redbirds, Joe Finegold went with them on the last road trip.

"We dropped four games in Candlestick Park," sighed Mrs. Finegold, who sees every night game with her husband.

"I wasn't worried," said Finegold.

"You weren't worried," said Mrs. Finegold, "you were sick."

Dr. Finegold fished a World Series ring from his pocket, heavy gold, the words "World Champions" circling a big stone. It weighed as much as three silver dollars.

Dock Ellis, the pitcher, poked his head from the dugout, caught Finegold's eye and asked, "If you get a chance, Doc, will you get me some peanuts?"

"He makes beautiful designs on the artificial turf with the shells," said Mrs. Finegold.

The Pirates play on artificial turf, which looks as if it were pasted down. "It's better turf than they have in the Astrodome," said Finegold. "Slip on it there and it's a third-degree burn. Here it's second degree."

Leo Durocher said of artificial turf that it was like playing baseball on a pool table.

Rick Wise of the Cardinals gave up a three-run homer to Richie Hebner in the first. The electronic scoreboard lit up like a menorah.

In the second, Mrs. Finegold worried about May 24. "Are you sure you can get the day off, Joe?"

"They're on the road," said the doctor.

"But are you sure?"

Finegold took the scorecard from Koskoff and showed her the schedule.

"Our son is being graduated from medical school on that day," said Mrs. Finegold.

"Pediatrics," said the doctor.

"Our younger son is entering Pitt in September. He and his brother are very good friends even though they're seven years apart. I just hope they marry girls who like each other," she said.

"Dear," said Dr. Finegold, "maybe the men want to watch the ball game."

Later, Koskoff asked what goes wrong with the ballplayers.

"They break their bones and tear their muscles and they catch flu. Otherwise, they're just like people. If they had a bad week, they don't feel so hot. Nelson Briles, a smart man, a college graduate, told me how sick he was. I said, 'Nelson, not one of these symptoms has ever been described in any medical text.' I gave him aspirin and the next day he struck out ten men and his symptoms are lost to medical science forever."

"Then why do they need a surgeon?" asked Koskoff.

"For the fans," said Finegold, waving his hand around the reaches of the ball park. "Fifty thousand people show up here on Sunday. There's a lot of towns with less than that in which people die every day in the week. People come out who shouldn't, people who don't know they have a heart condition, people who collapse from heat prostration. But the worst are the fans who scramble for the foul balls."

He pointed at Willie Stargell, who was digging in at the plate. "A left-hander can send a foul ball over here like a bullet. If it was fair, Clemente would have had enough sense to play it off the wall, but some fan will stand up on his chair and try to catch it. I've treated two people who lost their eye trying for a bullet foul."

From right field around center to left, the stadium has a double wall so that the kids cannot drop to the playing field. Only one small gate, specially inserted for Joe Finegold, lets from the reserved section to the diamond.

Above and behind us, in the second tier, stretching from first behind home to third, were cubicles with glass walls, many of them this night curtained.

Finegold pointed to them. "They are fully rented. You supply the popcorn and Crackerjacks. And for one of them you pay seven thousand a year for a minimum of five years."

There are some real sports in Pittsburgh.

Dave Giusti turned in three strong innings of relief and the Pirates won four to two. Finegold stepped through the small gate and, pumping his arms, skipped to the dugout. Mrs. Finegold took us to the Diamond Club, a restaurant with a three-story-high plate-glass window overlooking first base. The glass can withstand a batted ball traveling at 360 miles an hour. In right field, in the third deck, I had seen three prominent stars to mark where Willie Stargell had deposited homers the year before and in left field in the third tier was a fourth star where Clemente had parked one. I wondered if the glass could have withstood the speed of those balls, which traveled over 400 feet.

Members of the Diamond Club can enjoy their dinner while they watch the ball game below. Mrs. Finegold told us the practice was so popular that the dining tables in the evening were distributed to members by lottery.

This was the sporting scene these days. The members of the Diamond Club were elegantly dressed. One of the sports writers had just returned from a two-week vacation in Zürich. The women were stylish, but none of them of the bejeweled, befurred tootsie variety. I'd lay even money all of them knew about the skiing last winter at Aspen.

The walls were decorated with photographs of heroic Pirates, Pie Traynor, Bob Friend, and Ralph Kiner. An enlarged shot showed a 1960 Yogi Berra chasing Bill Mazeroski's ninth inning home run to the wall.

All in all it was about as nice a place to have dinner and watch a ball game as you could find. Of course, there are still some towns where the fans go to the ball game to empty the mind and fill the lungs.

"What's the only park in which no one ever pitched a no-hitter?" I asked.

"Forbes Field," said Dr. Finegold, who joined us. "What's the oldest ball park in the National League?"

"Wrigley Field," said Koskoff.

"I knew you'd know," said Finegold. "I was asking him."

"Candlestick is the second oldest," I volunteered.

"You're both big-leaguers," said Finegold.

"I once caught a foul ball with my bare hand," said Koskoff. "My surgical hand," he said, looking at it as though he were finding it for the first time.

"Speaking of which—" said Finegold.

"I cut in the morning, too," said Koskoff. Surgeons never say "operate."

On the ramp, I asked Finegold, "If you have to operate tomorrow at seven and go to the ball game tomorrow night, it makes for a busy day, right?"

"Doubleheaders make me even busier. But what the hell, I've got broad shoulders and a broad bottom. What else does a doctor need?"

PART II: CHANGING COMMITMENTS

NEW YORK CITY: In the Time of the Troubles

THE ATLANTIC WAS THEIR JORDAN
AND NEW YORK THEIR JERUSALEM

There have been four Jewish immigrations to America. All of them came first to New York.

They began in September, 1654, when twenty-three Jews, fleeing the Portuguese Inquisition in Recife, now Pernambuco on the coast of Brazil, landed in New Amsterdam. They had left Recife aboard the *Valk,* been driven off their course by pirates, and rescued by the French privateer, the *St. Charles,* whose captain, Jacques de la Motthe, promised to take them to the nearest Dutch port of call for 1000 guilders each.

Peg-legged Peter Stuyvesant, governing New Amsterdam in the name of the Dutch West India Company, told them they could not disembark. Stuyvesant wanted to bar these Jews not so much because he despised their beliefs but because if he set a precedent by admitting Jews, he would have to admit "Papists," Lutherans, and "unwanted immigrants," as he called Quakers.

The Dutch burghers overruled Stuyvesant and allowed the Jews to petition the company for the right to settle in New Amsterdam. In fact, after the worldly goods of the Jews had been sold at auction to satisfy the claims of de la Motthe, these burghers offered them shelter over the long cold winter, during which they awaited a reply.

The Dutch West India Company rescinded Stuyvesant's proscription. The directors of the company noted that many Jews in Holland owned shares in this enterprise, that Jews had suffered in the war with Portugal, and they went on to instruct Stuyvesant that he must "not force people's conscience but allow everyone to have his own belief, as long as he behaves quietly and legally."

In the spring of 1665, the Jews found themselves part of the New

Amsterdam settlement but unable to take much active part in it. Stuyvesant laid down the proscriptions that Jews could not bear arms, engage in retail trade, own estate, hold public office, or "exercise their religion in a synagogue or gathering." They also could not help their Dutch neighbors build a rampart to guard against Indian raids— a long, walled stockade which became the famous Wall Street.

On August 29, 1664, the Dutch burghers awoke to find four British men-of-war in the harbor, their guns trained on the fort, whose capitulation the English admiral demanded. Without a by-your-leave, Charles II of England had deeded all the land between the Connecticut and Delaware rivers to his brother James, Duke of York. There was little the Dutch could do about it. Peter Stuyvesant surrendered the fort a month later, and the British admiral allowed the garrison to embark for Holland with full military honors.

The English enjoined the same proscriptions against the Jews that Stuyvesant had but seem never to have enforced them. The Jews of what is now New York became tradesmen, acquired a burial ground, and in time built the Mill Street Synagogue.

The congregation called itself Shearith Israel—the "Remnant of Israel"—and in the last three hundred years the synagogue has moved from Mill Street to Crosby Street to West Nineteenth Street to its present home on Central Park West and Seventieth Street, built in 1897. The twenty-three Jewish refugees from Recife have become 2,687,680 Jews and to the Mill Street Synagogue has been added 1094 Orthodox congregations with over 400 buildings; 98 Conservative congregations with 53 buildings; and 100 Reform congregations with 70 buildings.

By the beginning of the Revolutionary War, however, Shearith Israel was one of only five Jewish congregations in the Colonies, which numbered 3105 other religious organizations. The other congregations were in Savannah, Charleston, Philadelphia, and Newport, the last in terms of affuence and numbers the premier Jewish community in the New World.

The "triangular trade" of rum, slaves, and molasses between Newport, the West Indies, and Colonial ports in the Carolinas and Virginia had made these Rhode Island merchants rich.

The Jewish merchants were rich enough to build Touro Synagogue in 1763, the oldest house of Jewish worship in the western hemisphere. The Touro Synagogue was designed by the English architect Peter Harrison, who imported 196,715 bricks for its outer walls.

Between 1776 and 1779, the British invested Newport, burning most of it, although they spared the synagogue, which later housed the first convention of the Rhode Island Legislature. Newport inhabitants fled, the Jews among them finding refuge in New York and Philadelphia. Only a small segment of Christians and Jews returned to the once flourishing city after the war.

Well before the turn of the nineteenth century it was obvious that New York would become the commercially preeminent city of the New World. Thomas Jefferson, viewing its great natural harbor, predicted as much, but he thought the New Jersey side was the harbor's future. Tea, wool, hides, wine, and machinery entered the United States through New York. Its banking resources doubled every year. The completion of the last stage of the Erie Canal in 1825 gave the Midwest and the frontier access to the Atlantic.

But the city did not have another synagogue until 1825. It was, however, the first city with enough Jews to support two congregations. In the whole of the United States at the time there were only 6000 Jews, collectively worth $10 million. B'nai Jeshurun was founded by English and Dutch Jews who wished to follow the Ashkenazic rather than the Sephardic ritual. *Ashkenaz* is the Hebrew word for Germany and *Sepherad* for Spain. The Colonial Jews had all been Sephardim. The Ashkenazim had not begun to follow in any significant numbers until 1820.

The Jews in Central Europe did not face the cruel extremes of the Spanish Inquisition. Nor had many of the people in Central Europe heard of America (it was the people in the maritime nations who heard most about the New World). America was also a land of unknown perils. Passage was expensive. In 1789, the year George Washington was inaugurated as the first American President, Europe exploded, first with the French Revolution, then with the Napoleonic Wars, which kept all in a tumult until Wellington defeated Napoleon at the battle of Waterloo in 1815.

Out of Waterloo came the Holy Alliance of Russia, Austria, and Prussia. Guided by the diplomatic skills of Prince Klemens von Metternich, the Holy Alliance denied the German-speaking people unification. Politically oppressive, the Holy Alliance drove many Germans, Jews among them, to emigrate.

In 1848, a wave of popular uprisings washed over Germany and succeeded easily in establishing a confederation. But the Habsburg monarchs in Austria and the Junkers in Prussia put down the insurrection in the fall of the year. What had been a steady stream of immigrants from Germany became a flood. Two million Germans came to the United States between 1848 and 1870.

The Jews of that immigration have been called the Forty-eighters. Some of them pushed to the frontier and became fur traders. Others became frontier peddlers. The Cherokees called the peddler *ju-wedge-du-gish,* which means "egg eater," for rather than eat nonkosher food the Jewish peddler subsisted often on a diet of hard-boiled eggs and vegetables.

The Forty-eighters were the first Jews many Western Americans ever met. A merchant who had ventured to Cincinnati in the eighteen-forties related how a housewife asked if she could feel his head. When he bowed it for her inspection she was disappointed to find he had no horns, an accouterment she thought the property of all Jews.

But, of course, many, many Jews stayed in New York. And many of those who had ventured forth returned to New York. Bernard Baruch's father, a surgeon in the Confederate Army, returned to New York City after the Civil War when he could no longer make a living in South Carolina. Lazarus Strauss and his four sons left their store in Talbotton, Georgia, for the same reasons. They started a wholesale china-importing firm, leased space to sell their wares in a store owned by Charles Webster called R. H. Macy's, and eventually became the owners.

By 1870 there were 250,000 Jews in the United States, 75,000 in New York. Since the eighteen-thirties and -forties they had formed a Jewish neighborhood on Bayard, Baxter, Mott, and Chatham streets, north of City Hall, east of Broadway, a square mile of city grids destined to become the most populous ghetto in the world.

This ghetto was created by the immigration of 2 million Jews and more from Central Europe. They came for the most part from the Russian Pale of Settlement. The Pale—the word means "fence"—extended across a third of Russia, for a thousand miles along the coast of the Black Sea, up through the Ukraine into Lithuania, north as far as Warsaw in the west and the Baltic Sea in the east. Millions of Russians lived within this area, but the Jews of Russian Europe could only live within the Pale. And within the Pale, they were restricted to their shtetl, a hamlet populated only by Jews which they could not leave unless bound on business for another shtetl. In the cities within the Pale, in Odessa, Kishinev, Kovno, Lodz, Jews were confined to the ghetto, in Russia a prisonlike community.

In these shtetls and ghettos, Jews worked as cobblers, tailors, black-smiths, tanners, hatmakers, butchers, bakers, draymen, and harness makers for meager earnings. They lived mean lives at menial labor. Conditions were no better for the Russian serf, peasant, or working-man.

Then in 1881 terrorists assassinated Tsar Alexander II. Alexander III blamed the Jews for the murder. He authorized a wave of pogroms, organized attacks and massacres, against the Jewish settlements. A year later, in 1882, he authorized the May Laws, which ordered Jews to move from their shtetls into much more crowded cities, where they were unable to find work and where families lived on the streets be-cause housing was so scarce.

Half the Jews in Russia over a period of thirty years left the Pale of Settlement, beginning the largest Jewish migration in history, into Europe and toward the wharves of Bremen and Hamburg for the ships which would carry them to America. Families trudged thousands of miles along muddy roads, hauling their few possessions in hand-made carts. Others carried what they could salvage in clumsy packs strapped to their backs.

Jews along their route made the pilgrimage possible. The Jews in Germany, Holland, Belgium, England, and France not only sent money, medicines, and food, but often shared their homes with the refugees, setting up cots in every corner of the house on which the wanderers slept in shifts. There was such a multitude of organizations in the United States that finally all agreed to merge into one, the Hebrew Immigrant Aid Society.

Passage to America cost thirty-four dollars. The Jews packed them-selves into steerage, the hold of the ship which once contained the steering mechanism and now contained tier after tier of cots, jammed close together. They spent as long as three weeks in this fetid darkness, subsisting on herring, black bread, and tea lest they offend their di-etary laws by eating food not kosher. The historian Moses Rischin quotes a widely distributed immigrant guidebook of the time which described the shipboard journey as "a kind of hell that cleanses a man of his sins before coming to Columbus' land."

Twenty million other emigrants from Italy, Ireland, Lebanon, and Poland also suffered through this hell. They poured into a country whose industrial expansion kept crying for new workers, whose grow-ing cities needed citizens to man its increasing services, whose fron-tiers kept expanding westward.

Jewish immigrants in those years differed from others in three respects. Among Jewish immigrants there was always a large number of women or children—44 Jewish women to every 56 Jewish men, and 24 children under fourteen to every 76 adults. More than 1 million Jewish women followed husbands and brothers and fathers into the New World—more women and children than in any other immigrant group.

They were also poorer than any other immigrant group. Not 7 percent of these Jews had fifty dollars on arrival. Fifty-five percent had no money at all. Nearly 70 percent of the Jewish immigrants had paid for their journey with money borrowed from relatives or Jewish agencies while millions of non-Jewish immigrants were imported by native American manufacturers to step into the growing labor market.

Before World War I, many immigrants returned to their native lands. But the Jews had come to stay. America was not an economic adventure. Less than 4 percent ever left America, compared to 19 percent of the Italians and 12 percent of the Irish. And most of the Jews who left went to Palestine which became Israel in 1948, not to their native countries.

They came speaking Yiddish, originally a German dialect spelled with Hebrew letters which over the decades accumulated not only scores of Polish, Russian, and Lithuanian words but also spawned its own dialects. It was a language the German Jews called "jargon." The shtetl Jews were Orthodox, an inconvenient apparatus with, however, some unseen advantages. For instance, at a time when most cities in the United States depended upon Chicago for meat, New York was still an important slaughtering center because of the demand for kosher cuts.

The city was able to accommodate the millions of immigrants who washed up on its streets by building multiple-family tenements, some of which had gone up as early as 1835 as a way of raising ground rents and housing greenhorns. The worst features of these jerrybuilt tenements were incorporated in the "dumbbell" tenements. These dumbbell tenements, which took their name from the resemblance of their floor plan to the weightlifter's dumbbell, were the creation of the architect James E. Ware, who won first prize in the Model Tenement House Competition of 1879.

They were tall, narrow apartment buildings, six and seven stories high, built without elevators or toilet facilities. Two apartments, each of four rooms in the front, were connected by a squeezed-in hallway to two similar apartments in the rear. Fire escapes, which served as an extra bedroom in the summer, latticed the building in front and back. The rooms were dark and airless—leading a Jewish child to describe them once to a settlement worker as "a place so dark it seemed there weren't no sky."

The tenements transformed New York and so did the inhabitants. By 1900, New York was the city of the foreign-born. More than three quarters of its people were immigrants.

The immigrants worked as peddlers, butchers, glaziers, carpenters, flooring men, roofers, bakers, and many of them still work at these trades. Thousands upon thousands of them found work in the needle trades, the "sweatshop system," known as the "Jewish industry" not because Jews owned it but because Jews were the workers. The manufacture of ready-made clothing was an American invention, an original industry developed in the big cities of the East. But clothing was a seasonal industry. Competition was fierce. The cost of maintaining a factory the year round wiped out profits. The entrepreneurs moved the manufacture of garments from the factories into the homes and small shops and lofts rented by the workers themselves. They were sweatshops because a dozen workers crammed into two or three rooms working the pressing machines in the blazing July weather while coal stoves glowed to keep the irons hot. They were sweatshops because the workers never ceased their toil.

The worker had become a threadbare contractor, an answer to the savage economics of seasonal manufacture, because he undertook many of the production risks as well as recruited the labor force. Buying sewing machines on the installment plan, obtaining materials on credit, paying little or minimal rent, the sweatshop proprietor had to drive his workers as he would drive galley slaves. These workers were his family and his relatives, and he worked them long and arduous hours and they were paid by the piece finished, not by the hours worked.

The profits were minimal and only increasing volume kept them turning. The sweatshop system has been described to a congressional committee investigating its abuses as "the most ingenious and effective engine of overexertion known to modern industry." By 1914, an industry which once employed Irish, English, and Germans was manned by shtetl Jews.

Five months of the year, the machines were silent, the knee-pants workers and the pressers and the blouse-sewers idle. Often the father of the house carried his machine on his shoulder and went from factory to factory asking for a day's work.

But then came the Socialists. With the failure of the Revolution of 1905 in Russia, hundreds of Jewish labor organizers, able, canny, and tough, joined the earlier immigrants. These sweatshop Jews founded the International Ladies' Garment Workers' Union in 1901, the Fur Workers' Union in 1904, and the Amalgamated Clothing Workers' Union in 1914.

These newly unionized Jews paralyzed the garment industry with mass strikes between 1909 and 1914, strikes which the workers won. The Jews won their strikes because they were determined and persevered, because workers elsewhere were winning strikes, and because the assimilated German Jews, wealthy industrialists, and publishers and lawyers like Jacob Schiff, Louis D. Brandeis, and Louis Marshall lent themselves to arbitrating strikes between Jewish workers and Jewish employers.

Many of the sweatshop workers wept when the industry became unionized. They were afraid they would lose their livelihood. In such ways does poverty feed upon itself.

The industry flourishes today. Wedged between Times Square and Herald Square and bordered by Seventh Avenue on one side and Broadway on the other but spilling east and west is New York City's garment district, which does $4 billion a year in women's clothing alone. More than ten thousand firms are squashed into a few dozen office buildings between Thirty-fifth Street to the south and Forty-second Street to the north.

Perhaps the two most striking changes in the garment industry in the past thirty years is that now the unions have more money than all of the employers put together and now the workers in the lofts are Puerto Ricans and blacks with only a small percentage of Jews among them. The union leadership is still in the hands of Jews and the entrepreneurs are Jews. The designers and cutters are Jews but the shop stewards speak Spanish.

Congress passed the first restrictive immigration law in 1917, authorizing the Department of Labor to deport aliens implicated in radical movements. It put an end to unrestricted immigration in 1924. The father of restrictive immigration was Albert Johnson, a newspaperman from the state of Washington whose twenty-year career in Congress from 1912 to 1932 was devoted to closing the gates. Johnson had proposed quota systems before, but in 1924, in collaboration with Senator David Reed, one of Johnson's bills became law. It limited future immigration to 2 percent of the nationalities present in the United States at the time of the census of 1890. The bulk of the American population in 1890 was from the northern countries of Europe. The quota system meant that the United States could offer sanctuary to only 168,000 Jews fleeing Adolf Hitler.

Of these 168,000 who fled from Germany, Italy, Austria, and Czechoslovakia before World War II ended all movement, most were men of immense reputation, achievement, and influence. Certainly they had money and sometimes great wealth, for to bribe their way past the Nazi bureaucracy demanded large payments. Probably this wave of immigrants was as sophisticated as the English Colonials. One reporter called them "the greatest flight of talent the world has ever known." More than a dozen of these immigrants had won or would win the Nobel Prize. In comparable figures, it is as though the city of Charlotte, would produce a Nobel laureate every other year.*

It was, however, the third migration that made not only the Jewish community in the city but New York itself what it is. Moynihan and Glazer remark in *Beyond the Melting Pot* (MIT and Harvard Presses), "Despite a half century of American life, which has made the grandchildren now coming to maturity very different from what their grandparents were, they retain much that recalls their origins."

There is still a Yiddish theater, though the actors and the audience are growing very old together, and there is still a Yiddish press, which yearly loses more and more money. Asked why they persevere, Yiddish editors shrug and say, "A man has got to make a living somehow."

And up until the mid-nineteen-sixties these Jews always supported the Democratic ticket. By the nineteen-hundreds, the Irish had coaxed the Jewish immigrants into the wigwam, as Tammany sachems like to put it.

There were occasional insurrections. The Lower East Side Jews voted for Theodore Roosevelt—"Tudder" Roosevelt, as my father called him—perhaps because his signature was on so many of their

* More than fifty Jews have won the Nobel Prize, six of them native-born Americans and one, Selman Waxsman, who emigrated to New York as a young boy. Hans Krebs, who fled from Germany to England, also won the Nobel Prize for Medicine.

naturalization papers. And they voted for Fiorello LaGuardia because Jimmy Walker had robbed the city blind.

When Alfred E. Smith lost in a landslide to Herbert Hoover in 1928, it is still instructive to remember that this was the first election in which the Democrats had carried *all* the big cities.

The cities were the home of the workingman and the immigrant, the home of the oppressed and the exploited. It was for these that the Democratic Party had an affinity. Whether Jews in New York identified themselves as Jews, workingmen, or the oppressed made little difference because their interests were the same. The chances were that the voting Jew identified himself as a member of a minority. Any social legislation from wages and hours laws to fair-employment practices aided minorities, and these were the causes championed by the Democrats.

But neither causes nor minorities endure *in perpetuo*.

MURDERING LINDSAY

What happened in Forest Hills, in the Borough of Queens, doesn't usually happen in New York, but it usually does happen in Queens.

"Lindsay Killed the Queens, Now the Queens Will Kill Lindsay," promised a placard, a guidon for Jewish middle-classniks parading in protest through the streets of Forest Hills.

This Jewish community fiercely opposed a $29-million low-income housing project to be built on 8.5 acres in the 108th Street and Sixty-second Drive area. This neighborhood is one of twenty stable middle-class Jewish neighborhoods in the city. Not only did these Jews picket, march, demonstrate, hurl abuse and a few stones, go to court, but they also chartered buses from which they heckled John Lindsay as he campaigned in presidential primaries in Florida and Wisconsin in early 1972. They undermined the mayor's popularity with the Jews of the city, thousands of whom do not live in Jewish neighborhoods but who nevertheless felt that if Lindsay would desecrate one, he would desecrate all.

The Jews in Forest Hills won their point. At this writing City Hall probably will compromise this project, if it builds it at all, cutting three twenty-four-story buildings which can accommodate 840 families—2495 men, women, and children—to three twelve-story buildings which will accommodate 432 families. City Hall may declare a moratorium on scatter-site projects.

In the beginning, of course, there were no Jews at all on 108th Street and Sixty-second Drive. "Architects," says the WPA handbook, "in Forest Hills, Long Island, made notable advances toward the creation of a homogeneous, protected, 'traffic free' neighborhood unit, a concept used increasingly in the design of modern residential communities."

A central boulevard, lined with modest stores, along which ran the Eighth Avenue subway, cleaves through Forest Hills. One- and two-story homes fill the community north and south of the boulevard. A bluff to the east once offered pedestrians and children an unobstructed view of the Trylon and Perisphere of the World of Tomorrow and later of the globe cast by United States Steel symbolizing "Peace Through Understanding" at another World's Fair also losing big money.

The Jews came with the apartment buildings which began to go up in the late nineteen-thirties and early forties. After the war, the apartments grew in profusion and height, some of them rising twenty-nine stories. By the nineteen-sixties Forest Hills was a completely Jewish community populated by young couples, living in their first suburban apartment, and by older Jewish families, the fathers small-business men, salesmen, teachers, or skilled workers who had left the Bronx or Brooklyn, intending to live and work in Forest Hills until they retired or died.

"The reaction to the housing development," said Ed Sadowsky, city councilman from Queens, "might have surprised everybody else, but it did not surprise me. Everyone forgot this same community staged a white boycott of integrated schools in 1964 that was nationally reported. My kids were involved. Two of these schools were only six blocks apart. The Jews won that fight, too. The concept of the 'neighborhood school' was born in Forest Hills."

Sadowsky is a Jewish lawyer with offices in Manhattan. Though he has been a councilman for over a decade, he doesn't look forty. He is broad-shouldered, and to the question did he mind being quoted, replied, "I've never yet said anything I wanted to retract."

Sadowsky explained that in 1964 the New York Board of Education, under pressure from civil-rights groups and the courts, announced a plan of "pairing" public schools to facilitate integration.

This plan involved transferring half of the students in a predominantly white school to the nearest predominantly black school and half of the black students to the white school. Pairing involved busing some, though not a majority, of the students.

Eighteen of these schools were in Queens, ten of them near enough to each other necessitating no busing. But it was the parents of the white students in these last schools who militantly opposed the plan and after picketing City Hall met together to form the Parents and Taxpayers Committee, which took the Board of Education to court.

PAT, as it was acronymically termed, argued that pairing would promote segregation by driving more whites from the city. A state court ruled that the Board of Education can rezone a school district as long as the children go to a school nearest their home.

"Forest Hills put an end to pairing," said Sadowsky. "The Board of Education these days slices up a black school district and sends one third of the kids to one white school, another third to a second, and a last third to a third. The black kids get paired, not the white.

"Why would anyone think Forest Hills was going to let a low-income development in without a fight?"

The Forest Hills-Rego Park development, as it is named by the City Housing Authority, is part of New York City's "scatter-site" housing program. Scatter-site housing is housing built outside an area of minority concentration, housing outside the slums. It is financed by the federal government. Fifty-one of New York City's 189 low-income public-housing developments have been built in just such middle-class neighborhoods as Forest Hills.

The Forest Hills project was originally planned for the Corona section of Queens, a middle-class Italian area. Corona traded it off with the promise to build a much-needed integrated high school (not yet begun). Forest Hills asked, "If not the Italians, why the Jews?" and blamed Lindsay for the muddy end of the stick.

Jews are also proprietary about their neighborhood, proud of it and comfortable within it. They reacted angrily to the prospect of its sudden transformation, a transformation subsidized and encouraged by the city administration.

These Jews had no particular objection to the poor. Sadowsky reminded me of the "matzah fund" to which Jews contributed pennies and nickels and dimes in the nineteen-thirties so that a philanthropy could buy a Passover meal for hard-pressed Jewish families. The objection of the Jews was that these new neighbors would be poor blacks and poor Puerto Ricans, which spelled crime and dope.

"They had genuine complaints," said Sadowsky, "and one of their complaints was about their own personal safety. The mayor told them this was the moral issue of our times. The administration promised to screen every family who moved into the project. But in this town there is no credibility between the citizens and their institutions. The people know the budget is a fiction and they know scatter-site housing projects will accommodate parole violators and heroin addicts. Simeon Golar of the Housing Authority told them that blacks within the project would suffer a higher incidence of crimes of violence. None of these answers allayed fears. Fears feed hostility. So the City and the Housing Administration consistently mismanaged the issue. They scheduled large public meetings between the opponents and the proponents, which was like trying to make lions and bears share the same arena."

Do not think Sadowsky bellicose, belligerent, or even partisan. He spoke evenly, dispassionately—analytically, as politicians should speak about the events which affect their constituencies. He was not, in short, advocating theory, he was describing practice.

"Mismanagement," he said, "is calling the leader of the opposition, Jerry Birbach, a rabble rouser. Birbach is a lot of things, but he was not leading a rabble. He was speaking with the assent of that community. The Queens Jewish Community Council—fifty-three member agencies—opposed the Forest Hills-Rego Park development. The rabbis opposed it. The local press opposed it. The elected representatives opposed it.

"There was one compromise which might have cooled it. That was on the height of the buildings. Jesus, they are big," he said, illustrating with arms on high. "They look like men-of-war coming up the channel. The state representative, the congressman, the borough president, and I met with Lindsay and Golar and urged them to scale them down. The borough president promised he'd find space someplace else in Queens for the overflow. But Lindsay and Golar wouldn't do it. And I am convinced Lindsay wouldn't do it because he thought a compromise on the issue would diminish his integrity as a presidential aspirant. The *Times* would say something mean about him and (God forbid!) the *Post*.

"If the City goes ahead with the project, the City will have won a Pyrrhic victory. The Jews said they would leave and they will. They are leaving now. The City will have created another slum out of what once was a middle-class neighborhood."*

Sadowsky leaned back in his chair and stared through the conference-room window, which overlooked Forty-second Street and Second Avenue. Opposite was the *News* building with its legend under the yellow marble frieze, "He Made So Many of Them."

"Everything we thought was constructive," said Sadowsky, "has proved *de*structive. We integrated our schools because that would bring us social justice. Go into one of the schools today and you see black boys eating their lunch with other black boys and white girls playing with other white girls. We thought it was a marvelous idea to tear down the slums. And we have spent billions to create new slums. Welfare would preserve the family unit. But welfare has perpetuated the worst conditions of poverty because slavery made sure there was no black family to begin with."

What started in Queens in November 1971 was really nothing more than one of the local neighborhood mutinies which occur daily in every city in the country. Residents, angry at the encroachment of the Forest Hills project, convened and staged a torchlight parade after an overflow meeting adjourned.

"For once there's a crowd and it's not a stickup," remarked a police lieutenant.

Out of this protest emerged a spokesman, rotund, aggressive Jerry Birbach, a real-estate agent with a thriving Manhattan business. Birbach had a gift for organization, a flair for winning personal publicity, and a talent for the hateful insult.

The efforts of Forest Hills to halt the housing project were attended—and encouraged—by widespread press and television cover-

---

* Ed Sadowsky proved prophetic. In June of 1973 Mayor Lindsay appointed Mario M. Cuomo, a housing expert, as mediator in the Forest Hills-Rego Park controversy. In July, Cuomo, after hearing arguments for six weeks, recommended that the City reduce the project by one half. He based his argument on the concern that the project would bring as its inevitable concomitant increasing crime, vandalism, and deterioration which had induced a widespread exodus; that the project as originally conceived would have created "precisely what it sought to avoid, another racially concentrated low-income community." Scaling down the project means the City will have to bear some of the costs. Still, Cuomo thought it was a good investment. Anent Jerry Birbach's political ambitions for the State Senate, Sadowsky had scoffed, "Bernard Kessler, who represented the Parents and Taxpayers Committee in '64, ran a primary against me and lost badly. Birbach will lose badly, too. They're smarter than that in Queens." Birbach, in fact, did lose and lose badly.

age. The protesters made news principally because they were sophisticated Jews who knew noise makes news and because the newspaper editors and the television commentators no less than John Lindsay and Simeon Golar had presumed that the Jews of New York constituted a reservoir of liberal sentiment.

Rabbi Josiah Derby, who tried to defend the housing project from his own pulpit, was roundly booed by a crowd of six hundred Jews who went so far as to wave their yarmulkas to shoo him from the lectern.

The agitation, which neither abated nor lessened, prompted an assessment of the Jewish commitment to civil rights. Some, like Judd Teller, argued that the actions and sentiments of the Forest Hills community were at odds with the Jewish prophetic destiny. To which many not-so-intellectual Jews replied, "What does he know? He doesn't live in Forest Hills!" Others, like M. Donald Coleman, a psychiatrist, who offered his assessment in the pages of *Jewish Congress Bi-Weekly* (March 24, 1972), more accurately gauges Jewish middle-class morale:

At this point, perhaps we should admit the possibility that scatter-site housing, with its undoubtedly laudable goals, is a piece of social engineering that may have to be abandoned, given the entire social fabric of cities like New York. There is just too much fear of crime based on substantial reality that must include factors such as the massive heroin problem, the breakdown of enforcement of most street crime (currently only a one percent conviction rate) and the breakdown of administrative authority in schools and housing administrations. The usual burden of people's prejudices against minorities might be overcome with difficulty, but not with the admixture of these realities.

Whatever courses we elect, we would do well to avoid doctrinaire attitudes towards solutions that appeal to us because of our ultimate hopes for society. Some things may just not be attainable in the form we would find most desirable. We will need all the social data from experts that we can get, but we should never allow them to use their position to throw dust in our eyes. I suspect a great many of us in the future had best reconcile ourselves to being called racist insofar as that term is being used to cover any attitude unfavorable to what is the voguish concept of how to help blacks. It may take a long while before we can respond to that kind of name-calling with more ability to dissect out that which is deserved from that which serves other interests.

Yet let us remember that the first public housing in New York City was built for Jews. In the nineteen-thirties, the Jews were the poor.

This information came from Val Coleman, the public-relations chief of the City Housing Authority. This Coleman is an Irishman in his mid-thirties, a Manhattan resident, for many years James Foreman's press officer. Val Coleman is the city official of whom Jerry Birbach asked, "Where did you study? With Joseph Goebbels?"

"Forest Hills," Coleman said, "is not a Jewish reaction to black housing. I've been in this business all my life and I have yet to meet an Irish Catholic priest who wouldn't break your heart.

"We're building several of these scatter-sites. There's one in the Bronx, the Fort Independence-Heath project, which has occasioned more violence than Forest Hills. There's been equipment destroyed and threatening telephone calls made. It isn't in the papers, thank God," he said, his hands in prayer, "because I don't think the press can handle two of these situations at once. And the Bronx papers suppress it. The violence isn't coordinated and they don't want to reveal that the protest isn't communitywide. In Forest Hills-Rego Park, the Jews are our enemies. In Fort Independence-Heath, the Jews are our friends."

Coleman is a coil of energy. He uses his hands for punctuation, he springs in and out of his chair—his whole being pulses.

"If you want to understand what happened in Forest Hills," he said, throwing his long legs on the desk, "it's this simple: there has been a profound change in the tacit supporters of civil rights. Crime in the streets, the riots, the militancy have something to do with it. But the real reason is that the pie is split more ways."

Scatter-site housing got its name in 1967 from the report of the National Advisory Council on Civil Disorders. The report recommended that low-income housing be moved out of the slums, which had few resources for the populace, into middle-class neighborhoods. The Forest Hills-Rego Park project was planned and budgeted by the Board of Estimates even earlier.

"The people said yes then and they say no now," said Coleman. "If the opponents of the projects can force it back to the Board of

Estimates for reconsideration, the Board invariably kills it. The City lost a million dollars on one of these when the Housing Authority couldn't get a variance on a dead-end street. When the Board got its chance, it cancelled the whole project."

The New York City Housing Authority is trapped by a cruel dilemma. Housing in the City is critically short. But the policy of the federal government, which provides all the funds for construction through the Department of Housing and Urban Development, demands an undeviating policy: city housing authorities must proceed affirmatively with low-income projects in middle-income neighborhoods. HUD also sets the ceiling on the cost per room. Because of this formula, and because of the high cost of realty and construction in New York, height and size are often excessive.

Or as Val Coleman put it, "A bungalow in Wyoming costs two thousand dollars. The same bungalow in Forest Hills costs two million. And it is not true that we refused to compromise. Forty percent of the apartments in the complex were reserved for the elderly—and in Forest Hills they are canny enough to know 'elderly' means 'white.'

"I know all about compromise," he said heatedly. "The only compromise the opponents will accept is our abandoning the project. Education doesn't work. Welfare doesn't work. Employment doesn't work. Housing doesn't work. We have to compromise. So okay, what are we going to do? Put 'em on a boat and ship 'em to Africa?"

SLOW BOATS, BAKED ALASKA, AND A NEIGHBOR-
HOOD STAKE

Past 145th Street, the subway exits from the tunnel and proceeds along the elevated structure, sweeping past Yankee Stadium to a stop at 161st Street.

From the seat beside me, an eight-year-old bolted from his mother, leaped across the car, pounced on the straw cushion to press his face against the window in ecstasy at the sight of the bank of blue seats soaring skyward behind third base, a reminder there are still gratuitous values in the world if you will but ride the IRT Lexington-Seventh Avenue often enough.

Alighting at 228th Street, you descend the steep stairs to Bruckner Boulevard. The west side of the boulevard is Irish. Bars, saloons, small stores, and groceries parade north. A poster on the elevated entrance and another pasted in the window of an orange-drink stand exhort, "Stop British Terror in Belfast!"

On the east side of Bruckner, past the elevated stanchions, is a low-income-housing development. That side is black. Farther up the block is a quick-food stand. A King Hamburger costs forty-nine cents garnished with a King Pickle.

A steep marble bluff to the west gives the area and the housing project its name—Marble Hill.

As late as 1913 Marble Hill and its northern neighbors were timber lands. They were also the scene for the first auto race for big money. In 1910, daredevils started at King's Bridge, zoomed along Broadway to Irvington, and doubled back for a purse of three thousand dollars offered by *Cosmopolitan* magazine.

Two Hundred and Twenty-eighth Street curves up from Bruckner to the Hudson River. Near its crest, opposite a deserted and barren playground, is St. Stephen's Methodist Church, its scored shingles dark brown from age and weathering. St. Stephen's is the pulpit of the Reverend William Tieck, pronounced "Tike," who knows more about the Bronx and its wildlife—floral, animal, and human—than any other man alive. Reverend Tieck has held this pulpit for twenty-six years, in which time he has published two definitive books on the Bronx, its geography, history, schools, and neighborhoods.

He is a wiry, small, ascetic man in his late fifties who emanates a vast kindness. He walked slowly up the steep hill, carrying a heavy bag of groceries for a colored lady, to whom he bid good day at the corner with a tip of his hat. He came back to the modest rectory, fronted by a high hedge. Steep wooden steps, with small lozenges of ice in the worn depressions, led to narrow double doors which let upon a small foyer, umbrella and hat stand at the ready. To the left was the reverend's sparsely furnished living room, a couch, two easy chairs, standing lamps, and handmade bookshelves. Characteristically, Tieck sat on the burnished piano bench which belonged to an old upright.

When he came to St. Stephen's over a quarter of a century ago, Marble Hill was a community filled with old-line Bronx aristocrats, patrician, influential, rich. Tieck's parish these days is 75 percent black and his Sunday school 100 percent. The whites are without exception childless. Imperceptibly, the neighborhood began changing in the fifties and then changed unalterably with the Marble Hill development and the advent of a large black population.

"Everything people warned would happen happened," said Tieck. "Realty values dropped. The neighborhood deteriorated. Discipline at the school collapsed. You see the ne'er-do-wells on the street corner. They make it unsafe for a woman to walk the streets in the evening. They will knock her down for her purse.

"But you must also understand nobody in Marble Hill, nobody ever made these people welcome. Nobody was ever neighborly with a black family, nobody ever invited a child to visit a nursery school or asked a parent to sign a petition."

Tieck rose and sprung a shade on his front window. "If you could see past the garage over there, you would see a Catholic church. Over that way, around the corner from the gas station, is an Episcopal church. Toward the river is a synagogue, an Orthodox synagogue, and the congregants are immigrants and first-generation Jews. There are no black Orthodox Jews that I know of in Marble Hill. Perhaps that is why the Jews kept their distance. But the black Catholics in the development worship in a church a mile from here, in the East Bronx. The black Episcopalians worship in Harlem. There was never room in Marble Hill churches for them.

"The only integration we ever had was when Martin Luther King was assassinated. We had a service here in St. Stephen's, marched over to the Catholic church for a eulogy, then to the Episcopal church for a benediction.

"And the people to whom law and order are important, the ones with the power and influence to command it not only from the precinct but from the City Council, were the first ones to abandon the neighborhood to the lawless."

The reverend took off his rimless glasses, wiped them, and waited for the next question, which was, "Why didn't *you* leave?"

"I love the Bronx and I love this parish."

"And what do you think will save the Bronx?"

"The only thing that will save us all—the grace of God. But we need the wit to see it."

He mulled over Val Coleman's alternative, that if we cannot salvage poor blacks we shall have to put them on a boat for Africa, and then Tieck asked, "But isn't that what we have done? Isn't that what Marble Hill is, a big brick boat which might as well be on its way to Africa?"

North of Marble Hill is Riverdale, still one of the most exclusive neighborhoods in New York City. Expensive developments throughout America borrow the name Riverdale, hoping to confer upon themselves the aura of wealth, prestige, and exclusivity.

The view across Bruckner Boulevard here does not let upon brick boats or King Hamburger but upon the verdant steppes of Van Cortlandt Park. The low-rise apartments have elegant canopies and there are some homes still staffed by servants. Big estates survive in Riverdale-on-Hudson, which faces the New Jersey Palisades. Wave Hill, for one, is regal enough for its occupant, England's United Nations Ambassador Sir Gladwyn Jebb, to have entertained the Queen Mother within. The Schwamm estate in the Fieldston neighborhood is also the home of a UN ambassador and U Thant in the years before his retirement lived in the Eugene Delafield palace. Many of the UN hierarchy make their American domicile in Riverdale. Turbans, saris, caftans, and chauffeured limousines make this Bronx neighborhood exotic.

Imagine what a scatter-site project would do to the resident's peace of mind.

Go no further.

On a six-acre tract of land between Mosholu Avenue and Fieldston Road owned by Robert Weinberg, an architect and professor of planning at New York University, the Association for Middle Income Housing intended to erect a superblock. Publicly aided housing involved a third partner, however, namely the City Housing Authority, which, whatever else it may do, is certain to doom exclusivity.

The project was called Faraday Wood because of its proximity to Faraday Avenue and because this particular tract was the last under private ownership with a virgin stand of great oaks, undisturbed throughout history.

Difficulties and delays attended the transaction. There were zoning revisions, architectural and planning changes, court injunctions and restraining orders. At one point, the Association for Middle Income Housing let its option lapse. Into the lists stepped an unlikely Ivanhoe, the Soviet Union.

The Russians bought the property for their permanent mission to the United Nations, paying as much for the land and its intended buildings as the United States paid them for Alaska, $7.2 million.

"Operation Baked Alaska," as the *Riverdale Press* called the sale in a red fifty-point banner headline, prompted huzzahs from the entire community.

"It was quite evident to me," wrote owner Weinberg in a by-lined story, "that the Russians have an unusual love of nature and consequent concern for the environment and were, in fact, attracted to this land for the very reasons we all cherish it for its unique character. They agreed to respect certain conditions in their treatment of the land which I spelled out to them and which I am confident they will live up to."

Maybe. It is hard to see how the Russians can preserve the forest primeval if they intend to throw up not only the mission, housing for the staff, a grade school, and espionage headquarters but also a parking lot for the air-conditioned Zims.

There are two Episcopal, one Congregational, one Presbyterian, two Baptist, and four Roman Catholic churches in Riverdale, plus ten synagogues and one Ethical Culture Society building. None of the above worried about either the plight of Soviet Jewry, the destruction of the capitalist system, or godless and atheistic Communism. But then the Jews, Catholics, Protestants, and Culturists were spared an *aliyah* into Riverdale of tenth- and eleventh-generation Americans.

Not far from Marble Hill and Riverdale is another scatter-site project, this in the Fort Independence area of the northwest Bronx. Fort Independence Street begins its graceful curve east at 231st Street. At the point where it crosses Heath Avenue is a 3.2-acre plot, a piece of land roughly resembling an uneven arrowhead.

Certainly the residents of the Fort Independence area cannot complain of the project's twenty-one-story height. Looming over the Bailey Avenue elevated stop are two forty-story concrete cylinders, apartment condominiums taller than the silos the government builds in which to let grain rust. An athletic tenant could hop from a second-story terrace to the platform of the elevated. These two apartments stand out like oil derricks in the Sinai because the Jerome Reservoir, which makes the lakes in Maine look like ponds, affords the pedestrian an unobstructed 180 degree view of the entire neighborhood.

Not long ago, the Jerome Reservoir turned the residents of the northwest Bronx into an army of Hans Brinkers. For reasons still impenetrable, the City drained this beautiful reservoir. The citizens of the northwest Bronx squeezed Robert Wagner's administration the way a housewife squeezes a dishrag and the City pumped the water back. But some assemblymen and councilmen lost election when the speckled swans never returned.

There was opposition to the housing project but the opposition did not command the universal loyalties of the community. Perhaps that is due to the mixed character of the neighborhood. It is populated by Italians, who live in rent-controlled apartments; Irish, who live in the two-story houses with glassed-in sun porches; and Jews, who live in high-rise cooperatives.

The opposition had splintered political and little clerical support. The Democratic committeewoman from the Eighty-fourth Assembly District spoke against the project, joined by Councilman Bertram Gelfand, Assemblyman Burton Hecht, and Algernon Miller, the executive leader of the Community Democratic Club. But the Reform Democratic Club, which had the clout, did not oppose the project, and Oliver Koppel, another assemblyman, favored it.

Roman Catholic bishop Patrick Ahearn had no interest in dooming or facilitating the project, but he told a City Housing Authority aide that he would fast from now until eternity to abolish New York State's abortion law. Father Zicarelli, a well-known neighborhood priest, told his parishioners to obey the law. The rabbis issued no public statements. One, to whom I promised anonymity, said that when he accepted this pulpit as a newly ordained rabbi, he had hopes of reinvesting the Bar Mitzvah ceremony with its pristine simplicity and dignity. "The congregation handed me my head. Later, I recommended that some of the money raised by our local philanthropy go to the civil-rights cause. Again, they handed me my head. On this issue, I counseled moderation. They could not hand me my head. Ergo, they were leaderless."

The Fordham Civic Association led the opposition. Its spokesman was one Fred Forman, an inveterate letter writer to the *Bronx Home News* and the *Riverdale Press*. The FCA staged several protest demonstrations, one of which took place in subzero weather on a Sunday in January. The turnout was disappointing until several chartered buses drew up and out onto Heath Avenue stepped Jerry Birbach and two hundred residents of Forest Hills, who had nothing better to do than applaud Jerry when he urged, "Stop our scatterbrained Mayor!"

The Fordham Civic Association did not have it all its own way. The Northwest Bronx Neighborhood Association, made up of dozens of tenant organizations, argued the following points cogently and effectively:

That many of the retired residents or those on Social Security were eligible for these apartments, which let at $21 per room;

That workers in the community were also eligible;

That the project would bring a day-care center with classrooms and a community center with kitchen and auditorium facilities to the neighborhood;

That the development had inspired the City to improve transportation facilities;

That the twenty-one-story project could accommodate 1100 tenants, which were not enough to dissipate the quality of the neighborhood.

The Northwest Bronx Neighborhood Association also persuaded the storekeepers that the housing development would materially increase business (which has heretofore always proved true when neighborhoods have remained intact). It pressured the City Housing Authority to give housing preference to the black and Puerto Rican maintenance men in the area's apartments who already play a role in the neighborhood (a concept the City Housing Authority calls "job-linked housing") and to the parents of black students who come from as far away as Brooklyn to the integrated high school.

A majority of the members of the Association were Jews. All of the letters to the editor in the *Home News* and the *Press* favoring the project were signed by Jews. What is the difference then between Jews in the Bronx and Jews in Forest Hills?

The difference was quickly explained by Mrs. Phyllis Heyman, an ex-actress, a stunning dark-haired grandmother, and Mrs. Elsie Brody, a city employee and an officer in the Reform Democrats, both prime movers in the Northwest Bronx Neighborhood Association.

Mrs. Heyman's apartment on Fort Independence Street let upon a small terrace. It overlooked the site itself and the streets, houses, and apartments behind it stretching north to Rose Hill, the home of Fordham University.

"The Jews in this neighborhood have it made," said Mrs. Heyman. "See all these apartments? They're union-built cooperatives. These Jews are union men. They're members of the Furriers Union and the Garment Workers and the Printers. A lot of them are retired."

"On those swollen pension funds," said Mrs. Brody.

"You saw the answer when you came into my apartment. I was saying goodbye to my daughter and grandchild. Thousands of other Jews live this way: the grandparents on one block, the sons and daughters on another, and the grandchildren on a third."

"Sometimes," said Mrs. Brody, "there are different generations of the family in the same apartment."

"The Jews are not atomic units here. They cannot make the ultimate threat, to move away."

"We have too big a stake in the neighborhood," said Mrs. Brody.

WHERE DID ALL THE YOUNG MEN GO?

It may or may not be true that the Jewish voting bloc always favored liberal candidates, the candidates who argued the primacy of rights over order and the duty of the government to provide shares in the social enterprise for everyone. The candidates *thought* it was true and stressed these principles in appealing for Jewish votes. Many Jews now, however, are of the opinion that the complexion of the liberal Jewish community has changed.

One of these is Norman Podhoretz, the editor of *Commentary,* a magazine without peer in the intellectual Jewish community. In *My Negro Problem—And Ours,* which he published in the magazine in 1963, Podhoretz was prophetic: "Thus everywhere we look today in the North we find the curious phenomenon of white middle-class liberals with no previous personal experience of Negroes—people to whom Negroes are faceless in virtue rather than faceless in vice —discovering that their abstract commitment to the cause of civil rights will not stand the test of confrontation."

The statement seemed outrageous in 1963, when liberalism was about to reach its high-water mark with the March on Washington, but it is simple fact in 1972. It is certainly a representative statement. And it is certainly true.

Another Jew, sage Alex Miller, for many years the community service director of the Anti-Defamation League of B'nai B'rith, says one of the watersheds which changed Jewish attitudes were the sit-ins which started in Greensboro and Charlotte, North Carolina, in the late winter of 1961. The sit-ins became black militancy and black militancy produced black anti-Semitism. More importantly, black militancy forced the policy of preferential treatment for minorities in civil-service jobs, educational complexes, and federally aided institutions. In New York City, Jews have massed in these areas. Sometimes the inefficient and unskilled have displaced and are displacing them.

"The Jews insist this is a situation of crisis proportions," sighed Miller, "but then the Jews are prone to see all situations as crises. They fail to realize the blacks in San Francisco have nothing nice to say about the Italians. They forget the immigrants slandered the doctors."

Lanky Haskell Lazere, savagely attacking a dainty cream cheese sandwich at his desk, impatiently answered an ever-ringing telephone. Lazere is the director of the New York region of the American Jewish Committee. "There are four reasons why the confrontation got the better of Jews in New York. The first is the vast social distance between blacks and whites. It has taken philologists until now to discover that 'okay' means 'yes' in Swahili. You can imagine how little the rest of us know about blacks.

"A second reason is intemperate black rhetoric. Blacks have heard so many meaningless promises that they put no value on rhetoric, not even their own. The Black Caucus in Gary, Indiana, passed a motion asking for the dissolution of Israel. They have succeeded in what they set out to do, namely, to keep this phone ringing all day with nervous Jews.

"A third is the insensitivity of the government response. The government threw blacks sops, never doing its share. The New York Telephone Company, for example, did its share. It tolerates inefficiency for the sake of training black employees in large numbers.

"And the last reason is black expectations. Exaggerated expectations must be realized at someone else's expense."

Preferential treatment in industry, subsidized housing in established neighborhoods, "affirmative action" guidelines in college hiring and admissions, formulated not to keep Jews out but to get blacks, women, and minorities in, intensify the Jewish disaffection with liberalism.

Writing in *Judaism* (not as widely read as *Commentary* but as prestigious), Seymour Seigal, professor of theology at the Jewish Theological Seminary, sums up the disaffection: "The liberals tend to favor an egalitarian society based on the equal possession of the goods of life rather than a society which makes possible individual achievement on the basis of effort and talent. They tend to favor that everyone finish the race in a dead heat, reaching the finish line at the same time rather than making sure that everyone start out at the same place and letting the race go to the swiftest."

The Jews want the fair start because they know they are faster; they cannot bear the dead heat because it means some of them must cross the finish line in single file.

The complaint against liberalism is not that it has changed but that it hasn't. Liberals still champion civil, economic, and social justice for all. Legislation and court rulings over the last twenty years have secured many individual rights, yet the disadvantaged minorities are still exploited and abused. Consequently, liberal efforts—and conservative efforts, too—have focused on group rights.

It is the Jews who have changed since the heyday of liberal politics because they are no longer one of the groups considered a minority. Their numbers are small, which is one way of being a minority, and they are not totally assimilated, which is another, but the latter is partially of their own choosing; indeed, many of the minority groups —Chicanos, blacks, Chinese, and American Indians—neither seek nor want assimilation.

The Jews manifest none of the other characteristics of the disadvantaged minorities. Their birthrate is low. With an average of 1.7 children per family they are barely replacing themselves.

Nor are Jews ill educated. Twenty-nine percent of the Jewish population has finished high school compared to 26 percent of the national population; 12.7 percent have one or more years of college compared to 7.3 percent; and 17.3 percent have four or more years of college compared to 7.5 percent.

Nor are the Jews in ill health, victimized by the diseases of poverty, diabetes, tuberculosis, rickets, malnutrition. The Jewish population, in fact, is older than the white population of the United States.

Lastly, the Jews are not poor. Thirty-five percent of the Jews are managers or proprietors compared to 13.3 percent of the national work force; 8 percent are clerical workers compared to 6.9 percent; 14.1 percent are sales workers compared to 5.4 percent; and not 1 percent are unskilled laborers compared to 7.7 percent.*

* "American Jewry, 1970: A Demographic Profile," by Sidney Goldstein. *American Jewish Year Book,* vol. 72, 1971. Jewish Publication Society of America, Philadelphia.

Jews also comprise the third major religious group in America, a courtesy honor, earned probably by their influence in the arts, philanthropy, education, and urban politics. In actuality, the three major religious groupings in the society are, in order of their size: 1) Roman Catholicism, the largest Christian denomination; 2) traditional Protestant fellowships—Methodists, Episcopalians, Presbyterians; and 3) evangelical Protestant sects—Seventh-day Adventists, Jehovah's Witnesses, Mennonites. Millions more of the folks are milling around with no religious affiliation at all.

In short, the Jews have become part of the white majority which the disadvantaged and the radical challenge and threaten to displace.

"The disquiet," says Bertram Gold, executive director of the American Jewish Committee, "is also the result of a rift within the Jewish community. The Great Jewish Consensus ended in 1967."

Gold should know. The American Jewish Committee is the oldest of the Jewish social-action organizations, the most conservative, and perhaps the classiest. It has always had a political orientation and it has always been able to make friends among the politicians.

"One of the events which caused a fissure," he continued, "was the New York teachers' strike in that year."

A great many grievances fomented the strike, but one of the central issues was the decentralization of the public schools. Decentralization was a policy devised by the Board of Education to give local communities autonomous control of their schools through neighborhood governing boards. The pilot school in this experiment was the Ocean Hill-Brownsville public school, which was in a black neighborhood. That governing board wanted black children taught by black teachers supervised by black administrators. Accordingly, the governing board notified nineteen white teachers and supervisors that their services in the district were terminated forthwith and that they were to report to the Board of Education for reassignment.

There are many more white teachers and administrators in the New York public-school system than black or Puerto Rican, although there are more black and Puerto Rican students in the system than white (because many whites go to private or parochial schools). Those white teachers who expected priorities in advancement by virtue of merit and seniority realized that decentralization threatened their interests. Almost half of these unionized (United Federation of Teachers) members were Jews.

The pros and cons of the strike flew like grenade fragments or fruit and vegetables when a tenor flats high C in Naples.

What the Jewish teachers did not get from their compatriots who help mold public opinion was sympathy. Intellectuals and politicians took the schools and the teachers to task. A school strike always creates a serious problem because the kids are underfoot. But the intellectuals and politicians also blamed the schools and teachers not for having failed to educate the disadvantaged, for failed they had, but with suppressing the fact of failure for a generation. Slum schools failed blacks not because they were different from other schools but because slum schools were too much like them. To the complaint that teachers could no longer handle troublemakers, the critics replied that their training in teachers' colleges poorly equipped them to handle anyone.*

The argument against the strike was that decentralization was a way of giving slum parents the same control over the education of their children that parents in the suburbs exercise over theirs, that the issue was not black principals or black curricula, it was whether schools and teachers will hold themselves accountable.

Decentralization will not save us. Few who joined issue ever thought it would. Something else motivated them. Another issue had emerged, an issue succinctly analyzed in a special *Commentary Report* (which is subsidized by the American Jewish Committee). Maurice J. Goldbloom, a former New York teacher, now a foreign policy expert, says: "But perhaps the most complicated issue which emerged out of the [strike] was that of the orientation of society to the problems of its least privileged sectors. There is a widespread movement now afoot to ally the bottom and the top layers of Ameri-

---

* No one ever doubted that the caliber of teachers in the thirties, when jobs were scarce, was appreciably higher than the caliber of teachers today. Schools of education, whose emphasis is on method rather than on command of a field of knowledge, had not proliferated. Schools of education are often classified as answer factories; they have indeed granted advanced degrees for a thesis on the variety of ways to bake a chocolate cake. But state boards will only certify as teachers those who have been graduated from such a school or who have accumulated a certain number of credits in education. No one has suggested that the way to improve faculty caliber is to certify as teachers the graduates of liberal arts colleges, like Yale or Kenyon, or those who hold advanced degrees from Stanford or Harvard in a subject like English or history. The caliber of the New York City primary and secondary teachers did noticeably improve during the Vietnam War when young men who taught in public schools gained exemption from the draft.

can society against those in the middle—and especially against organized workers. This strategy has its implicit assumptions; it stems from the belief on the one side that the first enemy of the man at the bottom is the man one step up, and on the other that the discontents of the most wretched can effectively be appeased without any expense to those at the top."

The black surge, the rift, are problems indigenous to the New York Jewish population. New York loves emphasis. It can convince the country that what happens there is sure to happen elsewhere soon. A fourteen-inch snowfall which delays Walter Cronkite's trip to the CBS studios convinces television newsmen that the entire country is immobilized.

The Six-day War also changed the attitudes of a large segment of American Jewry. The pride and relief Jews felt in the Israeli victory was dampened by the realization that they were in this alone.

When the Egyptians massed tanks in the Sinai and blockaded the Gulf of Aqaba, the Jews called upon their liberal friends, friends whose moral fervor they counted on, friends who owed them a favor, to muster quickly an intervening force to quell and subdue the danger. Whether that force was diplomacy, economic sanctions, or world opinion mattered less because Jews understood that the threat to Israel was annihilation. On this level, there are no national or cultural differences between Jews. The Jews ran to help Israel, and of all their friends only Martin Luther King, Jr., ran with them.*

After the war, the New Left mounted an unceasing barrage of anti-Israel propaganda which American Jews interpreted rightly as anti-Semitic sentiments. It was dismaying. As long ago as 1948, the Republican arch-conservative Senator Robert A. Taft had pointed out the areas in which the interests of the United States and Israel coincided. Israel is the one democratic entity in an otherwise Communist-influenced Middle East; it is the one developing country in an undeveloped area; it has the one politically stable government in a harem of hysterics. These were reasons enough to admire the Israeli victory. After all, everyone has a right to win a war and the

---

* It has since been established as a matter of record that the Lyndon Johnson administration knew through the Central Intelligence Agency that the Jews were sure victors. No matter how extensive and efficient their espionage network, there was no way for the Israelis to have learned the pinpoint location of thirteen Egyptian airfields except from satellite photographs. But Lyndon Johnson was never one to disseminate information along the Home Front.

Israelis had a moral imperative to save the Egyptians from perpetrating the crime of genocide.

The New Left, which believes that the grievous global inequities can only be righted by mobilizing the power of the subjugated and backward peoples of the "third world," accused the Israelis of aggression, barbarism, and the exploitation of innocents.

Doubly disappointing to the Jews were the reactions of the Catholic hierarchy and the Protestant fellowships. Jews had devoted forty years to the interfaith dialogue only to discover that Catholic and Protestant councils deplored the presence of Israeli soldiers in Jerusalem. Ranking and influential clergymen who had never expressed concern that the Jews were barred from the Western Wall and David's Tomb wanted the Israelis to abandon Jerusalem lest the Jewish occupation desecrate the sanctity of the city.

"We failed in our interfaith attempts," says pudgy, soft-spoken Harry Steinberg, executive director of the American Zionist Federation. "Instead of discussing brotherhood, we should have spent our efforts convincing Protestants and Catholics of the centrality of Israel to Jewish life. We have since made great progress with various Catholic groups. The Catholic laity is largely sympathetic to Israel and many priests personally sympathetic. The Pope has helped. He realizes the church has interests in Israel and that the way to protect those interests is by *Realpolitik*. Then, too, the Catholic hierarchy understands centrality. The centrality of the Catholic position is the divinity of Christ, the existence of the Trinity, and papal infallibility. They understand there are positions which cannot be modified.

"But the Protestants are stubborn. In the first place, they have an ax to grind. They have supported a large missionary effort in the Middle East which has converted thousands of Arabs. Unlike the Catholics or the Greek Orthodox, the Protestants never built shrines in Palestine. They consider the entire country the Holy Land, the cradle of Christianity, and the Jewish presence offends them."

He studied his hands thoughtfully. "We met with a Protestant group to ask their help in urging the passage of some federal legislation which would have aided Israel. They said they would help us if we would in turn help them send five hundred underprivileged kids to one of their summer camps. I said we would be happy to consider helping them with this project, but that Israel was not a *quid pro quo* matter. Israel is a nonnegotiable item. We wanted their support, but we would not buy it. The meeting ended then and there," shrugged Steinberg.

The Gentile response to the danger Israel faced, a response that was anything but urgent, does much to explain the turning inward of the American Jewish community, its continual reassessment of what is and what is not to its interests. There are intellectuals who unashamedly insist that political realism for the Jewish community is the question, "Is it good or bad for the Jews?"

Down deep is the knowledge that the Holocaust no longer protects us. The survival of peoples is a negotiable item for many nations. The Nixon administration was perfectly willing to cede the death of vast numbers of Bengalis in order to strengthen ties with Pakistan.

The Jews were the one people in history, however, consistently singled out from the rest for murdering. And the Bal Shem Tov, the Polish rabbi who founded the Hassidic movement, has himself remarked that the price of redemption is remembering. So, too, is the price of survival.

NOT THE DEBT BUT THE TERMS

Philanthropy in the United States in 1970 raised $17 billion. It is by far the biggest industry we have.

Of this, the Jews raised $420 million for Jewish causes. Obviously, Jews have no corner on philanthropy. Yet Jewish generosity is an eleemosynary landmark. One million Jews give money to Jewish philanthropy every year, one sixth of the total Jewish population, which includes the children, the poor, and the selfish. In addition, as neighbors, Jews contribute to the Red Cross and the Heart Fund, donate statuary to museums, endow chairs at universities, support the party of their choice, and buy Girl Scout cookies.

Jewish giving is not motivated solely by a religious impulse. All religions, from "I am as the tinkling brass" to "Alms for the sake of Allah," insist upon charity as a prerequisite for spiritual fulfillment.

Jewish giving came of age early because the hostile Gentile world insisted upon it. When the medieval popes locked Jews in the ghetto and the tsars in the shtetl, they told Jews that whatever they needed in the way of medical care, education, provision for the elderly and the orphans they had to finance themselves. Thus Jews never quarrel about the debt they owe to charity, but they will often quarrel about the terms.

The Dutch East India Company had also instructed Peter Stuyvesant that "The poor among these Jews shall not become a burden to the Company or the community, but be supported by their own nation."

The Jewish residency in America has been marked by a willingness to abide by this stipulation. Its charities have grown from a fraternal order which saw to it that no Jew was buried in a potter's field to gigantic Federations supporting hospitals, schools, old-age homes, and the State of Israel. Immigrant groups which have succeeded in this country have usually done so by developing an interior mechanism to help ease themselves into the mainstream. The Irish, Polish, and Italian Catholics developed a complex of parochial schools. For the Jews, the interior mechanism was the determination that the misfortune of one Jew should not disgrace all.

In this determination, Jews were supported by the government of the United States. No other government encourages charity the way ours does, which even grants a tax exemption for philanthropic contributions. No other people volunteer for good works like Americans. Frenchmen would say of drug rehabilitation that it was a serious problem for the Chamber of Deputies. But as our drug problem grew, RAP, REACH, Renaissance, and thousands of other drug rehabilitation centers proliferated, manned and funded by volunteers. The mechanisms of the society are oiled by the public-spirited who serve as elected members of the Board of Education and read to the blind for four hours every week or take in Fresh Air kids for a month in the summer.

No wonder Jewish philanthropy flourishes. It is as though a gardener transplanted a delicate rose from Europe into the most luxuriant soil imaginable.

One of the chief differences between Jewish and Gentile giving is that the Jew will give the big money while he lives, the Gentile when he dies. Giving confers upon the donor prestige and rewards him with gratitude. The Jew wants to enjoy these. But another truth is that giving is so ingrained a duty that no Jew who gives is ever called a sucker by his confreres. A Jew appointed the chairman for one of the fund drives will invariably double or treble his ordinary contribution while many a Gentile decides that his services and time make up his contribution.

One of the linchpins in the Jewish philanthropic effort is the local Federation. The other is the United Jewish Appeal. The Federation determines the needs of local agencies. To this, it adds a quota determined by the UJA for Israel. Sixty cents of every dollar collected by the Federation will go to the UJA. The UJA will provide a local Federation with everything from speakers to adding machines to enable it to meet its local and overseas commitments. The money is channeled by the UJA to the United Israel Appeal, then to the American Joint Distribution Committee, which has assigned priorities for how the money will be spent. None of the money goes to the Israeli government.

The offices of the UJA are at 1290 Avenue of the Americas and the tone within is that of a large corporation, not a General Motors type of corporation but a Rand think-tank corporation. The job is raising money and the staff goes about it with élan.

One of the UJA's divisions is devoted to the search for new "paper millionaires." Researchers go over every prospectus issued by the Securities and Exchange Commission, attentively study advertised stock offerings in every city, and plow through hundreds of year-end reports to the stockholders issued by major industries, always on the lookout for that Jewish name they have never read before.

Another division is Widows of Independent Means. These researchers comb the obituary and society pages for news about the bereaved widow whose husband might have left her well fixed. Very possibly, she might be persuaded to continue his good works.

Still another section devotes itself to contingency planning. Should the Russians, say, free twenty thousand Jews next month, these refugees would need transportation to Israel, food and shelter when they arrived, and processing. This money would have to be raised quickly and in substantial sums. One worker thought it would take between forty-eight and seventy-two hours to raise it.

A computer can produce the number of Jewish families in any American city and the amount that city raised in the last drive.

Fund raising is, of necessity, a constantly innovative industry. The UJA has subtracted the mystical overtones of Judaism from philanthropy and charity and made a perfect amalgamation with the American business process. This is not to be deplored. Philanthropy is essentially begging. The UJA has abolished servility.

Servility needed to go. Once upon a time, Jewish philanthropy was dependent upon the whims of the rich for its efficiency. Jacob

Schiff, for instance, the banker who was a partner of Kuhn, Loeb & Co., invented the concept of the "matching gift." Schiff would put up half the money for a worthy cause, which the rest of the community had to meet. Sometimes the community failed and Schiff saved money. When it succeeded, the community did a lot for Schiff's ego but little for its own.

A more successful technique is to recruit one rich Jew to convert another. The UJA constantly arranges for a merchant from Atlanta, who has contributed $100,000, to fly to New Orleans, where he will meet a contractor who wants to contribute $75,000. The merchant will tell the contractor, "This is not the year to cut back, this is the year to increase!" In addition to strengthening Israel by $85,000, this technique makes friends of strangers.

Trim, self-contained Irving Friedman, an executive vice-president of UJA, said, "Raising money for Israel isn't the hardest fund-raising job in the world. Raising money for a yeshiva from Jews who have no intention of sending their children to one is hard, but it's done every day in the week. American Jews have a profound dedication to Israel. Now and then we run across extremely wealthy Jews who insist, 'In my heart, I'm a poor man,' and will not contribute. The hard part of the job is to see that Jews help steadily, that they continue to help when there is no crisis because it is then that the Israelis get ahead of the game."

A successful philanthropy must do two things for Jews: it must serve a cause which has the assent of the community, and it must satisfy that community that the cause has indeed been served. That is why there is more communication between American Jews and Israel than there is between the residents of Kansas City, Kansas, and Kansas City, Missouri.

"More and more," said Friedman, "fund raising requires finesse. It is a delicate operation to convince a man who has recently inherited a million and a half dollars that it is to his interests to contribute $100,000 to Israel. You have to meet him under perfect circumstances, always through one of his friends who is responsive to this philanthropy. Then you tell him, 'We expect you to save Soviet Jews. It costs $35,000 to save one family. You can save four. It means more to those families if you save them tonight than if you save them next week. And it means more to everyone if you save five.' Usually he will want to talk it over with his wife and usually he will save three. We all like to bargain," Friedman said.

SIGNS OF LIFE IN THE OLD GHETTO

From the subway stop proceeding east, the south side of Canal Street is Chinese—food stores, restaurants, the Dot Gung Manufacturing Company, Fu Kee sportswear—and there are Chinese ideograms on the windows of ChemBank. The north side of Canal Street is Jewish—watch store after jewelry store lines the way to the Manhattan Bridge. Canal Street is headquarters for New York's wholesale watch and costume jewelry business.

Past the wide causeway which leads to the bridge, where men once dug the canal, begins the Lower East Side, once the ghetto of New York City. "Ghetto" now denotes black and Puerto Rican neighborhoods. Thus the Lower East Side since the end of World War II.

But there are still Jewish remnants. What makes you remember the old ghetto is the proliferation throughout the neighborhood of the Jewish religious stores. Over two hundred of them survive, enough to fill several columns in the Yellow Pages.

These stores sell Hebrew religious regalia—arks, ark curtains, atarahs, breastplates, candlesticks, chalofilm, huppoth, crowns, eternal lights, etz chains, menorahs, mezuzahs, Shabbas clocks and knives, talisim, tefillin, Torahs, and Torah covers. Some specialize in artifacts and objets d'art from Israel. Others sell only Hebrew prayer books and calendars.

One of the most prosperous of these stores is Ziontalis, at 48 Eldridge Street, its storefront facing the concrete playground of Public School 65. Ziontalis's proprietor is Marty Yaroslowitz, whose father opened the store in 1920. Ziontalis probably sells 20,000 mezuzahs a year, but 90 percent of its volume, Yaroslowitz, said is in talisim.

The mezuzah is a small cylindrical case which contains a parchment made from the skin of a clean animal on which are written two verses from Deuteronomy. The mezuzah is affixed to the right doorpost of every room in the house save the bath. Mezuzah means "doorpost," in fact.

The talis is a rectangular mantle which was worn in ancient times as protection against the desert weather. Our faith comes out of the desert. The meaning of "Messiah" is "The Anointed One" and the Messiah is anointed with water. The talis is worn at prayer. It is white and woven of wool, cotton, or silk (although Maimonides disapproved of the last), with blue stripes at both ends on which the benediction is embroidered in Hebrew letters. Tassels called *zizit* decorate both edges. Anyone can weave the wool or the cotton or the silk, but by law, strictly enjoined in Numbers 15:37–41, only a Jew can tie the zizit and appliqué the benediction. In Yaroslowitz's loft above the store and in his plant in Israel there are a lot of old-timers. Tying these tassels is a skill which reposes in the old.

Mr. Yaroslowitz was patiently explaining to a customer that Ziontalis didn't *charge* a sales tax, it simply *collected* a sales tax for the City.

The customer persisted in his outrage: the churches and the synagogues were tax-free institutions. Why then were the very implements which made a shul a shul taxed?

"If you are purchasing this menorah on behalf of a congregation, indeed it is tax-free," said Yaroslowitz. "But for me to forgive the tax means I must list your exemption number."

The customer quickly produced a Social Security number.

"No, no," said Yaroslowitz patiently. "An exemption number is prefaced by an 'EX.' "

Grudgingly the man paid over 7 percent and departed.

Two grandparents had selected a talis for their grandson's Bar Mitzvah. Traditionally, the talis is the grandfather's gift to the young initiate.

The grandmother, having finished her inspection, asked Yaroslowitz about a talis *zekel* (bag).

From beneath the glass-topped counter Yaroslowitz produced a blue zekel. He told the grandparents it cost $3.50.

"Doesn't the talis come with a zekel?" asked the grandmother. You could tell she would haggle over the price of war bonds.

"No," said Yaroslowitz, "the talis does not come with the zekel."

"Why not?"

"Lady," said Yaroslowitz, "when you buy whiskey they don't give you the glasses, do they?"

A talis at Ziontalis costs between $7 and $125. The one the grandparents had chosen was expensive. Shrugging, the grandmother said, "All right. So for the first grandson put the talis in the zekel."

Another customer interrupted to ask if he could buy a "new apartment house" greeting card.

"I don't stock them in English," said Yaroslowitz, "nor in Hebrew, but I have one in Yiddish. I buy them from Israel."

Yaroslowitz explained to me that this was a particularly busy morning. Ziontalis is a wholesale distributor, supplying talisim by the gross to synagogue and temple gift shops and to outlets in every major Jewish community.

"It used to be," he said, "that folks came in from the Island on Sunday or came over from Newark to do some shopping in the old neighborhood, flavor some *Yiddishkeit*. But no more. They can buy everything they need on the Island or in Newark."

Yaroslowitz's neighbor, at 58 Eldridge Street, is J. Levine, one of three brothers who maintain a Jewish bookstore. That store, too, is a wholesale supplier, shipping Talmuds and Chumashim and Kol Sifrei Maharalim to Talmud Torahs, seminaries, universities, and other bookstores. Levine Père also opened for business in 1920.

The books are, let us say, of inspired variety. They ranged from *Everyman's Talmud* to *Russian Jewry,* in two volumes, 1860–1917, and 1917–1967, edited by Aronson, Goldenweiser, Frumkin, and Lewitan. There was a shelf of Elie Wiesel, another of Martin Buber, and Chaim Potok, Herman Wouk, and Norman Mailer shared still another.

J. Levine, a short man, pleasant, wearing a yarmulka, as almost every wholesaler or supplier in this area still does, said that when his father opened the store, the people bought Hebrew theology, prayer books, and liturgical texts. "We carried an extensive line of Yiddish literature," he said. "People in the old days thirsted for Sholem Aleichem, I. L. Peretz, Abraham Reisen, H. Leivick.

"Today the business is English-language. The books in Hebrew and Yiddish are translated. People want Martin Buber, not Sholem Aleichem. The Hassidim and Hassidic Judaism, which is Jewish mysticism, has a wide audience. I can offer four different editions of the writings of the Bal Shem Tov.

"I also know there are more than thirty American universities which offer a course in the Holocaust. I supply the books. Every synagogue and temple, virtually every library has books on the Holocaust. Hannah Arendt's book on Eichmann and Raul Hilberg's on the destruction of European Jewry I cannot keep in stock for long."

He was a man who knew books and book lovers. He told me to browse, but there were so many books on so many crammed shelves that browsing had to be carried on at eye level.

Two blocks east of Eldridge is Orchard Street, once the crowded marketplace of the Lower East Side. Where pushcarts once lined the streets like caissons ready to rush across a captured bridge, now there is only a single lane through the file of cars parked along both curbs. Orchard Street still has Jews but the Jews are there in storefront warehouses. They are all distributors and suppliers—GMP Sales Company—Dress and Work Gloves; Goldman & Cohen—Bras and Girdles; Oxford Handkerchief; Victory Shirt Company. No more peddlers shout. The wares are announced by gaily painted signs swinging in a raw March wind. It is a parade of color. Feltley Hats is proclaimed by a Mondrian of red, white, and blue more expressive than anything nonobjective painters ever fantasized.

But on the corner of Orchard and Hester streets is Kaplan's Pickle Stand. Kaplan's Pickle Stand is not a store, it is a heavy board laid over several barrels behind which two old men wearing several shirts for warmth dispense horseradish at thirty-five cents a jar and quarts of dill pickles in Mason jars at eighty cents. Ripe olives are $4 a gallon. There are barrels of different-sized kosher dills. The roof of the stand is a canvas canopy, the cash register a worn drawer.

If you buy a single dill pickle, Kaplan or his partner will spear it with a little pick and hand it over in all its sour glory.

GREYLOCK

Almost two hundred of them came, well-heeled Jewish lawyers, accountants, dentists, school superintendents, lumber mill executives. One of them told me modestly he was the vice-president of a conglomerate. "But put down that it's a *small* conglomerate," he added, and for all I know he may well ride in a small Cadillac with a small chauffeur.

They were in their late forties or early fifties, a few of them with their wives, women used to formal parties by the look of their glittering gowns. Some of these men hadn't seen each other for thirty years, they were bald now, some of them portly but they didn't need the name tags to recognize each other.

The place was the Belmont Plaza Hotel, on the fourth floor, in the Baroque Room, red wallpaper flocked with fleurs-de-lis. The occasion was a Camp Greylock reunion.

Oberlin University doesn't coax two hundred alumni back for graduation week in June. The 13th Airborne wouldn't draw fifty ex-G.I.'s. But these two hundred men came from different parts of the country for a summer-camp reunion and they told me to a man they came because Camp Greylock had given them some of the most meaningful experiences in their lives; they were Robert Conroys who had beaten their way back to Shangri-La, for one evening at least.

Boys beyond number have gone to camp. They go as Boy Scouts or they go to the YMCA's Camp Mahackeno. The now defunct *Herald Tribune* in New York, and the *Chicago Tribune* have probably taken over a million boys from the slums and let them spend two weeks on the hills. The University Settlement sent me to a farm when I was ten. There are a variety of institutional camps sponsored by different churches. And there are private camps everywhere, from Aspen, Colorado, to Wingate, Maine.

But the private summer camp for Jewish boys, located for the most part in western Massachusetts, Vermont, New Hampshire, and Maine, became an American Jewish institution in a way the other camps did not become Christian institutions. They became Jewish institutions not through any religious orientation, for there was none, although most of the camps never served pork; nor through instilling an emotional allegiance to Israel, for in the nineteen-twenties and thirties American Jews were indifferent to the concept of a Jewish state; they became institutions because the sons and grandsons of immigrants, once removed from the urban milieu into the fresh air, realized intuitively that the American middle-class values of competition, clean living, camaraderie could be shared as fully by them as by anybody else.

William James of Harvard once noted that the American educational system was an eclectic system, borrowed from the Germans and the English. The one original contribution it made to education was the invention of the boys' summer camp.

One of the first of these was Camp Greylock, two thousand feet above sea level atop Mount Greylock near Becket, Massachusetts. This is one of the lushest areas in the world due to the geological curiosity of abnormally heavy spring and fall rains. King George III annoyed the Colonists when he proclaimed regal priority on all the ash and oak on this mountain for the masts of his ships. From nearby quarries came the marble for the United States Capitol. Ted Shawn founded his University of the Dance here.

Camp Greylock was founded in 1916 by Gabriel Mason, then a principal of Elijah Clark Junior High School, later the principal at Abraham Lincoln High School, and in his seventies and eighties a professor at Brooklyn College. Summer camps started to proliferate between 1910 and 1920, a response both to the feverish growth of the city and to growing Jewish affluence. In those first days, when a parent sent his boy to camp, he was in an imaginative sense sending his boy to the frontier. The boys, for example, had to eat their dinner while it was still light enough to see because there was no electricity. If the boys wanted a hiking path, they hacked it out. Over his Christmas vacation, Mason used to go up to Mount Greylock with two of his assistants, sweep the snow off the frozen lake, saw blocks of ice, and load them on a sled which a horse pulled up a causeway to an icehouse where they were packed in sawdust for the summer. At the reunion these men remembered Klaus Timberman, once Emma Goldman's associate, who lit the kerosene lamps along the main path years ago and who is buried at Greylock.

The Jews, an urban people, were never expert at woodlore. One of the reasons for Greylock's popularity was that Mason, who counted himself a disciple of Dan Beard, Ernest Thompson Seton, and Dean Gibson, the first educators who more or less institutionalized the outdoors, had as his partner his brother, George, a professional forester. Mason *frères* guaranteed that the boys would not only learn swimming in the lake and play plenty of ball, but go hiking and on their hikes learn to tell the difference between a pin and a copper oak. Once upon a time, before driver education became a requirement in the high school curriculum, hiking was dear to the hearts of city boys, probably to boys everywhere. Sixty years ago I made weekly forays to Van Cortlandt Park simply for the joy of scaling rocks. At Greylock the boys scaled mountains and they learned how to pack a knapsack and how to pitch a tent. Greylock may not have produced Daniel Boone, but it did produce boys who sooner or later guessed that Natty Bumpo was more a romantic than an accurate figure in the myth of the American woodland.

Schoolteacher Gabriel Mason added classes to the camp's activities. The boys studied surveying or mapmaking, and if they had done poorly the year before, they studied mathematics or geography. Listening to Mason describe his Greylock, an old man now, with clear blue eyes, his thick hair Scandinavian white from age, one senses he was trying to do quickly and expertly in the summers what he could only do tortuously and with great difficulty in his public schools in the winter.

Such ambition does not always succeed, but it succeeded at Greylock, succeeded in that the same boys came back summer after summer, and their younger brothers and friends followed them. Boyhood is the first and perhaps the only imperishable democracy we populate in life. Part of the affection these men still feel for each other must be from the realization that they became conscientious citizens in the middle class together.

"In the winters in Montgomery, West Virginia, I used to dream of those paths in Greylock," Bert Margolis told me. "The first classical music I ever heard was at Greylock and it was at Greylock I first studied French. All year long I saved my money as a kid so I could go to the Greylock get-together in New York in December. In fact, there was a time in my life when I spent every dime I ever earned so I could *buy* Camp Greylock."

Which indeed Mr. Margolis did in 1948 with two partners, the three of them bravely and Atlaslike struggling with a $250,000 mortgage. Margolis is a trim, stylish man, quite handsome in his early fifties. Since the tuition at Greylock last summer was $1500 and since the camp enrolls 365 boys, Mr. Margolis obviously is doing more with his purchase than simply trying to recapture the grace and happiness of his early youth. Part of the mystique about Camp Greylock is that Mr. Margolis is not a singular example. Twenty-seven Greylockers, unable to buy Camp Greylock itself, either bought or founded other camps.

"There might have been one hundred and fifty Jewish families in West Virginia in 1928," Margolis said. "I remember we had one traveling rabbi for the state. There was constant communication between us all. One of the families in Wheeling had sent their son to Camp Greylock, which was why my parents chose it for me. After my first summer—and I was seven—I knew I wanted to go into camping. When I majored in psychology at Johns Hopkins, my parents thought I wanted to become a doctor, like my brothers, but I knew exactly what I wanted."

It is different today, of course, he explained. No one ever shows a boy past seven something for the first time. The wonder and the innocence are gone, due probably to the schools, the input of television, and the attitudes of their parents.

"We have lectures on drugs and alcohol," said Margolis. "And when we tell the boys we don't have water skiing because we don't want boats polluting the lake, they understand. When I was in camp, the parents used to come for a two-week vacation in the bungalows.

Our boys aren't anxious to see their parents at all. They would much rather be separate. When Gabe Mason came up last year, I had to explain to him the forty parking spaces around the tennis courts weren't for the boys, they were for the counsellors."

"Tell them about no indoor basketball, Bert," said a wiry man interrupting us.

"I don't think boys should be indoors in the summer," said Margolis.

"Maybe you don't want to lay out the money for the courts," said the man.

"And I'm not putting in bowling alleys either," said Margolis.

"Listen," said the man, whose name was Oscar, "I was small as a kid, but a good athlete. On Sundays everyone in Becket used to come up to the camp to watch the counsellors play the semipro ball teams.

"We filled the bleachers every Sunday," said Oscar. "And the Becket people used to come up to see our plays, too. I remember when Margolis was going to be Peck's Bad Boy and came down with measles the night before."

"And that's what you remember about Greylock," said Margolis. "How to snap off a curve and how a great actor's career was nipped in the bud."

"A little more than that," said Oscar. "The first job I got when I left City College was in the office of a Greylock father. I married the sister of a Greylock counsellor and I spent my honeymoon at Greylock, in one of the family bungalows, working as a counsellor for two weeks. I've had the same doctor all these years because he went to Greylock and the same dentist for the same reason. And if I ever needed a psychiatrist, I would go to one who had gone to Greylock."

Later another man said, "I spent five years in the Air Corps during World War II. But you don't remember a war in terms of personal relationships. I didn't go back to my twenty-fifth college reunion because that was the weekend my daughter was getting married. Maybe I should have gone because she's working on her second divorce. I have recognized a Greylocker on a flight from Tanzania and I've recognized one who got out of a cab I wanted in front of F. A. O. Schwartz at Christmastime. If you ask me why I should remember the names of boys I went to camp with instead of the others, I'd have to say, 'Look at the caliber of these men.' "

Some of these men had gathered around an accordionist on the small stage, bellowing the songs they sang as boys thirty, thirty-five, and forty years before. There is something puerile about a middle-aged man working up a tear over a song he tunelessly shouted as a boy, but there is nothing puerile about good fellowship. In fact, we are often insistent that good fellowship is all that will ever redeem our society.

The Air Force officer put his finger on the Greylock mystique. I suspect some of the singing men had a son who dropped out of Michigan to live in a Seattle commune and some probably had daughters who are terribly unhappy. But once upon a time there was a community of values among middle-class Jews, values to which all subscribed; a time when Jewish fathers expected certain achievements of their sons, expectations with which sons did not quarrel.

There is still a community of values but we are never sure which of these values our neighbor holds dear and which our sons insist on discarding.

These men still measured up, not only to the expectations of their father but to the expectations they had of each other. There is a lesson all of us must learn and these men who had hiked together, played together, and sung together as boys had fortunately learned the lesson early rather than late. The lesson is that the obvious function of society is to get along with itself.

PART III: THE PRESS

"The *Jewish Ledger*," said Bert Gaster, its managing editor and publisher, "is the nearest thing there is to a nonprofit commercial enterprise in Connecticut."

That statement could serve as the epitaph for the Anglo-Jewish wire service press in America and would serve as its epitaph if the Jewish press weren't subsidized. It is my opinion that the press would be better off with the epitaph.

The subsidies are provided by the Federations, which underwrite publishing costs or guarantee the circulation or whose boards make up annual deficits. The Federations have turned the Anglo-Jewish press into a house organ, a house organ reporting on some extraordinarily dull employees who play a perpetual game of musical chairs with the chairmanship of the Special Gifts Division, ORT, and the presidency of the community center.

The Federations have become de facto publishers. Like most publishers without local competition, they have in their wisdom decided that hard news is the nonessential staple of a paper, an economic frill the Jewish community can readily do without. It is a sad situation but not on that account un-American. There are only three cities in America where publishers are in competition: Los Angeles, New York, and Chicago. Which is what led A. J. Liebling of sainted memory to remark, "There can be no schools for journalists until there are schools for publishers."

"We are the most censorious people in the world," said Jack Fishbein, editor and publisher of the *Sentinel,* whose masthead boasts it has been the voice of Chicago Jewry for over sixty years. "There is no reason why we should have a good press. You can buy most of the editors with a two-inch ad. The Jewish press is trying to reflect what is not the actual fact but the Federation wishes were, that we are a monolithic community, all subscribing to the same beliefs. But the Federation is separated from the mass of Jews as the Pope is separated from the mass of Catholics."

Albert Bloom, the executive editor of the *Pittsburgh Jewish Chronicle,* said, "Our forte is communication. Jews have plenty of money with which to train social workers and even more money to retain them, but there is not one fellowship or scholarship to train a Jewish newspaperman. There is not one prize for a Jewish journalist."

Herb Brin of the Los Angeles *Heritage,* who used to write the Rosh Hashanah and Yom Kippur greetings for Jack Kennedy, said, "The Jewish press seems no longer willing or interested in the big story. Can the plight of Soviet Jewry be unknown to a single American Jew? But week after week Soviet Jews are the page-one layout. In California there's a professor canned every week for the exercise of his conscience; a Jew named Dave Barrat has unexpectedly become premier of the province of British Columbia; a Jew who travels with Dr. Fred Schwarz's right-wing Christian Anti-Communism Crusade has formed a Jewish Citizens Council to fight for the Nixon-Agnew ticket. These stories belong on the front page and that is where I put them."

Fishbein and Brin, of course, own their papers—which return profits. Fishbein travels all over the world and writes knowledgeable articles on the Falasha Jews in East Africa and the Jesus freaks in East Chicago. He is such a profiteer that he insists that he sit on the dais for any Bonds for Israel banquet he attends.

The *Sentinel* was the first and, with the exception of the *Heritage,* the only Jewish newspaper to treat as newsworthy the Schroetter charges made in October 1972. Leonard Schroetter, a Seattle attorney who had worked in the Israeli Ministry of Justice, made a trip through Russia after Richard Nixon's conference with Brezhnev. In a confidential memorandum circulated among the White House staff, Schroetter argued that Nixon's summit conference in Moscow, far from relieving the distress of Soviet Jews, compounded their difficulties. "It is the conviction of Soviet Jewish leadership," wrote Schroetter, "that the President's trip gave the Russians the impression he was more interested in selling corn than in protecting human rights and freedom."

These charges may or may not be true. They may even be frivolous, but certainly they were newsworthy. If true, they dictate a change in strategy for the American Jewish community in its efforts to save Soviet Jews; if false, rebuttal and disclaimers; if frivolous, dismissal. It will not do to headline, as the *Cleveland Jewish News* and dozens of others headlined ISRAEL PLEASED WITH SUMMIT RESULTS—*Nixon*

Raises Jewish Issue in Moscow and then proceed to wax enthusiastic on these developments on the basis of *one,* mind you, one Henry Kissinger statement.*

Herb Brin's *Heritage* is located on the outskirts of Watts. It is a new, one-story brick building. Inside hang paintings by the Los Angeles artist Eric Ray. Heavy gates, however, always locked, protect the interior, and the building is without windows to discourage burglars who prowl by night and saunter by day. Brin, who came to the business in the early fifties from one of the Los Angeles dailies and had a hard time of it for ten years, said everyone begged him not to put up a new building where he did. "But I think this is where the *Heritage* ought to be," he said. "It is better off here than in Orange County besieged by Jewish reactionaries. The *Carolina Israelite* did all right by making integration a Jewish fight. I think we'll find the right kind of fights here."

Brin is a lanky guy who writes poetry. Poetry that is published.

The *Sentinel* and the *Heritage* are the best of them. The rest are almost wholly without a redeeming feature. And to top it off, they are utterly without humor. The Jewish press is solemn. It need not be so. The daily press is not solemn. I remember when my son, Harry Golden, Jr., covered the Reverend Billy Graham's first tent meeting in Charlotte, North Carolina, in the late nineteen-forties. Billy came to town at the end of the tobacco harvest and Charlotte was filled with farmers who had sold their crop. While these farmers sought salvation, pickpockets mingled freely. Harry Jr.'s headline read, "Some Rolls Are Called Up Yonder."

There is simply no reason why out of our history and tradition we should produce a press so lackluster. The name of a Jewish journalist has passed into the language itself: Joseph Pulitzer, the first publisher to use verbs in a headline, who invented the Sunday supplement, and perfected the use of color in newspaper, and whose "yellow journalism" made papers readable, appended a confidential memorandum to his plans for endowing Columbia University with a School of Journalism. "I strongly wish the college to set aside a sum of money for annual prizes for particular journalists and writers for their various achievements and accomplishments of excellence."

* Joseph Polakoff. Moscow (JTA) . . . "We did what we said we would do in Salzburg," Dr. Kissinger remarked. . . . "You have to consider the problem of discussing in an international forum what one side regards as an internal issue." He did not elaborate.

The Yiddish press was virtually a social force in the country. Its exemplar was Abe Cahan, who edited the *Daily Forward*. The immigrants said the *Daily Forward* was a university which cost two cents. Cahan explored every aspect of American life, once headlining a story THE FUNDAMENTALS OF BASEBALL EXPLAINED TO NON-SPORTS, in which he included a three-column diagram of the old Polo Grounds.

But there is a vital and vigorous Jewish press. It is the "underground" press, written and published by Jewish college students in universities across the country. It is an underground press not in any Belfast or Weatherman sense but because it is virtually unfunded. Jewish philanthropies here and there give these papers minimal support, for which the kids do not bother to thank them at all.

These journals, which are often no more than two four-page folds and more likely than not set in cold type are beginning to proliferate. There are enough of them to have called into being the National American Jewish Students Network with offices at 154 West Twenty-seventh Street in New York City. For "offices" read "unconverted loft." The Jewish Students Network is not a membership organization, it is an umbrella organization helping the variety of campus organizations keep track of what each is doing. Among these organizations are fifty-eight newspapers.

These papers range from *Genesis 2,* published at Harvard, to *Chutzpah,* published at the University of Chicago, to *Ha'am,* published at UCLA.

Their content is editorials, frankly opinionated yet on subjects which rarely quicken establishment interest. They report on activities as diverse as the ruling of *Beth Din* of Boston that chemical additives in food are not kosher to the good news that the College of Letters and Science at UCLA will establish a new major in Jewish studies. There are articles on DEATH AND DAVENING IN VIETNAM and TEACHING THE HOLOCAUST TO AMERICAN CHILDREN.

And they cover hard news, too. An example, from *Ha'am* (I wish I'd written the head):

UNICOPS GO CRACKERS OVER MATZAH MOBILE
The Day They Raided the Matzah Mobile
BY PHIL METSON

Wednesday, April 5th was the seventh day of Passover. About noon that day Mrs. Joyce Green, Coordinator of Student Activities of Hillel Council at UCLA, drove the "matzah mobile" (her car-in-disguise) to the front of Ackerman Union. Riding with Joyce was Rabbi David Berner, Co-Director of Hillel Council.

The purpose of the matzah mobile is to provide Kosher L'Pesach lunches for students on campus. The need for the matzah mobile lunches arises from the failure of the UCLA Food Service to provide lunches for students who observe the special Pesach dietary laws.

Joyce and Rabbi Berner had been distributing lunches from the matzah mobile for about ten minutes when a police car drove up. The two Unicops who emerged from the car were immediately joined by a representative from the Office of Environmental Health and Safety (EHS). The raid was on.

The police can act against a vendor on campus who does not have a permit from the Business Office to sell his goods. The Pesach lunches were merely being distributed and were not being sold on campus. Thus, the whole incident should have ended with little fuss.

While the Unicops were deciding what action to take, the man from EHS took over. The EHS man thrust his hand into the lunch bags for an inspection tour. Joyce quickly informed him that the bags contained macaroons, fruit and matzah. These bags of food that had seemed to him mighty in potential danger were really mighty innocuous.

The EHS man then directed his attention to the gefilte fish salads carried by the matzah mobile. He told Joyce they could not be served unless they were kept cold in a refrigerator or warmed to 142 degrees.

During this discussion, one of the Unicops had reentered the police car. Emerging from his car once again, the Unicop approached Joyce. He told her that he had spoken with his supervisor at Headquarters who decided that the lunches could not be distributed, even without charge. Both policemen returned to their car to watch the matzah mobile to insure against further distribution of food.

Subsequent investigation has revealed that the police and EHS were called to the scene by someone in the Food Service. This anonymous "someone" witnessed the matzah mobile's activities the previous day. One can only wonder why "he" did not approach the matzah mobile on that Tuesday to investigate the situation, and thus, avoid Wednesday's tragic-comedy.

PART IV: SOME DAUGHTERS

Some incidental intelligence gleaned from traveling:

> Our language has become blue, a hangover from World War
> II. Obscenity between men is not only casual but common parlance;
> The telephone is the greatest menace to the uninhibited dialogue
> since the invention of eavesdropping;
> If you talk to Jewish leaders about their Jewish community, you
> would be lucky if you guessed half of that community are women.

There are Jewish men who love their wives, delight in their daughters, and honor their mothers. There are probably even Jews who adore their girl friends. But no Jewish alderman in Chicago recommended a woman for my enlightenment although Ellen Sapperstein is a state representative from the North Side; no Federation official in Cleveland interrupted his litany of superstar fund raisers to name a woman, although Jewish women raise millions of dollars every year; only Irwin Goldberg, the director of Montefiore Hospital thought to mention Lois Michaels' dissertation which is a history of Jewish medicine in Pittsburgh.

Men often think of women as little cobras or little bonbons. There are, indeed, women who can kill a kangaroo with a single blow and there are others who collect love letters (it is unwise ever to write a letter to a woman you can't cool a beer on).

But not all Jewish men subscribe to this truth.

Naomi Levine is now the executive director of the American Jewish Congress; Gloria Schaeffer, prettier than any weather girl you'll ever see on television, is Connecticut's Secretary of State and a likely candidate for her Democratic Party's nomination for governor; and Mary Kaufman is probably the leading legal authority on war crimes and cold-war conspiracies.

One must ascribe a Pacific Ocean of good humor to Jewish women like these. Unchanging male attitudes, far from reducing them to nervous states of hypnotic imbecility, seem instead to generate intelligence, patience, and good works.

Ande Manners has the face and characteristics of the devoted nurse who never appears careworn, only compassionate and professional. She is the author of *Poor Cousins,* an account of the immigration of the Eastern European Jews to America from the viewpoint of the assimilated German Jews.

Ande Manners, née Miller, is married to the writer Will Manners, the author of several novels, a biography of LaGuardia, and the estimable history, *TR and Will,* the story of the break between Theodore Roosevelt and William Howard Taft, which made Woodrow Wilson President in 1912. The Manners are the parents of three daughters and they live in Norwalk, Connecticut, on a secluded acre on East Rocks Road. Adjoining their land is the home of Will Manners' brother, David, and his wife. The two couples bought the land jointly several years ago and have from year to year constructed what are now large, comfortable houses.

Will and Ande had just finished another addition to their home. Sawdust and wood chips ringed house and the living room was suffused with the smell of cedar. One side of the Mannerses' living room is glass overlooking a wooded hill which slopes south to the Norwalk River two miles away.

Mrs. Manners prepared the coffee. The greatest economy of motion in this world is a woman in her kitchen.

She has an unblinking gaze and an uncluttered mind and her book is one to put beside *The Spirit of the Ghetto, Strangers in the Land,* and *The Promised City.*

As for any disadvantages she suffered as a woman, she said, "There are too many good writers and too many good editors who are women to consider the question seriously. There are disabilities, but I think they exist for our generation, not my daughters'. Many times, the older men I interviewed were condescending. They'd ask me if I was married and did I have a family and when I told them yes, I was married and yes, I had a family, there was a silence in which they wondered why wasn't I home caring for them?"

The former chairman of the New York UJA, presently a vice-chairman of the Joint Distribution Committee as well as the national chairman of the Women's Division of UJA, is Mrs. Burt Siris. None of these posts is honorary or nominal. Mrs. Siris has raised millions of dollars from Jews for philanthropic and overseas agencies.

Elaine Siris is blond, trim, hazel-eyed and gracious. She is, in short, comely. She is energetic and well-spoken, delights, in fact, in talking, but she is always to the point.

Her home is in Rye, New York, in Westchester County and from her living room one can throw a stone into Long Island Sound. A pier juts into the water. Between the house and the shore is a swimming pool, forlornly abandoned on this cold drizzly January day.

"I built three swimming pools in Israel before I built that one," she said.

We talked over a table at one end of the living room beside a two-way fireplace where wet wood spat and popped. "There's a difference I want you to know," she said, "between the balabatim and the Zionists. I am a Zionist. My father made me a Zionist. He was a well-to-do man. He was the founder of Howard Clothes but he became a Zionist in the thirties.

"He was ill and the family went with him to Carlsbad to consult with specialists. We went through Germany on a train where we had to keep the window shades down. The evil was omnipresent. We could feel it. But once exposed to it, my father vowed he wouldn't die until he had done everything possible to save the Jews of Europe.

"After the war, the Jews who were left were the DP's. Then he worked even harder. And he lived long enough to see Israel become a state. I was a little girl before we went to Carlsbad and I used to say to my friends, 'I'm not ashamed of being Jewish,' which is a terrible thing for a child to need to say, and Zionists don't say it."

Then she laughed. "Going to Carlsbad made me a Zionist and my sister met a Scotchman on the golf course who was a Jew and married him."

Mrs. Siris goes to every part of the country to talk to Jewish groups. She had the day before returned from Kansas City, where she spoke despite an impacted wisdom tooth. She means business when she says she likes to talk. It is strenuous volunteer work. She is asking people for money. She must, accordingly, be absolutely informed as to why that money is needed and for what specific purposes it will be spent and why it must be this particular group to give it.

She has made twenty-five trips to Israel and trips to Rumania,

Morocco, Iran, South America. "I've been in Paris," she said. "Jewish Paris, where the newcomers from Algeria live.

"I have on occasion seen money spent poorly and on other occasions spent wisely. The accommodations for the elderly *olim* in Israel, in fleabag hotels and collapsing apartment houses, are sometimes hazardous and demeaning. I think we could do something better. I have suggested that these people are lonely, ill at ease, and frightened. I would like to institute a program to train Israeli housewives who don't work to take one of these families under wing and help ease them into their new and rigorous life. I think we need such a training program because there's no concept of volunteerism in Israel like there is here. In Rumania, where the Joint Committee maintains a department store for Jews, purchases are made by buying credits. On Hanukah or on one of the happy holidays, the Joint Committee sends a letter to the single aged, the elderly widows or widowers, without family now, often without friends, telling them they have 350 credits to spend in the department store. Because these are credits, no shopper and no clerk knows the purchases are charity. It is smart spending."

She made no bones about the discrimination against women in the UJA and the other fund-raising organizations. "Men are shortsighted," she said. "Seventy percent of the money will come into the possession of Jewish women who live longer than their husbands. Men find the work exciting and exulting. They still think women do it because they are dutiful. But the women I know exult in the work, too."

While she was the chairman of the New York UJA in 1969, Elaine Siris received an invitation to accompany a Prime Minister's Mission to the Suez and the Sinai. "The invitation said 'RSVP Israeli Consul,' which I did, and he said I couldn't go. He said the invitation was a courtesy invitation extended because I was a chairman. But the trip was too arduous and dangerous for a woman.

"I said, 'Your Prime Minister's a woman,' and he said, 'That's different.' To make a long story short, I was the only woman among sixty men who made the trip. On the Canal, Moshe Dayan spoke to me."

As well Moshe Dayan should!

The mother of three children, Mrs. Siris said that what has encouraged her work and her zeal is the admiration of her husband, who rejoices in her accomplishments. "He likes to introduce himself as the husband of the speaker," she said. "The work takes disproportionate amounts of time and money. Our annual gift is $50,000, but I spend another $10,000 in traveling. If my work ever menaced my husband, I couldn't do it."

Since Burt Siris is an ex-Navy deep-sea diver and a manufacturer who has built up a business which has recently gone public, the chances are that Elaine Siris will never menace him unless she embezzles from the UJA.

Congresswoman Bella Abzug's New York office is at 252 Seventh Avenue, in the Federal Building at Twenty-fifth Street. Two-fifty-two has all the angularity and discomfort of any building ever approved by the chairman of the House Public Works Committee.

Mrs. Abzug represents New York's Twentieth Congressional District, which runs along the Hudson River from the northern part of Greenwich Village up Manhattan's West Side and into Riverdale in the Bronx. Though the district has a heavily Jewish population, it also has a heterogeneous mix of blacks and whites, Puerto Ricans and Protestants, rich and poor and those in the middle.

Howard Brock, Mrs. Abzug's aide, a young man but reticent, thoroughly informed but cautious, told me the district has many groups of varying degrees of political sophistication.

"And many of her constituents," he said, "come here for service. They want to lodge complaints against a slum landlord or they want help with food stamps or they need advice on how to apply for Medicare. Mrs. Abzug has become so adept at helping these constituents satisfy their needs through local New York agencies that other congressmen call her on behalf of *their* constituents. Our office has become a clearinghouse."

Mrs. Abzug was late this foggy Friday afternoon. Her telephones kept ringing and other aides kept rushing to answer them. As a matter of fact, the place was as busy as the old-fashioned horse room.

An overalled service man brushed by the desk carrying a paper-wrapped bundle. "I'm here to install the curtains," he announced peremptorily.

"You were supposed to be here Monday," said the receptionist. "Monday morning. You can't hang curtains in there now. Mrs. Abzug has several appointments this afternoon."

The man shrugged and hoisted the long bundle to his shoulder and backed out.

"Is there any chance you could come next Monday?" asked the receptionist.

"You gotta ask my boss about that, lady," said the man.

In New York, even the clearinghouses need clearinghouses.

Mrs. Abzug came in, burdened by a heavy overcoat and a heavy briefcase and her big hat.

"I'll be with you in a minute," she said, not stopping, then over her shoulder to the receptionist at the desk, "Did this man get a cup of coffee?"

This is Mrs. Abzug's second term in the House. In 1970, after winning a primary, she was elected the representative from the Nineteenth Congressional District, which the Republican Legislature in Albany gerrymandered. She waged a primary for nomination as the representative from the Twentieth against the incumbent William F. Ryan, which she lost in the spring of '72. Two months later, however, Mr. Ryan died of cancer and the party named Mrs. Abzug as its candidate to succeed him.

She is the second Jewish woman to serve in the House of Representatives. Some years ago, a Mrs. Adele Meyer was elected to fill her husband's unexpired term when he died in office.

I sipped hot coffee from a plastic cup in her office while she dug out vanilla ice cream from a Dixie cup with an old-fashioned double-bladed wooden spoon.

In discussing women's rights across a steel-sided desk, I found none of the militancy I expected. She spoke evenly and dispassionately even though one suspects she might be a compulsive talker. But the more she talked, the more arresting her face became until at last I realized that Bella Abzug has a beautiful face.

"There is no question," she said, "but that the Jewish organizations have not yet realized that women have a public position. I doubt that any organization in New York or elsewhere has thought to count the number of Jewish women, say, in the State Legislature.

"Last week," she went on, "I spoke at the Riverdale Federation. Afterwards, the men congratulated me and offered the information I was the first woman ever to address them. I speak before a great many Jewish groups and the men are always telling me I am the first woman.

"Jewish men need to get used to women in different roles. And they will have no choice about it," she said. "There are already three or four women rabbis. The politicians are getting used to women. Women did all the work and now they want some of the offices."

I hazarded that the religious subjugation of women in Orthodox Judaism might be a contributing factor for Jewish male indifference. "I am a Conservative Jew," said Mrs. Abzug. She stared past me toward the window the curtains should have by now been gracing and perhaps she was thinking that men didn't need Orthodoxy for their indifference.

"Jewish groups often bring pressure on Jewish congressmen," she said. "A Jewish group has to come to me perforce because I am the congresswoman. My womanhood is no obstacle to them nor is it to me. We perform together.

"There are twelve Jews in the House of Representatives. We meet from time to time to consider the concerns of American Jewry—aid to Israel, Soviet Jews, more recently the election; we're Democrats and Jews and we have to inform our Democratic constituency that Richard Nixon isn't better for the Jews than George McGovern. George McGovern is better, but that's water under the bridge. Of these twelve, I am the only Jew who studied Hebrew and I am the most fluent in Yiddish. If it were possible to be the most Jewish member of Congress, which it is not, I would be elected.

"And I am the least passionate," she went on. "We met with Henry Pottinger of the Department of Health, Education, and Welfare to discuss the affirmative guidelines policy.

"You're aware that there are Jews exercised over these guidelines because they think it results in reverse discrimination. They fear that quotas applied to the able and the qualified to advance the cause of the disabled and the unqualified penalize Jews. The Jewish groups want blacks to advance but not at the expense of Jews.

"But Pottinger convinced us that these guidelines are indeed affirmative, that they will produce results, that they will realize legitimate goals. We urged Pottinger to establish an ombudsman so that those who feel discriminated against can have redress. Pottinger agreed. Unless we wanted to scuttle what was a positive program, I can't think of a more reasonable solution."

Then, for the first time, her fist clenched and her voice rose a decibel. "The problem isn't that a woman has to be chief of surgery in a hospital or that blacks must have precedence over Jews in getting into medical schools. The problem isn't that a Puerto Rican must be the head of a science department in a university or that the disadvantaged must have priority in housing. The problem is that we need more hospitals and more medical schools and we need more universities and better housing for all income groups in the middle- and low-income range. But we cannot have these because we keep sinking our money into military hardware."

I bid Mrs. Abzug *shabbat shalom*.

Feminist movements recur every fifty years. Florence Nightingale and Clara Barton went into the hospitals in the nineteenth century and suffragettes chained themselves to fire hydrants in the twentieth. In this decade a woman will sit on the Supreme Court and another will run for vice-president. The gains made by a feminist movement are never lost. Seven hundred wives and princesses and three hundred concubines broke King Solomon's heart when they turned to other gods. God was wroth, the Bible says. He forgot that Solomon was an old man with some old-fashioned ideas.

PART V: ZAYDIM AND BUSH BURNERS

CHARLEY WEST

The escalating concern over the pollution of our environment had one of its first alarms in Charleston, West Virginia.

There, in 1806, the Ruffner brothers, Andrew and Thomas, drilled the first salt well in America. By 1815, the Ruffners were pumping 2500 gallons of brine daily, which they boiled over 52 salt furnaces.

In drilling for brine, the Ruffners and other salt kings not only tapped natural gas deposits, which were later used to fire the furnaces, but also petroleum, for which there was no commercial use. They let the oil drain into the Kanawha (K'naw) River, which West Virginians nicknamed "Old Greasy."

Charleston, or "Charley West," as the airlines call it to distinguish it from its namesake, "Charley South," was founded by Virginia planter Colonel George Clendenin as Fort Lee in 1788. He named the fort after his father when the Virginia Legislature chartered it as a city in 1795. Daniel Boone was Charleston's first representative.

Slavery was never useful in this mountain area. After Sumter, Charleston and Wheeling representatives nullified Virginia's Act of Secession of 1861. West Virginia, along with Delaware, Maryland, Tennessee, Missouri, and Kentucky, became a border state. Confederate troops occupied Charleston at the beginning of the war but retreated in November 1862, when Union general William Rosecrans secured the lower Kanawha Valley at the battle of Gauley's Bridge.

On April 20, 1863, Abraham Lincoln admitted West Virginia to the Union as the thirty-fifth state. Among the soldiers in the Ohio regiment stationed in Charleston who cheered the proclamation were Colonel Rutherford B. Hayes and First Lieutenant William McKinley, to whom John F. Kennedy bore an uncanny resemblance.

Seventy thousand people live in Charleston, the state capital and the second largest city in West Virginia, whose total population numbers 1.7 million. Kanawha County is one of the chemical centers of the country. Union Carbide, Monsanto, Goodrich, DuPont produce chemicals ranging from chlorine to urethane foam.

Charley West has a Southern flavor but it is not a Southern town. Only 4.5 percent of its citizens are black. At the venerable Daniel Boone Hotel, a West Virginia Teachers Convention was in process when I was there. Black teachers casually took elevators up and down to the seminars. Traveling around the country, one always sees more and more blacks in hotels, restaurants, and especially in airline terminals—and not black businessmen or salesmen, but black families.

In school desegregation, Charleston was well ahead of its neighboring Southern states. Governor William G. Marland was the only political leader below the Mason-Dixon Line to make a public declaration that the 1954 Supreme Court ruling on school desegregation was the law of the land and would be implemented. He saved the state a great deal of agony. A few years ago, Marland turned up in Chicago driving a hack, an ex-alcoholic on the way back. Sadly, he succumbed to cancer a year ago. He had a telling effect. For example, West Virginia State College was a black school in 1954. It integrated. It has more whites than black students today.

Many things have changed since Jews from the Lithuanian village of Popilan began coming to Charleston in the late eighteen-nineties, but many things have not.

On Summers Street, across from the movie house and beside the poolroom, is B & B Loans—The World's Smallest Department Store. Guitars and ukuleles hang from the ceiling as straight in their rank and file as a regiment of West Pointers. Hi-fi transmitters pyramid on the shelves. Luggage bulks along the walls. Jewelry, opera glasses, binoculars, and nowadays, of course, chess sets await inspection beneath sliding glass panels in display cases.

B & B's president is Edwin Masinter, a big fellow in his fifties, with black eyebrows and a barely perceptible drawl. B & B, for all its advertised smallness, is an eight-clerk operation.

"This was my father's pawn shop," said Masinter. "He came to West Virginia as a peddler, selling buttons and needles and pots and pans in the mining camps and the coal fields. Then he opened a saloon, which Prohibition closed down. So he started up B & B Loans, a pawn shop.

"Nobody borrows from a pawn shop any more. B & B is a retail business, but I try to preserve the old myth that you can get a real bargain in a pawn shop. We do an awfully good business in musical instruments and electronic equipment. But I have to buy it all in New York.

"That's the idea behind the slogan 'The World's Smallest Department Store,' which I invented. In fact, the slogan was once a subject of scrutiny by Wall Street lawyers. No one, not the newspapers, not the Yellow Pages, not the SEC, likes 'The Biggest Store in the State,' or 'The Greatest Dollar Volume in West Virginia.' These statements may or may not be true. But when I incorporated 'The World's Smallest Department Store,' the lawyers said no one is ever going to challenge the claim."

Masinter is the treasurer of the B'nai Jacob Synagogue, the Orthodox congregation, and he is a member also of Temple Israel, the Reform congregation. Throughout the South, the traveler will often find Jews who belong to as many congregations as there are in town, Reform, Orthodox, and Conservative, on the ground that the shul needs all the members it can get.

"None of us are pawnbrokers or peddlers any more," said Masinter, reviewing Jewish history in Charleston, "but some of us are still doing things our fathers did. My father took care of the traveling *schnorrers,* the Jewish drifters who demanded a handout from every Jewish storekeeper on the route. I was always humiliated when my old man made me lead these bums over to the hotel."

Incredulously, he pointed his finger at himself. "*I* take care of them today. *I* maintain the family tradition."

"The schnorrer still comes, but in a different package. One fellow ran into the store one afternoon and told me he had a wife and three kids stranded in the car. He was out of gas and had no place to sleep. 'What do you need?' I asked him. 'Could you spare a twenty?' he begged. I said, 'Here's ten. Fill up on gas. Get the wife and kids some food, then come around with them and we'll see what we can do for the night.' Never saw him again," laughed Masinter.

"Usually I take them over to the poolroom and see that they get a meal and listen to their story. The Jewish community puts up money to help them out. We call it the Little Federation. Two kids came in one day and in the poolroom I heard their story. One of them wasn't Jewish and the other was maybe Jewish. His mother was a Christian and his father had remarried and she's a Christian, too. The two kids are on their way to Pensacola to see a buddy about

a job," Masinter shrugged, "and they are starving. But I wanted to
know so I asked, 'How did you hear about me?' And the maybe-
Jewish kid says, 'My father told me when I left that if I got into
trouble in the South go to the Jewish store on Main Street.' That
was very good advice and I gave them a couple of bucks to get to
the next town and filled the back of the car with bread because I
wanted to be sure they didn't starve going over the mountains.

"It's a good thing they come to me first. Because if they reach
the rabbi, he gives them everything. He'd pay for psychiatric counseling if we let him."

Masinter smiled. But I had the distinct impression that if the Jewish
community let him, he'd pay for psychiatric counseling as quickly.

In its way, Charleston is the world's smallest department store,
too. It offers great bargains. It supports a symphony, several little
theater groups, and a minor-league ball team. Within a four-hundred-
mile radius are Chicago, Cleveland, Pittsburgh, New York, Philadelphia, Richmond, Jacksonville, and Atlanta. The real buys are
unlimited geography—unspoiled and undeveloped—and the prospects
of intensely enjoyed leisure.

American leisure is no longer a family trip to the church social.
Leisure is a weekend on the water in a pleasure craft or a camping
trip in a well-appointed trailer. Hunting rifles come equipped with
telescopic sights and reels on fishing poles do everything but scale
the trout. And as these pleasures multiply, so does the congestion.

Yet West Virginia hasn't made as good a thing of Charleston and
the surrounding mountains and waterways as Ed Masinter has of
B & B Loans. With every census, the state loses a congressman. Since
1966, Charleston has lost 1000 citizens. The population loss in West
Virginia and in this city is not, as it is in many other Southern cities,
a loss of the unemployed, the blacks, and the poor whites trekking
north to industrial centers. The loss is among the skilled and the
professional. It is a loss of the young who do not come back after
college, of the adventurous who seek risk in the big city, and the
competent who seek greater if faceless security in megalopolis.

A CENSUS

There is no Jewish enclave in Charleston.
While several smaller towns surround the city, notable among them

Nitro, built instantly in 1917, named for the explosive it manufactured to win World War I, there is no suburban complex. "And anyway," sighed Rabbi Samuel Cooper of B'nai Jacob, "it is hard to have enclaves with only twelve hundred people."

Orthodox Rabbi Cooper came to this, his first and only pulpit, forty-one years ago, at a time when there were more Jews in Charleston than there are now. The Jewish population of Charleston reached 2000 in 1950, but since then Jews have hiked out with the mountaineers.

A rapidly diminishing community is an unsettling experience for Jews. They lose more of their people proportionately than any other segment of the population. The departure threatens the investment the remaining have in B'nai Jacob and Reform Temple Israel, whose rabbi is Samuel Volkman. The departure diminishes as well a way of life and a place in the community. For the Jews in Charleston are a singular group. There is no Greek Orthodox community in the city as there is in Charlotte or Irish community as there is in Savannah. The fewer the Jews, the more vulnerable they feel, vulnerable in the worry that their heterogeneity will be subdued and made meaningless.

In 1959, Rabbi Cooper began keeping a comprehensive record of every identifiable Jew in Charleston. He collected his data from births, deaths, arrivals, departures, marriages, Bar Mitzvahs, conversions, and apostasies. In these thirteen years, Cooper has become a skilled demographer. Though it is small, he can trace the complete nervous system of one Jewish community. His research and statistics are widely quoted by Jewish sociologists and demographers elsewhere. The reasons for the Jewish attrition are obvious reasons: more Jews die than are born; many Jews marry Christians and abandon their identity; and the young, trained for the professions, are no longer interested in the family store.

Rabbi Cooper publishes his report on March 1 of every year. His fourteenth annual report, 1971–72, lists 26 Jewish deaths and 6 Jewish births. Between March 1959 and March 1972 there were 229 deaths and 149 births.

Where the birthrate of the general population of the United States is 17.7 children per 1000 and the birthrate of the general population of Charleston is 17.3, the Jewish birthrate in West Virginia is 5.1 per 1000. Where the mortality rate of the general population of the

United States is 9.4 deaths per 1000 and that of Charleston 10.3, the Jewish rate is 22.1.

Demographers cite as the replacement level for the family 2.1 children, which takes into account the number of adults who never marry, the number who marry but remain childless, and the number of children who do not succeed to adulthood. Where the average size of Catholic and Protestant families is at least 2.1, the Jewish family size is 1.7.*

Jews have the smallest families because they marry late, because they do not desire large families, and because they have uniformly favorable attitudes toward contraception; i.e., Jews are more likely to practice contraception *before* the birth of their first child.

Many have advanced clever and almost persuasive reasons to explain the low Jewish birthrate which range from the fact that the Jews are an insecure minority to the desire of the Jewish mother to lavish love and affection on her children and consequently she has fewer in order to lavish more.

Rabbi Cooper waved these considerations aside. He is a medium-sized man whose movements are as impulsive as electric charges. I thought I heard an accent—no, he speaks so quickly that his words are clipped.

"Our birthrate," he said, "is falling because of our social mobility, our desire to realize to the fullest the middle-class values. Social mobility involves educating children, which a large family precludes. Social mobility involves obedience to prevailing mores and large families are not the vogue. Even in the most expensive developments, houses are rarely built to hold six or seven children.

"And the second reason our birthrate is low is due to the changing image of the American woman. No one today thinks a woman plays only a maternal role. No one thinks she owes everything to the children. The common expression is that she owes it to herself. These ideas affect every American, but we see them at play first among Jews because Jews are more mercurial."

The college generation has disappeared from Charleston. The young are always on the lookout for green pastures. If there are any in Charleston, they do not see them. Rabbi Cooper's sons have left and so have Rabbi Volkman's daughters, and Ed Masinter does not expect his boys to join the smallest department store.

* *The Growth of American Family Studies*, Princeton Fertility Studies, and *Detroit Area Studies*, quoted in *American Jewish Book* (1971), pp. 16–17.

Birds taking wing is not a new phenomenon. But more than birds are flying.

Of the original 1626 Jews Cooper counted in 1959, only 839 still live in Charleston. These represent the hard-core second- and third-generation Charlestonians, who still maintain family establishments. The professional composition of the Jewish community has changed radically. Once it was a community of entrepreneurs. Now it is a community of professional employees. One hundred and two Jews work in government, state, municipal, and federal, where thirteen years ago none did; 42 Jews are teachers, where thirteen years ago only 18 were; 91 are now professional employees, accountants, chemists, sales managers, where none were in 1959.

"It's sad," said Rabbi Cooper, "because it means these Jews have their roots in the organization, not in the community. The organization is designed to exist into perpetuity while a community is made up of mortals making mortal assumptions."

The salient characteristic of the Charleston Jewish community is that where the rest of the country is growing younger—50 percent of all Americans are twenty-four years of age or under—Charleston is growing older. Sixty percent of its Jews are over thirty-five. There are six times as many Jewish widows as there are Jewish widowers.

The older Jews in Charleston are socially and religiously self-sustaining but the younger Jews are not. Forty-five percent of the Jewish marriages in Charleston in the last thirteen years have been with a Christian partner. Outside the enclave, the rate of intermarriage among Jews is always high. In Iowa, over 50 percent of the Jews intermarry and in Indianapolis 35 percent. Sometimes the Christian partner converts, more often not. Conversion of the Christian partner is a more likely prospect in areas where there is a heavy Jewish concentration, in Cleveland or Boston, but it is not a likely prospect where Jews are few in number.

Intermarriage may be one of the reasons compelling Jews into the enclave, which offers concentrated Jewish activities. But the enclave may prove futile, too, when children disperse into other cities and into professions.

Rabbi Cooper, like most rabbis, is anxious to entertain the visiting fireman in his study. The interview concluded, the rabbi shows off the sanctuary and the classrooms.

But Rabbi Samuel Volkman came to the Daniel Boone Hotel

and over a table in a dining room made livid with mycotta discoursed on the fate of his congregation, Temple Israel.

"Cooper's annual report is demoralizing," said Volkman, who has been in Charleston now for twenty years. "I don't mean he shouldn't issue the report—he should. I mean that it is hard to escape the conclusion that there is an apparent willingness in many Jews to defect from Jewish responsibilities."

Rabbi Volkman, graying, dour, and stylish, is not a man to waste time on overcooked hamburgers or frost-covered glasses filled with right smart ice and Coke when he sees consequences.

"I do not think all Jews should be Democrats nor all of them Republicans. And I do not think all Jews should live in metropolitan areas. Jews have been valuable to Charleston. There are other marginal sects in the South which have thrived and burgeoned by virtue of a proselytizing mission which our law forbids.

"What's to be done? I think the national organizations who are casting about these days for something to do ought to decide that keeping the Jew in the boondocks is a high-priority necessity. The enduring pattern of Jewish scholarship in America is a subtle propaganda aimed at redeeming the Jew by proving he is a contributing force in American culture. Outside of metropolitan areas, however, we are liable to become a community devoted to the care of the aged . . ."

There have been ghost towns and I suppose there will eventually one day be a ghost state. It is hard to see what the national organizations can do when the local Jews can do virtually nothing to arrest the exodus.

During World War II, the Jews in Charleston recruited a kosher butcher. They wrote to a young man in the Navy that the community not only offered him a competition-free market, but they were willing to offer him a low interest rate. He turned it into a good deal, too. And the board of B'nai Jacob rescued a Jewish businessman when his credit was cut off by heartless banks.

But B'nai Jacob has been without a cantor for several years and nearby Huntington cannot find a rabbi. The city of Charleston has a Committee of 100, businessmen, clergy, teachers, and politicians who try to attract intellectuals and teachers and artists. The one émigré from the Eastern establishment has been Jay Rockefeller, who settled in West Virginia because there he thought he would most quickly and most meaningfully realize his political goals and ambitions. But how many young men are there in the whole American community with Jay Rockefeller's talents and vision?

One of the congregants at B'nai Jacob, Simon Meyer, a businessman and lately a historian, has ventured the as yet embryonic suggestion of a Jewish Committee of 100. But there are imponderables. A kosher butcher is a known quantity, but a Jew who is, say, a newspaperman is not.

The prospect for Charleston Jewry in the next decade is that it will steadily diminish to a point where the two congregations will have to merge. To Jews of the post-Depression and postwar generations this seems a necessary and in many ways a desirable course. In the Southern town, the synagogue or temple is the focus of almost all Jewish activity. From the synagogues and temples emanate Jewish influence.

But in the South there is often an attenuated bitterness between the Reform and Orthodox congregations, as though one set of Jews had a right to be jealous of another set's credentials. Some of this bitterness has been fostered by the rabbis and some of it has been fostered by the nature of the South. Southerners thrive on gradations. It is hard to live long in the South before learning that there are important distinctions between high, middle, and low Episcopal services. Southern Episcopalians will insist on elucidating these differences whether the respondent wants to learn them or not. Other Southerners will limn the gradations among their McCosh, Stewart, and Cannon relatives. The novelist Hamilton Basso said the South was a Shinto culture. He was right. Ancestor worship is endemic in the region and the hoarier an institution the more venerable it becomes. The Daniel Boone Hotel is a prime example. One would think Holiday Inns and Hilton Travel Lodges would have put it out of business long ago. It offers the kind of room traveling salesmen fled at night. Yet it is going strong. The number of times an Orthodox rabbi explains to Southerners the difference between his congregation and a Reform congregation and a Reform rabbi the difference between his and an Orthodox is enough to inspire most men with the notion that there really is a profound difference.

Probably the rabbis have fostered bitterness unconsciously, fostered it because the older the Orthodox rabbi the greater the chances that he was educated in his seminary by Eastern European scholars and Talmudists, unfamiliar with the American impulse. America is a secular society. The U. S. Constitution insists upon it and the Chamber of Commerce insists on rabbis, priests, and ministers weekly delivering benedictions and convocations and occasional "Get up and go" talks. The native-born Reform rabbi, educated by the native-born teacher, cannot help but believe his congregation is an integral part of the general community.

This is not to insist that Orthodox rabbis are parochial—indeed, Rabbi Cooper leads the peace parade in Charleston—but there is often a feeling among the Reform that the Orthodox insistence that the letter of the law is the only prescription for the Jewish life is simply a placebo.

In most Southern towns, too, the chances are that the Reform temple will be the older or the oldest congregation. Temple Israel in Charleston was founded by German Jews in 1863 and B'nai Jacob by shtetl Jews in 1897. And, in their way, once upon a time German Jews were snooty and selective.

The meld between all the Jewish sects, which has transfigured Jewish communities elsewhere in America, which has produced Federations, community centers, and Hebrew high schools is just beginning to affect the South. And only the larger cities, not the smaller ones.

One who will not hold dual membership is Reform Jew Stanley Lowenstein. Over a meal of broiled flounder and roasted corn, Lowenstein said forcefully, "I do not like an Orthodox rabbi telling me I am not a good Jew. I do not like the Orthodox telling me they are the observant Jews, the religious Jews. You can quote me."

Lowenstein, an investment banker, a quondam manager of the championship Choate football team, on which Joseph Kennedy, Jr., played, is a third-generation Charlestonian. His new home, high on steep Louden Heights Road, has an encircling wooden deck which offers a view of the Kanawha River below and, beyond, the downtown lights of Charleston.

Canvases hang in every room. "None of it is big-name stuff," said Lowenstein. "We have three paintings by a Haitian named Botello and two small pieces of sculpture by James Rosati, whom I met once and liked very much. We buy canvases we like and admire at local art shows and we have been accumulating them for years."

When I asked him about the Lowenstein Fountain in front of the library, he explained that the money for the sculpture had come from various members of the Lowenstein family and was given to honor his father, Joe Lowenstein.

"By virtue of the gift," he explained, "I was asked to serve on the committee and did not select the work personally. It was done by Robert Cornbach, a Long Island sculptor, who specializes in fountains."

The Lowensteins have a married daughter in St. Louis, a son at Wesleyan, and a younger boy who is a freshman at the Kansas City Art Institute.

"The boys," Lowenstein said, "think my animus about the Orthodox-Reform distinction is silly. They call it 'irrelevant.' " Then he thought awhile. A dry mountain wind rustled the dry leaves on the mountainside. "I hope their view prevails," he said.

STRIP MINING IN TOWN

West Virginia is the nation's leading coal producer. Metallurgists estimate that there are 4 billion tons of coal still up there in the hills. Pit mining is the state's biggest industry. There are, however, areas where the operators gouge coal from the surface, the notorious strip-mining process.

Though strip mining is not as widespread in West Virginia as it is in Kentucky and Ohio, there is enough of it to make it a campaign issue in the gubernatorial election, Arch Moore for, Jay Rockefeller against. "The land is there for us to use," said Moore. He won.

Flying down from New York or up from Atlanta, the traveler sees none of the strip operations. Even if the airlines offered a tour, he would probably devote much of his attention to the alarming vision of the Charleston airport, which is a filled-in runway between two mountains.

Strip mining is, among other things, a bad habit which not only desecrates nature's loveliness but now threatens the center city's stability. The engineers and their bureaucratic allies find it as fulfilling to tear up a city street as they do to tear down a mountainside.

The state has destroyed valuable precincts of the city, victimized by the "Southern Highway Syndrome." When the United States Congress appropriated millions upon millions of dollars for highway construction, Southern legislatures ran to grab it. They laid down superhighways east, west, north, and south until it dawned on them all they were doing was facilitating the passage of tourists through the state with blinding speed.

But the authorities can always find one more reason to raze a neighborhood. So daily the bulldozers lumber to the lots and level homes. Strip mining might have run rampant in Charleston but for the fact that now and then the Jews got in the way.

Several years ago, eighty Jews banded together to found a country club with tennis courts and a nine-hole golf course. Stanley Lowenstein, who recited this history, explained that the purpose of the Jewish country club was not necessarily to emulate the Gentiles but in some respects to avoid them. The "five-o'clock shadow" between Jews and Gentiles, or "segregation at sunset," is an actual prevailing condition: Jews and Christians meet in commercial or community interests only. It is also true that many Jews desire no more. They have little interest in social integration.

This Jewish country club, named South Moor, went its parochial way until the Charleston Board of Education needed a new school and dispatched a team of surveyors to find the flattest land, which is at a premium in Charleston. The South Moor Country Club, while it was no mesa, was still not a precipitous bluff. The Board of Education exercised its right of eminent domain and condemned the property.

Understandably, the Jews were nettled. They conceded the right of the state to expropriate the property of some for the benefit of all, but there was only one Jewish country club and very possibly, if the surveyors had applied themselves, they might have found more than one tract of flat land.

Ed Masinter said if the Jews had demonstrated, parading around City Hall with placards and shouting slogans, they might well have saved South Moor. "But," he added, "the ground was undeniably flat and we have more important priorities than mustering heroic efforts on behalf of a country club."

What was annoying was not that one cultural institution of dubious worth was about to be razed but that no one in Charleston gave a damn where the Jews were to golf and play tennis in the future. Harry Hoffman, an editorial writer of rare gifts who philosophizes for the *Charleston Gazette,* took the country-club set to task because none had offered haven to the Jews in this crisis.

So things remained until . . .

Until the Board of Education announced it was proceeding with the purchase. The only way to purchase a country club is to buy it from the owners. In this instance, the members of South Moor were the owners, each of whom was a shareholder. The shares had originally cost $2500. The city paid $7500 per share.

This redemption value prompted an ecumenical gesture from the Edgewood Country Club, the ritziest in town and one whose threshold no ethnic had ever crossed. Edgewood issued a blanket invitation to the Jews of South Moor to come on over. All they had to do to become members was surrender their share in South Moor and the pool, the tennis courts, the golf links, the riding to the hounds—everything was theirs.

The Jews thanked Edgewood but said they wanted to think it over. Edgewood, like most country clubs, was engaged in chasing the endless spiral of increasing costs. Obviously it needed new members. What the Jews mulled over was the cold statistic that it cost a Gentile $1500 to join Edgewood but it was going to cost them $7500. They said no thank you.

The story has a happy ending. Spurred by brotherhood, several other country clubs offered memberships without strings to the dispossessed Jews.

Ecologists have warned that if you strip-mine, you are liable to rend yourself on occasion, a prophesy brought home cruelly to Governor Arch Moore and the Legislature.

Governor Moore wanted to build a science and cultural center by the State Capitol, hereinafter referred to legally as the "Capitol Complex." It would include office buildings populated by state agencies, an archive, a history annex, State Police Headquarters, an auditorium, and parking facilities.

Stanley Lowenstein wondered why Charleston needed another auditorium when the perfectly good ones it already has are usually half empty.

To build this complex meant literally devastating a neighborhood in the east end of Charleston, a neighborhood bounded by Quarrier, Washington, Duffey, and Greenbriar streets. The people who lived there loved it. It was an old neighborhood, an established neighborhood, a stable neighborhood, and its proposed disappearance naturally distressed the residents.

Among these residents was Rabbi Cooper. The man next door loved his house no less than the rabbi, but the rabbi by virtue of his calling had to live in a house within walking distance to the synagogue. This sorely afflicted citizenry, led by Cooper, went to court to fight City Hall.

The wails of the summarily displaced are nothing new in the land. But in this instance, Charlestonians did not wail. Instead they argued that the Capitol Complex was illegally financed. To build and maintain the complex, the Legislature had authorized bonds which rents would retire. But the rents were paid by state agencies with appropriations made by the Legislature, which constitutes state debt on which the constituency had not voted.

The court agreed with the plaintiffs. It ruled that no matter how the Legislature sliced it, it was still debt. The state constitution required a vote of the people before such debt could be incurred. If the ruling embarrassed West Virginia financially, the judges said, that was not the fault of the court. It was not the wording calculated to make Bache & Company, who had purchased the bonds, particularly happy.

In hurried convention, the Legislature decided to avail itself of the annual $3.6 million in liquor profits to let Bache & Company live happily ever after. The state was in a bit of a jam here because it had already constructed two of the buildings.

The litigants met in the Rose City Cafeteria to plot subsequent tactics. A reporter asked Rabbi Cooper for a statement. "Having won our first battle," Cooper said, "we are ready to enter the fray again. Many people here are upset because it looks like an 'edifice complex' is more important to some of our state officials than homes for people and businesses operated by small private entrepreneurs who are struggling to keep their heads above water."

This time the plaintiffs charged that financing the Capitol Complex from liquor profits was as unconstitutional as financing it through rents.

The most interesting aspect of this episode is that Rabbi Cooper, one of the leaders of the movement, could not have become a litigant without the express consent of his trustees. B'nai Jacob owns the house the rabbi lives in. When the Capitol Complex was announced, the trustees bought their rabbi another house. He told them he didn't want another house, he wanted the house he had, next to the neighbors he enjoyed.

Obviously, his trustees thought he had a case. Had they chosen, they could have called him off legally. It is a measure of the confidence these Jews have in Charleston that they told the rabbi to go ahead and fight.

But there are rabbis like Cooper and Volkman who are not deferential to their congregants. After all, both of them have made a lifetime commitment to this city and its Jews. It is they who must make this small segment *stand for* something, ideals which can feed pride and establish identity because the community is too small to share in the tumult of fund raising and too remote to borrow energy and ethics from the more concentrated Jewish communities.

SAVANNAH

Savannah was the civilized world's first attempt to solve the perpetual problem of welfare. It was founded by Major James Edward Oglethorpe, not only a professional soldier but the son of a professional soldier.

In 1731, Oglethorpe, then a thirty-five-year-old member of the House of Commons, headed the King's Commission to investigate the conditions in English jails. The practice of imprisoning debtors was by this time almost five hundred years old. Ten thousand Englishmen were serving indeterminate sentences because they owed other Englishmen money. Citizens, particularly those who had to borrow the rent money from month to month, were beginning to wonder where it would all end.

Oglethorpe found English prisons uniformly infested with filth, vermin, smallpox, and fever. Mothers in prison bore children who perished immediately. Jailers killed more debtors than they hanged thieves. Thumbscrews, shackles, floggings, and the iron skullcap were punishments meted out indiscriminately. Reforming a prison system then no less than now, however, was an intractable proposition.

Oglethorpe told George II he thought the way to relieve these conditions was to transform these debtors into the colonists of a new Southern settlement below the Carolinas whose climate would accommodate orchards of mulberry trees for silk and vineyards for Málaga wine. Oglethorpe proposed to call the colony Georgia. He finally persuaded the King by pointing out that such a colony would serve as a buffer for the Carolinas against Spanish aggression from St. Augustine.

With 120 settlers, Oglethorpe founded the city of Savannah on February 12, 1733. He chose a site ten miles upstream from the ocean at a point where the Yamacraw flows into the Savannah River. Savannah sits on a high bluff because colonists in Charleston, two hundred miles north, suggested the plateau had few swamps and might be malaria-free. The city takes its name from the Spanish word "zavana," a treeless plain.

It is a myth to suppose that Georgia was originally settled by the impecunious, the lawless, and the abandoned. The settlement on the Yamacraw was not peopled by renegades, nor was Savannah an earlier Botany Bay. Indeed, once Oglethorpe announced the venture, so many honest citizens down on their luck petitioned for passage that the trustees made sure no one went to Savannah without a certificate of past good conduct.

The first thing these settlers had to do was build a crane to haul their equipment from the *Ann* up the steep bluff to the fort site. It could not have been easy. It is not easy today to walk from the river up the stairs to the bluff. To imagine struggling up that bluff burdened with tenting and axes and barrels of gunpowder is unendurable.

Oglethorpe remained an exemplar to the colonists as long as there was hope for silk and wine. Neither proved practical.

The colonists chafed under his strict prohibitions. Slavery and rum were against the law. Without slaves the colonists said they couldn't compete with the other colonies and without rum they said they didn't want to. In 1743, George recalled Oglethorpe.

Thirty-two years later, George II's successor, George III, offered Oglethorpe the command of the British armies in the colonies to put down the incipient rebellion. Oglethorpe agreed on the condition that the King grant him the powers of concession and conciliation. George III replied that if he wanted a general to lose the war, he could find one easily enough.

When Oglethorpe left Savannah, the city numbered 700 colonists. Nor is it a large city by today's standards—118,500 according to the 1970 census. But it is the largest port between Baltimore and New Orleans, served by 114 steamship lines with a gross tonnage of over 6 million.

Before the Civil War, its chief export was cotton, King Cotton. Its exports now are naval stores, paper board, iron and steel scrap, machinery, and vegetable oils.

Its largest industry is the Union Camp Corporation. The Savannah operation is the world's largest pulp-to-container plant. To a degree,

Union Camp helped stunt Savannah's industrial growth. UCC was one of those Southern industries always at pains to keep other industries out and by so doing exploit the labor pool to its best advantage. Sooner or later, Southern industry learned that this was not to its advantage, and there are 191 manufacturing industries in Savannah presently, employing 15,500 workers with a $108 million annual payroll.

The Savannah economy is also augmented by nearby Fort Stewart and the Hunter Army Airfield, which comprise another subcommunity of 18,000. Parris Island, the Marine Corps recruit depot, is in nearby Beaufort, South Carolina. Many military personnel stay on in Savannah after their discharge. Savannahians, with typical Southern provincialism, call these men "immigrants."

Still, Savannah is a cosmopolitan city. It boasts a genuine *haute cuisine*. Its museums take more than twenty minutes to traverse. Its architecture is endlessly interesting, original, and utile.

Eli Whitney invented the cotton gin near Savannah in 1793, and the cotton economy brought prosperity. Savannah was the great port city of the antebellum South. The prosperity coincided architecturally with the English Regency period—the simpler home made of stucco with windows always balanced, balconies ringed by filigreed iron railings, stairwells sweeping from the ground to a second-story entryway, pastel shades emphasizing the delicacy. Regency was a particularly convenient style for Savannah. Tabby, a building material made of oyster shells, lime, and sand, was invented in Savannah. These Regency houses belonged to the English, Yankee, and Southern cotton brokers—factors, as they were called then. The island plantation owners also built these as townhouses. The Carolinas and Georgia have two coastlines: one formed by the near-shore islands and the second by the mainland.

The supreme example of Regency architecture in Savannah is the Owen-Thomas House at Abercorn Street facing Oglethorpe Square. It was designed by William Jay in 1816, and from its front porch the Marquis de Lafayette addressed a crowd come to honor him when he stayed in the city in 1825.

Twenty years ago, these Regency homes constituted Savannah's slums: the houses had to accommodate three, four, and often five black families. Mills B. Lane, the president of Citizens and Southern Bank, perhaps the richest in the South, began to acquire some of them, which he renovated and let to the rich at pretty good rentals.

His example made the historical societies bestir themselves. Both Lane and the societies were spurred in their endeavors by the low 3 percent interest rate with which the federal government favors urban-renewal projects. As a consequence, the old section of Savannah is as fresh and fancy today as the Georgetown area in Washington, D.C.

These houses surround fifty-two one-acre squares. The squares boast fountains or statuary and greenery but, more importantly, offer open space and a perspective on the neighborhood. Savannah was the first planned city in the western hemisphere. Its streets and squares were laid out for Oglethorpe by Colonel C. W. Bull, the then governor of South Carolina.

Esplanades filled with oak trees divide the broad avenues. Long festoons of Spanish moss drape the branches shading the street below. Spanish moss is a plant nurtured by the sea. In Savannah's newer neighborhoods to the west, however, the developers had no more appreciation of the mossed oak than they had of any other organic plant. Recent housing projects sit on bald land soaking up the sun, which in the summertime is as pleasant as soaking up sulfur.

Savannah was the one important Southern city not devastated and broken by the Civil War. Sherman spared it. In December 1864, when he took Fort McAllister to the south of the city, William Tecumseh Sherman had completed his March to the Sea. He entered Savannah on December 21 to find that the Confederate brigades had withdrawn across the Yamacraw River toward Charleston. Savannah held 20,000 people then, and rather than burn it, Sherman decided it was to be his Christmas present for the President.

Savannah preserved its pristine uniqueness. Its citizens speculate that the United States would look far different if the post-Civil War pioneers had passed through Savannah and transported its architecture westward. But even these proud Savannahians admit after reflection that it would have been a roundabout trip.

The Ku Klux Klan also spared Savannah—a fact noteworthy because the modern Ku Klux Klan was born in Georgia, occasioned by the murder of a fourteen-year-old factory girl named Mary Phagan, whose mutilated body was found in the basement of Atlanta's National Pencil Company on Confederate Memorial Day, 1913. Her employer, factory superintendent Leo Frank, a twenty-nine-year-old Jew, a Northerner and, as the red-necks charged, a capitalist, was arrested, tried, and convicted of the crime. In 1915, Governor John

M. Slaton, knowing Frank to be innocent, commuted his sentence to life imprisonment. Immediately afterward, Slaton fled the state for his life. Virulent anti-Semitism swept across Georgia. The hills howled with masked men, one hundred of whom, calling themselves the Knights of Mary Phagan, vowed to punish Frank.

Twenty-five of these Knights stormed the Milledgeville Prison on August 16, 1915, kidnaped Frank, drove him over 100 miles of back-country roads, then hanged him from a tree in Marietta, not far from the murdered girl's home. On Thanksgiving Day, 1915, these men climbed Stone Mountain outside Atlanta and from its crest burned a gigantic cross as they reincarnated themselves as the Knights of the Invisible Empire of the Ku Klux Klan. Only in Georgia in 1915 did a Jewish community in this country ever fear for its livelihood and safety. Jews left Georgia by the hundreds—except the Jews in Savannah.

There are a variety of reasons why the Jews in Savannah felt secure, and paramount among them is the fact that Savannah did not have a homogeneous white Protestant constituency. Savannah had then and has now a large Irish population. After New York, Boston, and Chicago, the St. Patrick's Day Parade in Savannah is the largest in the country. The Church of St. John the Baptist on Abercorn Street by Lafayette Square is the cathedral of the bishop of Georgia.

The Klan, who terrorized foreigners, Jews, Catholics, and blacks, had some of the ground cut from beneath them.

The Jews and the Irish in Savannah were natural allies and split up many offices in city and state government.

No doubt the port made the city cosmopolitan, which mitigated some of the Klan's ferocity, but there was another mitigating factor as well. That is the gentility of the city, the devotion to the enrichment of human experience which shades the quality of life in Savannah as Spanish moss shades the streets.

John Wesley, the inaugural minister of Christ and Holy Trinity Church, taught the world's first Sunday school in Savannah. His successor, George Whitfield, chartered Bethesda, America's oldest existing orphanage.

Juliette Gordon Low founded the Girl Scouts in Savannah in 1912. Her home on Oglethorpe Avenue and Bull Street is a National Historic Landmark, as is all of old Savannah, the only city so designated. The first black Baptist congregation was formed in Savannah in

1788 and so was the first black hospital, the Georgia Infirmary, established here in 1832.

Savannah was, after all, the first city in the world founded to relieve social distress and give the have-nots equity in the future.

It sells history and tradition, Colonial history and Colonial tradition.

A statue stands on the spot where Sergeant William Jasper fell in 1779, trying to rescue the colors as the Continental Army fought to retake the city from the British. Casimir Pulaski, the Polish nobleman who fought for Washington, also fell before Savannah. There is a statue to Pulaski but no tombstone because his corpse stank so badly it was thrown in the river. His memory is also perpetuated in the name of Fort Pulaski, the Army's first Pentagon, built in the eighteen-twenties with 25 million bricks. Fort Pulaski was Robert E. Lee's assignment after he was graduated from West Point and until Union forces trained a new weapon in it—the rifled cannon—it was considered impregnable.

The Confederates abandoned the fort in 1862 rather than have the Union fleet reduce it to rubble.

It has been a city blessed with the good sense to save itself when it got the chance.

"THIS SOUTHERN ACCESSION . . ."

When George II gave Oglethorpe Georgia's charter in 1732, there were 6000 Jews in London, more than half of them Spanish and Portuguese Jews fleeing the Inquisition. These Sephardim were without resources and dependent upon London Jewry's Honen Dalim, a philanthropic society, for sustenance. Savannah looked like a good bet.

A board of trustees administered the settlement in Savannah. This board appointed commissioners to solicit funds from the general populace to finance the liquidation of debts, charter ships, and pay for the tools, livestock, seed, and gunpowder the colonists needed.

Three rich London Jews, Moses da Costa, Joseph Sequeira, and Jacob Suasso, applied for and received commissions from the trustees to solicit money from the Jewish community. But Da Costa, Sequeira, and Suasso did not turn over their collection to the trustees: instead, they chartered a ship, outfitted it, and embarked forty-two poor Jews for a venture in the New World, the first Jews to settle in an English crown colony.*

The leader of these Jews was Benjamin Sheftall, who had been born in Germany on the west bank of the Oder River but had been raised in England. Abraham Minis, his wife Abigail, and his daughter Leah were also German, as well as one Jacob Yowel. The rest of the Jews were Spanish or Portuguese refugees with names like Nuñez, Henriques, D'Olivera, or Delmonte.

They landed at Savannah on July 11, 1733, not knowing what to expect, their only advantage that Oglethorpe did not expect them. Oglethorpe was nonplussed. He did not know whether to admit them into Georgia or not. He sought a legal judgment from the King's barristers in Charleston, who advised him the charter banned only "Papists." Oglethorpe did not quarrel with the ruling. Besides, he was a pragmatist, and one of the Jews, Samuel Nuñez Ribiero, was a physician. Typhoid that July was epidemic in Savannah.

The trustees, however, were outraged. They instructed Oglethorpe to pay the doctor for his ministrations but to deed no land to the Jews. By the time the letter reached Oglethorpe the settlement of the Jews was a *fait accompli.* In explaining himself to the trustees, for he had deeded land to the Jews, Oglethorpe wrote, "This accession of Israelites far from proving a detriment has proved a boon." He went on to say that the Jews had appreciably increased the population of Savannah from 275 to 317; that they were thrifty, honest, and hard working; and that to expel them was to violate the charter, which provided for religious freedom.

Two weeks after the Jews landed, Mrs. Moses Ledesma delivered the first white child born in Georgia, and a year to the day of the Jewish accession, Abigail Minis delivered Philip, the first white child *begotten* and born in Georgia. In 1740, King George naturalized all the foreign Protestants and Jews in the colonies.

Much of what we know about the settlement of these Colonial Jews descends to us from a diary Benjamin Sheftall kept in Hebrew which was continued after his death in 1767 until 1808 by his son, Levi.

Sheftall started to keep the diary when the Savannah Jews formed Mikvah Israel, the third oldest congregation in North America.

---

* Jews had landed in New Amsterdam when it was Dutch; a little later had come to Newport, Rhode Island, when it was a settlement of dissident Protestants led by Roger Williams; and to Philadelphia when Pennsylvania was still a Quaker preserve.

Mikvah Israel was formed in 1735 because for two years religious differences separated the Sephardic and German Jews.

Many of the Sephardim were *marranos* (the word means "pig" in Spanish), Jews who had converted to escape the inquisitorial pyre. They were more relaxed in their Judaism, keeping the spirit rather than the letter of Hebrew law. Nuñez's sons, for example, used to drop in on the Anglican services on Sunday.

Sheftall, Minis, and Yowel, on the other hand, were strict in their observance. Reverend Bolzius, who led a Lutheran group from the German city of Salzburg to Savannah in 1734, confided in *his* diary, "The Spanish and Portuguese are not so strict in so far as eating is concerned. They eat for instance the beef that comes from the warehouse or that is sold anywhere else. The German Jews on the other hand would rather starve than eat meat they do not slaughter themselves."

What brought the two groups of Jews together was the proselytizing energies of their Christian neighbors. One of the Jews converted and the assimilated Sephardim and the ghettoized Ashkenazim put aside their differences to come together in a rude hut which passed for a synagogue. Later, they added a mikvah (ritual bath).

By 1742, almost all of these original Jewish settlers had abandoned Savannah. When Oglethorpe in an abortive move failed to take St. Augustine, the Spaniards moved north. The threat of the Inquisition frightened the Sephardim. They left. Though Oglethorpe held the line against the Spaniards at Fort Fredrica on St. Simons Island and then moved to beat them at the battle of Bloody Marsh, there were only two Jewish families in Savannah at the end of 1742—the Minises and the Sheftalls.

But Sheftall continued making entries for the next twenty-five years until his death. Some of the original Jewish settlers drifted back and new Jews came to Savannah from London. Afterward, Levi Sheftall continued the entries, a more entertaining diarist than his father: "On the 12th day of January 1803 Abraham Sasportas was married to Leah or Charlotte Canter of Charleston. Her age was between 19 and 20 years and his was at least 57 but he must be 60."

Benjamin Sheftall's house, built before 1775, stands in Savannah. The Unitarian Universalist Fellowship completely restored it in 1971. It is a three-story clapboard dwelling with a brick foundation and a hip roof, now radiant with a pastel-green exterior gloss.

Benjamin Sheftall married twice. A son by his first marriage, Mordechai, became a Revolutionary War hero and was captured by the British when the Redcoats took Savannah. Mordechai's son, Sheftall Sheftall, was captured with his father but after his parole guided the sloop *Carolina Packet* past the British blockade into Charleston. Sheftall Sheftall practiced law in Savannah until he died in 1848. He was known as Cocked Hat Sheftall because he always affected the tricornered hat and knickerbockers past the day that tailors made the fitted suit fashionable.

Levi, a son by Sheftall's second marriage to Hannah Solomon, stayed home in 1776 and accumulated money by a variety of enterprises which ranged from skinning deer to keeping store. When he died in 1809 he was the United States Agent for Fortifications.

"Like leaves are the races of men," says Homer. They scatter. Yet these two families, the Minises and the Sheftalls survived in Savannah, though not all of them survived as Jews. Laura, Mordechai, and Henry, the children of Mordechai and Virginia Russel Sheftall, perished in the yellow fever epidemic of 1854 which claimed the lives of 1040 Savannahians in four days. Abram "Bob" Minis is a broker in Savannah today and there are Sheftalls living in nearby Gaffney, South Carolina.

There are still Sheftall descendants in Savannah itself. One of them is B. H. Levy, a millionaire lawyer, who urges visitors jovially, "Call me B.H." Levy has offices in Armstrong House on Bull and Gaston streets. Armstrong House is impressive enough a marble mansion for the tour bus to stop in front of it. But B.H. told me it was built by a shipping magnate in 1919 who died two years later, leaving his estate to Armstrong College. When the college moved to bigger quarters, Bouhan, Williams & Levy moved in.

The house itself may be more impressive than its history, but it is still an impressive place from which to run a law practice. The anterior reception area, with two marble staircases sweeping up at one end, could pass for a Roman atrium. There is a fireplace big enough to roast a wild boar in every room. Levy's office, wood-paneled and warmed by a Persian rug, offered access to what had once been a greenhouse. The firm was obviously doing business because where plants once blossomed now stood typists' tables and file cabinets.

B.H. took me to luncheon at the private Chatham Club, a penthouse dining room atop the DeSoto Hilton. The Chatham (Savannah is in Chatham County) offered an unexampled view of the port and the city. Everybody at the Chatham called B.H. "B.H."

A World War II Air Force colonel, B. H. Levy is sixty, humorous and well-mannered as only Southerners are well-mannered. He apologized for not being a direct descendant of Ben Sheftall. His wife is the direct descendant, but he has, over the years, become more interested and more familiar with the Sheftall family history than she. He has cared for and collected the Sheftall Colonial artifacts. When his wife dies, these will go to the University of Georgia.

B.H. himself is the grandson of an immigrant who came to Savannah and opened a small store which eventually grew into Levy's, the largest department store in the city. An only son who intended law as a career, B.H. had no interest in the store and some years ago it was acquired by the May's chain.

His law practice is corporate and very little of it Jewish. "There isn't enough Jewish business in Savannah," he said, "to pay for the heat in one room of Armstrong House in December." He is an officer of Temple Mikvah Israel and sighed as he told me of the temple's problems.

"We have just hired our third rabbi in two years. Rabbi Starrels was here for twenty-five years, all of them productive. But his successor had wife trouble and the next successor fell sick."

Over cocktails, B.H. confided that he and his wife pray before every dinner. "But that," he said, eyeing the waiter, who was busily engaged in serving us a shellfish salad, "does not make me feel I am part of an ethnic group."

I allowed as how if you ate lunch often at the Chatham Club you wouldn't feel that way at all.

B.H. worried then whether I'd learned enough that noon about the Sheftalls and Savannah.

I told B.H. not to worry. I just wanted to find out which way the leaves blew.

Another of the Sheftall descendants is Harry Eicholz, the president and owner of the Ben Sheftall Company, at 346 West Broad Street. Mr. Eicholz assured me that the name "Ben Sheftall Company" is copyrighted, protected, and secure from any encroachment. The company wholesales black barber and beauty supplies—wigs, pomades, face cream, hair dryers, mirrors, etc. It does a thriving retail business as well. Eicholz and I talked while seated on two beautician's chairs and three times we moved so that clerks could extract goods from the shelf behind us. Harry Eicholz waved hello to everyone who came in.

Through the display window, I could see the cranes working on the wharves. West Broad Street has warehouses, wholesale establishments, and a black neighborhood along its length.

Benjamin Sheftall, the Sheftall who lived in Gaffney, started the business. He was Mr. Eicholz's cousin. "Benny was a star basketball player at Alabama. And he was a gentleman. His family raised me. I remember a Bible they had. It had the whole record of the Sheftall family but I have no idea what happened to it. I know Benny's widow, who has remarried, has all the Sheftall china and silverware. Benny started this company in 1932. It was a chain in South Carolina. I became his partner in Georgia, his *oral* partner. I've been at it ever since. Bought Benny's share out when he died. I'm not rich, I want you to understand, but you can make money at this business."

He made money, I realized, because he thought nothing of rising from his chair to help a young girl select a twenty-five-cent comb.

Eicholz has three sons. The eldest, Benjamin Sheftall Eicholz, is a junior at Tulane University. "Smartest boy you ever saw," he said. "Hard worker. His idea is to go into politics and help the disadvantaged."

Another son, Richard, who was working in the store, tall, swarthy, muscular, is a freshman at Georgia State and hopes to succeed his father.

Mrs. Eicholz, a personable blond, told me a third son, Tony, thirteen, is a student at the Hebrew Day School in Savannah.

Did the Sheftalls have money? Great money?

"No," said Eicholz, "not great money. They were workers and they made their living working hard but they were never big rich. Waring Sheftall, Benny's father, was a thirty-second-degree Mason but he would be what you'd call a junior eye-zecutive in a wholesale clothing firm here along the river."

With innate courtesy, Eicholz insisted on driving me back to the hotel so that he could show me the old Sheftall home. "Not the reconstructed house, but the family house where the Sheftalls lived for fifty, maybe sixty years."

In August, Atlanta broils. Getting into Eicholz's car was like squeezing into a hot waffle iron. Then the air cooled us as we proceeded a short distance west from the river through a neighborhood half slum and half reconstructed Regency. The windows in the reconstructed houses had curtains and spanking-white paint outlined the trim. The fences were new and rot hadn't gotten the better of the porch posts. The slum houses had broken panes. Black women bulged from the open windows.

The Sheftall house was a four-story structure, its brick turned muddy brown from discoloration. "Mills B. Lane's going to do a jig when he finds that house. Few houses ever built that substantial, you know what I mean?"

We drove through the old city, Eicholz pointing to the Green Mansion, where Sherman set up his headquarters in January, 1865, near a corner drugstore where Robert E. Lee had his prescriptions filled.

Waving goodbye to Mr. Eicholz, I wondered how many family names of the Christian colonists who came with Oglethorpe on the *Ann* survive? There are, I discovered, a great many family names which descend from the plantation society, but only MacIver and MacIntosh descend from the Colonial period. The original MacIvers and MacIntoshes were Scotch Presbyterians Oglethorpe settled in Brunswick, a fort to the south.

It wasn't a far walk from the drugstore to Temple Mikvah Israel. Among the artifacts in Mikvah Israel are two scrolls of the Torah, one of which was brought to Savannah on July 11, 1733, and the other sent by Benjamin Mendes of London which arrived on July 12, 1737.

By 1786 there were once again enough Jews in Savannah to form a congregation. These Jews re-established Mikvah Israel. "We opened the snogo," reads Levi Sheftall's misspelling, "and the following persons were coshen [sic!] for the head of the congregation. . . ."

Mikvah Israel differs from all other Jewish temples in America in two respects. It is a cruciform, probably the only Jewish edifice in America built in the shape of a cross. There is a simple explanation for this. The Jews of Mikvah Israel were forced to build a new temple in 1875, when an older temple had burned. But they were broke, unable to afford an architect. So they borrowed the plans for the cathedral from their buddy the Catholic bishop, and told the builder to reduce the plans to fit their modest lot.

The Jews in Savannah were often broke. In 1911, when they determined to found a Jewish Educational Alliance, they raised the necessary $25,000 among themselves by purchasing the bricks at one dollar apiece.

They are broke no more. Mikvah Israel also has an endowment, a large endowment. Just how large an endowment it enjoys is hard to discover since the officers suspect that publicizing the amount might discourage some of the members from the punctual payment of their annual dues.

Much misinformation has circulated about the Jewish Colonial settlement and about Mikvah Israel. The Savannahian who has helped set facts straight is David A. Byck, a retired printer turned historian. A lifelong member of this Reform temple, Byck is also a former president of the congregation.

Byck set himself the task of finding the congregation's original charter. After years of poking through musty records he came upon it filed away with receipted gas bills in a folder dating from 1918.

It was Byck who uncovered the whereabouts of the translated Sheftall diary. Word had passed from generation to generation about the existence of the diary but no one knew how or when it had disappeared.

With the devotion that only historians muster, Byck spied a one-inch news item to the effect that the Americana collection of Keith Reid, a Savannah businessman and noted bibliophile, had been purchased by the University Library at Georgia. Byck contacted the curator at the library and asked if any of the manuscripts had Hebrew lettering on one of the end pieces. He had found it!

Byck is a tall man in his sixties who speaks with a soft Southern drawl. No word better describes him than courtly. He wore a Panama hat, a gray summer suit, and a properly restrained necktie. When he walked through the electric-eye doors of the Hilton, he looked for all the world like a Southern squire striding on a columned portico. He carried a heavy leather binder in which was neatly arranged all the research he had accumulated.

"Savannah," he told me, "calls the Jewish cemetery the 'De Lyon' cemetery. The assumption is that it was the De Lyons' private burial grounds. But that is not true. The De Lyon tombstones were the only ones which didn't sink and which remained upright. In the nineteen-thirties, a WPA project uncovered many more of the stones.

"Nothing is ever static with an old institution. We had a moribund board of trustees who were supposed to administer any property the temple owned. We thought we owned nothing. But that board ceased being moribund the day the Southern Railroad discovered Mikvah Israel owned a forgotten lot over which they wanted a right of way."

One cannot help but feel a wonder in talking to a Jew who can trace other Jews back into the early American beginnings. Family history for most American Jews commences with a grandfather or father who immigrated. And that immigrant is the family's only source because if he left relatives behind in Europe, Hitler killed them.

My companion, Byck, though not a Sheftall or a Colonial descendant, came from a family that had lived for several generations in Savannah. The man was as familiar with Savannah and its times as the archivist at the Georgia Historical Society on Whitaker Street.

I asked him about his relationships with his Christian neighbors and Byck replied matter-of-factly, "Frankly, Ah don't have many relationships with mah Christian neighbors. Ah'm more comf'table with mah own. Ah puf-fer the Yudim."

BEEBEE JACOB

"Our biggest problem in Savannah," said Irwin Giffen, "is that every Jew in the city will insist the community is 5000 strong. That is wrong. There are 2900 Jews in Savannah. We, too, are a diminishing community."

Giffen should know. He is the executive director of the Jewish Educational Alliance and the director of the Federation, both located in the same building on Abercorn Street, a mile or two from the old city.

Giffen's office was as cluttered as a Collier brothers' alcove but he was as deft as W. C. Fields at digging papers out of the morass.

"Savannah is an affluent Jewish community," said Giffen, "but the young Jew doesn't feel opportunity here, or he wants to break family ties, or he finds no opportunity in his profession. And these young Jews are right. There are Jews here in business and in professions and in investments but none, not one, in management. Next door, an hour by air, is Atlanta, the biggest city in the South.

"But Savannah gets a small Jewish influx as more and more malls are built and we also find a small influx of Jews settle here fleeing the congestion of the North."

There is every reason why Savannah should offer a nesting place for Northern refugees. It is no city for the extremist. Hosea Williams, for example, the black militant leader, comes from Savannah but found the national scene more amenable to his talents. The Savannah

City Council and its Human Relations Commission always found a way to meet Williams' demands for justice without provoking violent protest.

This is not to say, however, that the 2900 Jews of Savannah do not have their differences.

Bearded Abe Eisenman, who met me at the airport, was the only Jew in Savannah worried about the fate of the Democratic Party. "Everybody loves Nixon down here," said Abe. "Nixon loves the military posts and so does Savannah."

Abe is a native-born Savannahian who published the *Savannah Sun,* a personal journal, for many years until rising postal rates and astronomical printing costs did him in in 1962.

Eisenman spent thirty-two years in radio broadcasting working in cities as diverse as Newark, New Jersey, and Columbia, South Carolina. During the sixties, he was the sales manager for WSOK in Savannah, a black station, until the demands by the black community for an all-black staff forced him out.

"Ah could get a job in a store selling suits," said Abe, who was born in 1914. "But what the hell. One of the boy's a professor at Temple University and the other's a professor at Yale. Ah'm going to stay home and write awhile."

Abe is beetle-browed and wears his hair in fair imitation of Ben Franklin. He is the author of volumes I and II of *Why I Should Be President,* published in 1963 and 1969, both of which, Abe insists, scooped the Pentagon Papers.

On another evening, I met Dr. William Wexler, a Bull Street optometrist, the ex-president of the B'nai B'rith, an international Jewish service organization engaged in educational and philanthropic programs. Wexler is one of the co-founders of Democrats for Nixon.

A big man, balding, in his early fifties, Wexler has traveled all over the world on the behalf of both the B'nai B'rith and Israel.

Dr. Wexler's first wife died a few years ago and he has recently remarried. His wife is an Israeli, a doctor fulfilling her residency requirements in Atlanta. Some day, confided Dr. Wexler, he hopes to live in Israel.

We discussed integration in Savannah, a subject more congenial to us than politics. The city has progressed more than most, Wexler thought, because the National Association for the Advancement of Colored People was and still is the influential black voice. The NAACP seized upon the federal voting laws and antidiscrimination statutes to advance the cause of the black materially. The postal workers are all black and so are many of the longshoremen. Blacks work in all of the stores although there are still hundreds upon hundreds of domestic workers, few of whom, Wexler added, are paid the federal minimum wage.

Eisenman and Wexler represent the political spectrum in Savannah and they represent as well different life-styles. Dr. Wexler flies back and forth to Israel as often as Abe Eisenman enters tennis tournaments. Abe is the senior men's champion.

These differences, however, are not divisive differences.

Nor can you find many divisive differences in Savannah. Ninety-two percent of these Jews are affiliated with either Mikvah Israel or Agudas Achim, the Conservative temple or B'nai B'rith Jacob, the Orthodox synagogue, which claims the largest membership, 55 percent of the affiliated Jews.

BeeBee Jacob, as it is called, was founded in 1860 by members of the new B'nai B'rith. Its present rabbi, the tenth in its history, is Abraham I. Rosenberg who has spent the last forty years in Savannah.

"Once upon a time," Rabbi Rosenberg said, "holding a conference on the future of the Jews in the South was like holding a conference on the future of agriculture in the desert. But now young boys in Savannah wear their yarmulkas to public school."

The rabbi affects a carefully trimmed Van Dyck and spectacles over whose rims his eyes search for signs of intelligence. If a rabbi can dress as formally as a Philadelphia lawyer, then Abraham Rosenberg does.

"Maybe Savannah is different from other Southern towns," I suggested.

"Indeed Savannah is different," he said. "Do you know what the difference is? Savannah has no Jewish country club. That makes the difference. There are twenty Jewish millionaires in Savannah and the only place they can meet other Jews is in the synagogue or the temple. That makes them not only better Jews but better millionaires."

Clemenceau waged war; Rosenberg fights country clubs.

Rabbi Rosenberg is one of those strong-willed, authoritarian, and intelligent rabbis who find a pulpit in the South a favorable office. Like Samuel Cooper in Charleston, Rabbi Rosenberg tells his congregation which way to look and when to march.

"And now," said Rosenberg, "we are going to a funeral."

Rabbi Rosenberg marched west on Abercorn Street, protected against sunstroke by a Homburg. The shoulder of the road was made scraggly with weeds. Heat waves hula-hulaed from the scorching cement. We crossed to a large, white, tastefully simple funeral home, whose chapel was filled.

"The man who died," said Rosenberg, seating himself, "was Joe Waldman. His daughter is married to a Friedman, one of the premier families in Savannah." The rabbi looked around, nodding to friends. It was an airy, bright chapel with only the Mogen David across the coffin for effect.

"This is not a Jewish burial home," said Rosenberg. "There isn't one in Savannah. This mortician came to me several years ago and said he thought he could bury Jews properly. He wanted my advice. I told him it was easy to bury Jews. All the coffins are the same price."

After the eulogy, the rabbi and I followed the mourners outside. He held his hand to restrain me from passing the hearse. We waited until the cortege moved off. Then the rabbi walked to a small outdoor faucet and held his hands under the running water.

"Do you know this custom?" he asked, not wiping his hands but letting the water dry. "We wash our hands, not of the dead man, but to say we hope we have had no part in his death. Our hands are clean."

Back at BeeBee Jacob, Rosenberg showed me the immense mural which covers one wall of the sanctuary. Its prevailing tone was brown because its background was the arrangement of stones of Jerusalem's Western Wall.

The mural was a puzzle. There were symbols for the Tribes of Israel—mandrakes representing Reuben, a lion Judah, a gazelle Naphtali. A leopard and an eagle represented the boldness and ease with which a Jew obeys the bidding of God. Two challah loaves on a silver tray with a cloth cover and a wine cup represented the Sabbath. The obverse and reverse of an Israeli Bar Mitzvah coin represented the year in which this new BeeBee Jacob was built.

"Only the artist and I know what every symbol means," said Rosenberg, "and I probably know more than the artist."

I gave him a searching glance.

"I think I know more," he said.

Thus Savannah, one of those Southern towns where the Jewish community becomes in effect a family, attending each other's funerals, weddings, Bar Mitzvahs, visiting the hospital at a new Jew's birth.

One Jew knows all others and every Jew knows the gossip. The gossip I heard about Rabbi Rosenberg was that he had become more Orthodox as he became more entrenched. But he has probably saved the congregation of BeeBee Jacob from itself, from dissipating its considerable energies into social diversion and from secularizing the mystic significance which makes Jews a wonder to themselves and to the world around them.

WALTHAM

IN THE KINGDOM OF THE ACADEMY

Brandeis University is so new, only twenty-five years old, and its buildings so contemporary and functional, that the architectural feature of the campus is Usen Castle. With its turrets, embattlements, archways, and ivy-covered stonework it looks exactly like a medieval fortress out of Disneyland. The Castle was once the home of Middlesex University, whose buildings and 100 acres Brandeis acquired.

Brandeis is on the outskirts of Waltham, Massachusetts, ten miles west of Boston and southeast of Concord and Lexington. From its boundary on the Charles River, the grounds sweep upward to Boston Rock, where Governor John Winthrop once made a survey of the Massachusetts Bay Colony.

Since 1948, seventy new buildings in expanding perimeters have climbed the steep hills of what is now a 240-acre campus. The university's first president, Abram Sachar, told its founders, "If you insist on a small university that is as good as Johns Hopkins, you have got to provide facilities and salaries that will attract brilliant teachers. You need books and you need libraries. It won't do to present someone with a master plan that shows how great the place will be in twenty years. You won't get the best teachers and you'll only get the students that were turned down elsewhere. So any group that is thinking of starting a small university had better make up its mind to build fast or forget it. You have got to create a well-equipped university almost overnight."

The Jews did all right by Abram Sacher. The university started without distinguished graduates from whom it could importune gifts, yet in dollars raised Brandeis is only behind the UJA. Over 30 percent of its present operating costs are met by contributions from those the Development Office calls "foster alumni." One hundred and more

Jewish women's groups sponsor kickoff meetings and teas to support the library. Every building on the campus is named for a donor— the Grunebaum Astrophysics Observatory, the Slosberg Music Center, the Wolfson-Rosensweig Biochemistry Building. In this, it does not differ radically from other universities. Princeton, for example, has the Firestone Library, Pyne Hall, and Palmer Stadium. The difference is that Palmer, Firestone, and Pyne are dead and Grunebaum, Slosberg, Wolfson, and Rosensweig are alive.

Brandeis was a gift of the Jews, a corporate contribution to American education. It was "in the tradition," as the catalog puts it, "of great American secular universities that have stemmed from denominational generosity."

The Jews got into university building late and only once. Aside from their seminaries, the Episcopalians founded Kenyon, Hobart, and Trinity Colleges and the University of the South. The Jesuit Order of the Roman Catholic Church founded and maintains twenty-eight American colleges and universities, among them such prestigious institutions as Fordham, Canisius, Holy Cross, and Georgetown, not to mention the Catholic Bishops, who maintain Catholic University, and the Order of the Holy Cross, which maintains Notre Dame.

There is, of course, no dearth of Jewish seminaries: the Hebrew Union College in Cincinnati and the Jewish Theological Seminary in New York City are world-renowned centers of Jewish study. Nor is there any dearth of yeshivot, including Yeshiva University with its Albert Einstein School of Medicine. But Brandeis was the first Jewish-sponsored nonsectarian institution of higher learning in the western hemisphere.

The founders chose Brandeis for a name because it was Louis D. Brandeis, the first Jew appointed to the Supreme Court of the United States, who articulated what may conveniently be called Jewish political liberalism in the first half of this century. Nor is the university the one institution to bear his name. In the Jezreel Valley in Israel, in the kingdom of the kibbutzim, Ein Hashofet is also named for Brandeis, for Brandeis was also among the first American Jews to see that Zionism was part and parcel of Jewish liberalism. Ein Hashofet, founded and mostly populated by American émigrés, translates as "Fountains of Justice" and honors Brandeis for the financial and moral contributions he made to it. Ein Hashofet is also called the millionaires' kibbutz.

A statue of the famed jurist in his robes stands on the Brandeis campus facing north. In this instance, he rather resembles a Supreme Court justice dribbling an invisible basketball.

The university shield bears three Hebrew letters spelling "truth" and its motto, "Truth even unto its innermost parts," is taken from the Fifty-first Psalm. In the tabard are the three hills of Old Boston, a beacon flaming on each.

Brandeis is one of the few small private universities in the United States (Princeton, again, is another). It is coeducational enrolling 2200 in its undergraduate college, 700 in the Graduate School of Arts and Sciences, and 100 in the Florence Heller Graduate School for Advanced Studies in Social Welfare.

Since it enrolled its first class in 1948—it was accredited in 1954, record time—Brandeis has graduated nearly 7000 students, 1200 of whom are teachers, 600 lawyers, 500 doctors, 600 social workers, and 100 clergymen.

The first students of this pilot class to receive degrees were Sanders and Phyllis Acker, who met as freshmen and married as seniors. Eleanor Roosevelt was the first commencement speaker, and the Korean War was the worrisome concern of the times. Two other members of the pioneer class are now university trustees: Paul Levenson, a Boston attorney, and Dr. Gustave Ranis, a member of the Economic Growth Center at Yale University.

Roughly 65 percent of the students are Jews. Among them, one group has published a children's book, *A History of the Jews of Russia,* under their own colophon of Modi'n Productions; another group ventures into Dorchester, once the Jewish center in Boston, now a black neighborhood, to hold Sabbath services for Jewish remnants who remain; another group works with the Spanish-speaking poor of Waltham and has established a preschool program.

The school has succeeded in attracting ambitious, capable, and active students who as a body hold dear the cause of academic freedom and civil rights.

To say the money which produced the efficiency and comfort of the physical plant brought them there is shortsighted. Brandeis was in the right place, for one thing.

There are over 100 colleges in the Boston area, enrolling 31,000 students. In Waltham itself, there is Bentley College. Within a ten-mile radius of Brandeis are Wellesley, Boston College, Boston University, Harvard, Radcliffe, MIT, Tufts, Northeastern, and Simmons.

Among these students are 6000 Jewish boys and girls—more Jewish students in Boston than there are Jews in Savannah, Charleston, and Charlotte combined.

Students came to the university, too, because of its distinguished faculty. Marshall Sklare, the preeminent expert on Jewish patterns in suburbia, is the Nathan Appleman professor of American Jewish studies and sociology; Nahum Glatzer, Martin Buber and S. Y. Agnon's editor, is the Samuel Lane professor of Jewish history; William A. Johnson, the Protestant theologian, is the first incumbent of the Albert V. Danielsen chair in Christian thought; Adrienne Rich, the poet, is the Fannie Hurst visiting professor of creative literature.

Lastly, Brandeis presidents have provided leadership and direction in troubled times. Marver H. Bernstein, who was inaugurated in 1970, has served on several presidential task forces and been as well the dean of the Woodrow Wilson School at Princeton. His predecessor, an interim appointment, Charles E. Schottland, was Eisenhower's Commissioner of Social Security and is presently the dean of the Florence Heller School. Morris Abrams, the Atlanta lawyer who won the argument for reapportionment before the Supreme Court served as president, succeeding Abram Sachar, the guiding light of the enterprise, its Plato and Meister Eckhardt.

Sachar, long a professor at the University of Illinois and a noted Jewish historian whose *History of the Jews* was a definitive work for its time, was in retirement in California when the presidency of Brandeis was offered him. He served the university from 1948 until 1968 and he was well into his seventies when he became chancellor.

The post put an end to his scholarly and literary career. "There were books I would have written, if I had had the time," he said in a summing up. "But I have made it possible for others to write books. That gives me tremendous satisfaction, almost as much as if I had written them myself."

ROUTE 16

Waltham, once the "Watch City," fell upon hard times when the watchmakers, along with the mill owners and other industrialists, chased profits south, where there were more of them because of the cheaper land, the salubrious weather and mill rate, and the large pool of unorganized labor. Along with the watchmakers, the mill owners, and industrialists went the potato-chip peelers and the brewers of Chelmsford Golden Dry Ginger Ale, so effervescent you didn't need rye whiskey in it on New Year's Eve.

Polaroid picked up some of the slack, and Raytheon, and the electronics industry lined all too thinly along Route 128.

The 75,000 people in Waltham work mostly in Boston, which has the third largest insurance complex outside of Hartford and Texas (to sell insurance in Texas, a company must locate its home office there). The leather industry in Boston is still healthy, although shipping is minimal.

Proceeding from Waltham along Route 16 through Belmont, Cambridge, and into Somerville, one sees that the populace also works in the service industries. The route is lined with gas stations, television-repair shops, laundromats, and plumbing-supply outlets. There are no shopping centers along the way, at least not along the main streets of these towns, which are the hedge of the Expanded Boston Area. There are, it seems, still cities where the folks drive downtown instead of to a shopping center for their needs. A drugstore adjoins a shoe shop beside a children's clothing store, tinted cellophane lining the windows to protect the clothes from fading by the sun.

Even though it is Christmastime, the cheap neon lighting cannot dispel the dreary atmosphere. Traffic is congested. Ahead a bus lumbers, its pulley bouncing along the grid of electrified wires which provide the power. Neither parks nor playgrounds interrupt the clapboard-and-brick façade. The Roman Catholic churches which command the corners look like prisons designed by Puritans.

These suburban towns around Boston—Medford, Arlington, Everett, Newton—and Boston itself are Irish now, heavily Irish. For a century the Irish, who came to Boston because steerage was nine dollars cheaper than to New York, contended with the Brahmins for hegemony. The Irish outproduced the Brahmins. Of all the immigrant groups, the Irish were the most politically sophisticated, probably because they arrived in command of the English language. The traffic cop's headache in Boston is Sunday when everyone goes to mass.

Finding your way from a flailing traffic cop is a maddening experience because the brogue and the Boston accent conspire to produce a heretofore unexperienced dialect.

"You'll want to keep your car heading east on sixteen" becomes "Yull wahnt to keep yer cah heading east on sixteen." It is uttered with the rapidity bored priests once reserved for the singsong Latinity of the mass.

I nod my thanks for receiving this information made worthless by the fact that the car doesn't have a compass, there is no sun, and the cop has put his hands in his pocket to warm them.

Cambridge is more interesting because Route 16 sweeps by the open spaces around Harvard Stadium. Dormitories are on the left and the stadium on the right, across the Charles River, in which an obviously demented youth sculls past ice floes. There are boutiques and clever gift shops and bookstores in Cambridge. There are black students in dashikis and white students in motorcycle helmets.

Somerville is a town of 70,000 whose chief industries are peanuts and Tufts University. I want College Avenue.

"Far traffic lights ahead, thin make yer left on Day. Yah cahn't miss it, there's Mi Lady of Lourdes on the cahrner. Follow Day till yah cross a squa-a and that's Collidge where the rich people usta live."

FELLOWSHIP IS A DIMENSION IN TIME

Between the Masonic Temple on College Street, a new three-story building, its square and compass glinting in the moonlight, and a frame house with a widow's walk and rounded cornices, every window bright with Christmas lights and candles, is the Havurat Shalom Community Seminary.

The address is 113 College Avenue, not far from the Woodbridge Inn, the last motel in America where the guests still share a single bath.

Little distinguishes the Havurat from the other homes on College Street. Tufts University is only a few blocks to the north and many of the houses on College Street are converted dormitories. The other homes in this neat, middle-class neighborhood are occupied by the denizens of the middle class, the insurance men, teachers, and sales managers.

The Havurat Shalom still posts its screen door, which is rent so that you can reach your hand through and poke the bell with your finger.

The *havurat* is a coming-together. It is an adjective. *Havurah* the noun means fellowship and a *haver* is a brother—a brother in the sense that he worships with you. The Havurat Shalom Community

Seminary is chartered by the Commonwealth of Massachusetts as an educational, nonprofit corporation. Its members, in fact, may receive 4-D classifications since the havurah is recognized by the draft board as a rabbinical seminary. Since few of the members in this or other havurot have availed themselves of this privilege, the haverim are obviously not seeking pulpits.

The Somerville Havurat Shalom was founded in 1968 by some Conservative rabbis, chiefly inspired by Rabbi Arthur Green, now a professor at Smith; and Albert Axelrad, the Reform Hillel director of Brandeis University. This fellowship, or community, provides its members with opportunity for an intensely personal concentration on Judaic studies in which to realize the individual's relationship to God.

It is important to note that the Havurat Shalom, the Havurah in New York, and the Fabrangen in Washington, D.C., the only three classical havurot, modeled on the Pharisaic havurah which evolved in biblical Jerusalem, are not communes. The members of a commune are dependent upon one another for their sustenance as they pursue the same transcendental goal. The members of a havurah share tasks and chores, and they pay dues, but they independently pursue their own livelihoods and interests in the outside world. Nor do they necessarily live in the havurah, though some do, but they hold *at least one* Jewish ideal commonly: that ideal is the sanctity and importance of the Sabbath.

Mark Sandor admitted me to the Havurat Shalom living room, bare, three couches flush against the wall, a small rug, embarrassed by its failure to cover much of the floor, standing lamps, and five-and-dime shades on the windows. A coat rack stood in the entry hall beside a mammoth Duncan Phyfe table. The stairs supported a heavy wooden bannister.

What was once this home's dining room was now the havurah's synagogue. A cat fled at our approach. The synagogue, too, was bare save for cushions on the floor arranged in unordered semicircles. The pulpit was a lectern and the handcrafted ark, a small wooden cabinet, hung on the wall. On the fireplace mantel was a hand-made menorah, cups fashioned from cigarette foil in which Wesson Oil burned.

Sandor, in his early twenties, with a red beard, explained that there were between twenty and forty members of the Havurat Shalom, of whom only four presently lived within it. Sandor said he was one of them. A graduate of Bucknell, Sandor is preparing for medical school with some additional science courses at Tufts. I had interrupted his study of an anatomical text.

Another of the residents came downstairs. He was Nehemiah Polen, a newly ordained rabbi from the New Israel Seminary in Baltimore. He was a tall boy with dark hair and a chubby face who apologized for not being typical. He was not sure he wanted a pulpit, not sure he wanted to continue as a rabbi. But indeed none of the haverim are typical save for this: they are one segment of what Jews call the counterculture, a youth movement, to which the insurgents come either during or right after college. They are not only informed and articulate but well bred. Though not deferential, they are invariably polite.

Soft-spoken, patient Sandor explained that the haverim were not compulsive about Halakah, Jewish law. They did not follow kashrut guidesheets. Their structure was loose. "There are," he said pointing to the cushions, "no assigned seats for Sabbath services."

The members come from diverse Jewish backgrounds. Sandor explained that his religious upbringing in New York City was almost casual. But he went on to say that the Havurat Shalom was a closed community. One can volunteer, but the volunteering does not make one a member. "The havurah is not for everyone," Sandor said, "and sadly we have had to tell people it is not for them."

One of the considerations for membership is that the new haver either read or be willing to learn to read Hebrew for the liturgy of the service, and the subject matter of the courses demands fluency.

On the bulletin board beside the front door, in pencil, was a list of the new semester's classes: religious poetry; Jeremiah; music workshop; and Liturgic Kommentar Schriebund Gruppe.

The next morning my Cicerone was Bill Novak, another soft-spoken twenty-five-year-old graduate student. Bespectacled, affecting a bushy mustache, Novak is a Canadian, a graduate of York University in Toronto and currently completing a thesis at Brandeis in contemporary Jewish studies (he is writing on the political diversity of *Commentary* magazine since 1960). Novak is also the editor of *Response,* probably the most informed and well-written journal of the counterculture.*

* *Response* is far from apolitical, although its politics are not "Whither the Jewish Vote?" Its contributors, who remain unpaid, are writers like Sylvia Ozick, theologians like Jacob Neusner, and historians like Leonard Fein. It was founded by Alan Mintz, now a doctoral candidate at Columbia, and Novak succeeded

Even in the daylight, the Havurat Shalom was more than reasonably presentable despite its inhabitation by four bachelors.

It was a Thursday and the haverim were planning for their by now traditional communal meal that evening. One had the feeling that this joyous repast, so intrinsically important for the union of the members, was prepared in pots atop the range rather than in casseroles or roasting pans within the oven. The stemware, to give it charitably a generic designation, boasted no twins; nor was there any Preem for the instant, and there was only one communal spoon for the sugar and stirring; yet there were no dishes in the sink, nor was coffee coppering in abandoned cups, and the linoleum floor was newly scrubbed.

"I do not mean to suggest the Thursday meal is a last-minute enterprise," Novak said, "only that there are several last-minute expeditionary parties to the nearby stores.

"On Friday evening we have Sabbath services. It is the traditional service, and usually it is read entirely in Hebrew. Before it starts, we either sing a *niggun* or meditate in silence. The chazzan may read a chapter from the Song of Songs before it starts.

"The service, particularly the opening psalms, is slow and deliberate. There is a low-keyed, restful, almost sad mood which nobody can explain. The service ends with a niggun but now it is Shabbat and the world is somehow different than it was an hour earlier."

As many as seventy guests sometimes visit the havurah in addition to the twenty or so haverim. On Saturdays, Novak went on, the haverim take more liberties with the service. They replace the liturgy of the opening section with singing and the Shacharit (morning service) which follows is spiced with still more singing.

"Then," said Novak, "we spend some time in explaining to curious guests what a havurah is."

---

him two years ago. One of its tables of contents reads: "Is Our Schizophrenia Historically Important?"; "Jewish Survival and the New Priorities"; "On Reforming the Philanthropies"; and "The Jewish Student Exchange Movement." It is, of course, like most magazines, in perpetual financial distress. It accepts no advertising and as a Socratic gadfly to the Jewish community it is hardly likely to endear itself to a patron like the American Jewish Committee, which sponsors *Commentary* to the tune of $100,000 a year. *Response* lists only twenty-three sponsors at fifty dollars a head, among them Rabbi Armond Cohen of Cleveland and the Havurat Shalom of Somerville. Its publication is assisted by a grant from the Jewish Student Projects, Inc., of the Combined Jewish Philanthropies of Greater Boston. Four thousand subscribers pay six dollars a year or eleven dollars for two years.

The Havurat Shalom is not so complicated an endeavor that it eludes ordinary understanding. What is confusing about this havurah and the others is that they are not programmatic. The haverim are not out to reform Judaism or redirect it or provide for its survival, nor are they missionaries with a message for Boston Jewry. They are no more than they say: a community devoted to the realization of deeply personal urges and impulses. The Havurat Shalom is a fellowship, and Bill Novak quotes the theologian Jacob Neusner on the subject: "Fellowship has no substance. . . . Fellowship is a dimension of time: one cannot say fellowship is, but rather, fellowship happens. It is created and re-created from moment to moment when certain elements, namely, radically isolated individuals, coalesce to create it. . . . The components of fellowship are individuals coming together out of radical self-involvement and isolation from one another, to pursue a purpose that transcends their own individual lives."*

Jewish men and women do not usually congregate for the purpose of exploring the self. Jews no longer expect a burning bush to signal their spiritual liberation as the burning bush in Sinai signaled Moses. Instead Jews spend an inordinate amount of time obtaining pledges, recruiting members, and selling tickets. The serious criticisms leveled by the youthful counterculture, of which the havurot movement is a most moderate part, is that middle-class institutionalized Jewry has an obsession with performance, overprotection, and the suppression of authentic emotion. It is intent on the desanctification rather than the canonization of experience, to borrow terms from a nearby religion.

In its nature, then, the Havurat Shalom is anti-institutional. It is also apolitical (though this is not true of other counterculture groups). Bill Novak intelligently suggests that the havurah is an alternative for young Jews no longer concerned with a physical or political revolution. Others echo this. Erich Segal, the author of *Love Story,* a Yale professor with whom I once regaled a Hadassah group, replied to my query about student quietude after Kent State, "No student at Yale, and they are smart or they wouldn't have gotten into Yale, thinks for one moment that his demonstrating will advance or serve any cause."

---

* A thorough and varied discussion of the havurot movement can be found in *Contemporary Judaic Fellowship In Theory and Practice,* edited by Jacob Neusner, KTAV Publishing House, New York, 1972.

Those who see the Berrigans as models of ideal religious person-alities, Novak has explained elsewhere, experience a disappointment in the Somerville havurah. Members have left because of the group's lack of interest in anything but the most inconsequential engagements. "We have been accused of being anti-Zionist," Novak said, stirring black coffee. "Which is not true. But we are more likely to treat the prospect of living in Israel as part of our lives rather than as part of our thought, if indeed living in Israel is a prospect for some of us. We have no ideology. We are not ideologues. We have no adminis-tration."

There are young Jews of the counterculture who are militant ac-tivists, many of them, in fact, not so young. They have allied them-selves in the past with progressive and leftist causes and discover in the mysticism of Judaism spiritual nourishment for their radical beliefs.

The most eloquent of these radicals is Arthur Waskow, of the Jews for Urban Justice in Washington, D.C. A lawyer by profession, Was-kow is the author of several books on military strategy and political repression in the modern superstate. He is also the author of the popular *The Freedom Seder* and in *The Bush Is Burning!* (Macmillan paperback editions, 1971) writes: "Slowly, slowly, those of us who have been 'political' but had been cut off from the 'religious' tradition began to understand the 'political' dimension of the Shabbat as fore-taste of the Messianic Age—Shabbat as a present moment of the future 'revolution.' More important, we began to experience in our own lives the sense of peace, completeness, community, created by a Shabbat communally celebrated—and therefore to understand more deeply what the 'revolution' was that we were seeking."

Counterculture is not a widespread or popular movement but it is vocal and more than vocal, it is intelligent. This one small corner of the movement, the Havurat Shalom, does not proceed amid cheers, applause, and admiration. Indeed the havurot movement has proved itself an indefatigable critic not only of the synagogue but of the Fed-eration—the haverim have no hesitation in telling the Federation how it misspends its money—and it would be curious if its criticisms pro-voked no reaction.

There are serious complaints to be lodged against the havurot movement, and the most thoughtful and reasonable have been leveled by Jacob Neusner, the theologian who teaches at Brown University. In *Contemporary Judaic Fellowship* Neusner prophesizes: "This observer tends to believe that the significance of the havurot has been highly exaggerated, partly by the need of some Jews to convince themselves that, like the church, Judaism has produced radical dissenters. I am inclined to suggest that this artificially inflated dimension of the youth culture will prove to be a passing fad remembered nostalgically by those who are easily seduced by slogans and fashions which promise instant eschatology, and by schools where students and teachers are interchangeable, love is God, and the greening of America is inevitable."

Novak acknowledges the justice of these criticisms. The Havurat Shalom is a temporary setting, he admits. The havurot were established by dissidents who had found little encouragement within the Jewish establishment. They may develop into a community which serves the needs of adult members for the rest of their lives, but in a society in transition, this is unlikely.

"People," Novak concludes, "are always asking us questions, saying, 'That's fine for now, but what about the future?' It's hard enough making something that's fine for now, after all."

PART VI: AD ASTRA

CHICAGO: This Ain't No Sissy Town

TOUGH-TOWN FIRMAMENT

The flag of the city of Chicago: two equidistant blue stripes divide the white field into three equal panels representing the North, South, and West Side. Every place in Chicago, however, is to the west, toward the frontier, because Lake Michigan, a vast landlocked sea, is the east.

Four blue stars occupy the center panel of the flag. These stars symbolize the founding of Fort Dearborn in 1803 (whose entire garrison as well as the women and children were ambushed by marauding Indians during the War of 1812); the Chicago Fire of 1871 (which consumed a shanty town from which sprang an alabaster city); the World's Columbian Exposition of 1893 (celebrating the quadricentennial anniversary of the discovery of America); and the World's Fair of 1933, the Century of Progress Exposition (celebrating Chicago's hundredth year).

A lot of tough men put those stars in the flag.

And at least three good women: Jane Addams, Chicago's first Nobel Prize winner, the founder of Hull House, an innovative social settlement; Sally Rand, who made the esoteric fan dance a popular diversion; and Frances E. Willard, who transformed her birthplace, nearby Evanston, into the world headquarters for the Women's Christian Temperance Movement.

Some of the tough men were the bootleggers who hung out in Cicero and made Chicago notorious during the nineteen-twenties. Hundreds of thousands of Americans who will never visit Chicago still feel it is a familiar city by virtue of having seen Jimmy Cagney, Humphrey Bogart, and Edward G. Robinson movies. The locale of these movies was always Chicago and, according to the late film critic Robert Warshow, these films transformed the gangster into a tragic hero, an Oedipus whose Thebes was the North Side and whose Jocasta was the American Dream of the Bitch-Goddess Success.

Television has also made Chicago familiar. The networks have four times re-created the detailed mechanics of the St. Valentine's Day Massacre of 1929 because few men have ever managed a mass murder with the finesse of Al Capone (to whom history has dealt a bum rap, say some Chicagoans, under the mistaken impression that Al kept the soup kitchens open during the Depression).

The city's politicians, particularly its Democratic politicians, have always proved hard and tough men. German-born John Peter Altgeld, who vaulted from the Cook County Superior Court to become governor of Illinois in an unexpected Democratic victory in 1892, not only pardoned four anarchists unjustly imprisoned as a result of the Haymarket Riot in 1886 but also told President Grover Cleveland that his use of federal troops to break the Pullman Strike was unconstitutional, a criticism of his party's leader which earned him predictable defeat.

Three-time mayor William Hale Thompson, "Big Bill" to the electorate, promised his Irish constituency that if the visiting Prince of Wales showed his nose in Chicago, he would personally punch it in. The Prince, later Edward VIII, still later the Duke of Windsor, carefully considered the threat and sedulously avoided the city.

Anton Cermak, who won the mayoralty in 1931 by assembling an ethnic coalition, took the bullet intended for Franklin D. Roosevelt while accompanying the President-elect in an open car in Miami on February 15, 1933.

There's a fifth star in the flag, an invisible star symbolizing the Democratic convention of 1968, a star planted by Richard J. Daley, City Hall's incumbent, who is not only tougher than all the gangsters and politicians put together, but probably tougher than Frances E. Willard.

Daley presides over the only city in the Midwest with a vigorously growing downtown, the only city in which business and industry seek to enter rather than leave. New buildings rear skyward. The foundations are dug for more. And they are not the office buildings of the speculators, as they are in New York, but the headquarters of established industry—John Hancock, Xerox, the *Chicago Sun-Times*.

He presides over a city whose budget is $1 billion. One of the City Hall reporters in the press room impressed the astronomical proportions of this sum upon the rewrite man with these instructions:

"One billion dollars. Nine hundred million from local taxes and $100 million from the feds. To understand how much this is, I want you to clear your mind of everything. In one half of your now empty mind visualize the new John Hancock Building, a hundred stories high. In the other half imagine crisp new $100 bills. Stand on the sidewalk and put one $100 bill on top of another. You keep putting one bill on top of another until you reach the 100th floor. Then you take the elevator down as fast as you can and you start another pile of crisp $100 bills. When the second pile reaches the forty-third floor, you stop. That is $1 billion."

Daley also presides over a city which once a week produces a municipal scandal. During the last week of September 1972 a grand jury indicted County Clerk Edward J. Barrett, a jolly professional Irishman, for thirty years active in state, county, and city politics, on charges of accepting $180,000 in kickbacks from a voting-machine manufacturer.

A former governor, Otto Kerner, a recently appointed judge of the U. S. Court of Appeals and a one-time Daley protégé, has been found guilty of fraud, bribery and tax evasion for the fraudulent manipulation of $300,000 worth of racetrack stock, a payoff for giving the Illinois racetrack queen, Mrs. Majorie Lindheimer Everett, favorable racing dates.

State Representative Harold Washington was charged with and admitted evading $66,000 in income taxes by not filing returns for four years; his colleague, State Representative Bernard O'Hanrahan, also admitted failure to file returns. He told the judge he was so harassed by his official duties that he simply never got around to it.

The newspaper *Chicago Today,* with the aid of the Better Government Committee, disclosed that Cook County taxpayers lost $500,000 a year in potential earnings on massive county funds in noninterest-bearing bank accounts, banks in which several politicians had an interest. And at this writing Alderman Thomas Keane faces indictment on charges growing from this disclosure.

The *Sun-Times* revealed that the photograph of the bullet holes which proved that two slain Black Panthers, Fred Hampton and Mark Clark, had fired first through the door at raiding police were in reality thumbtacks. State Attorney General Edward V. Hanrahan was tried for conspiracy to obstruct justice. He was acquitted of putting the thumbtacks in the door and of taking the photograph. But the newspaper publicity probably was responsible for his defeat in the 1972 election.

The week prior to Eddie Barrett's indictment, the FBI arrested Fred Hubbard. Hubbard, a black Second Ward alderman, disappeared in 1971 with $110,592 he had embezzled while chairman of the Chicago Plan, a federal program for creating jobs for minorities. At the time of his arrest in Gardena, California, Hubbard's total assets included $60 plus $151 he had just won at the poker table with a full house, threes over.

This is not all that occupies Daley. While friends and acquaintances were going in and coming out of trial court, the cops staged a citywide job action to win sympathy for higher pay scales. They handed out traffic tickets the way Santa hands out toys. Every motorist in Chicago got a ticket either for not signaling properly or for parking more than three inches from the curb or for having only three whitewall tires.

Cops even ticketed City Council member Vito Marzullo, who is rumored to have "connections." Marzullo promised to fight the ticket and pointedly asked what was wrong with the cops fighting crime and drugs.

Hizzoner told the press that if the policemen, who are the highest paid in the nation at $14,000 per year, thought they could threaten the city, they had another think coming. He was as good as his word. The next day the precinct captains ordered all cops to patrol their beats on foot. Pedestrian locomotion is an inhumane punishment to Americans. The inhumanity of the precinct captains brought home to the sensitive patrolmen their own inhumanity to motorists. Also, it is harder to ticket a motorist on foot than it is in a patrol car.

IMAGES THAT YET FRESH IMAGES BEGET

The poets have always taken Chicago seriously. Carl Sandburg described it as "Stormy, husky, brawling / City of Big Shoulders," and Allen Ginsberg as ". . . a smoking winter city / under that fogged flat / supersky of heaven."

In this poetic instance, Ginsberg has the better of it. He suggests Chicago's weather is not all it should be. It is always preparing to rain in Chicago.

Chicago used to talk about itself so much, about its stockyards and industries, its two hundred square miles of city, about the tonnage in and out of its port (now over 3.5 million) that outsiders called it the city of "beef and brag."

It is a city which has been well described, perhaps overly described, but it is a city which lends itself to description.

The Chicago River cuts a broad V through town, its North Branch running east to a point at Lake Street and Wacker Drive, then the man-made South Branch running west through a ship and drainage canal to flow into the Des Plaines. There are, accordingly, bridges everywhere, 57 of them movable, 30 fixed, and 74 viaducts. At both ends of the bridges, in glass cupboards—life preservers.

At night, the view from the Lake Front offers a paradise of light. The cubes and silos of the new apartment houses and condominiums march north along the shore on Michigan Boulevard outlining the Gold Coast. Chicago has twenty-nine miles of shoreline, half of it Gold Coast, the other half containing thirty beaches, parks, the Art Institute of Chicago, a planetarium, the Chicago Museum of Natural History, the John C. Shedd Aquarium, and Soldiers' Field, where Gene Tunney took the long count in 1927 and where the College All Stars almost never beat the pros.

In the center of the city is the Loop, the business and entertainment district. It takes its name from the elevated transit structure which makes a rectangular loop around this core depositing commuters from the north, west, and south.

It is not the Loop or the lake or the Gold Coast which has inspired the novelists. It is the fact that Chicago looks like Everycity, U.S.A. Which is to say it looks like Elizabeth, New Jersey. Past the lake, behind the façade of the Loop and the Gold Coast, Chicago is a flat expanse of nondescript, drab and probably unwholesome dwellings.

The poets treat Chicago as a hero and the novelists as a bum. Chicago is both.

On the way to its premier Jewish restaurant, the Ashkenaz on Morse Avenue, called the Ashcan, the elevated passes Wrigley Field, where Ferguson Jenkins year after year turns in twenty-game seasons and the Bleacher Bums terrorize the kids who root for Cincinnati; then the el roars over a cemetery whose concrete fence bears in sloppy black letters the hortatory graffito, "All Praise to the Lord Christ."

Richard Wright condemned the city in *Native Son* and so did James T. Farrell in *Studs Lonigan*. Sherwood Anderson described its grotesques and Ben Hecht found it heartless. Chicago spawned a school of writers; but curiously, the two local boys most admired, Ernest Hemingway and Archibald MacLeish, for some reason never mention Chicago at all.

It is one of two publishing centers in America, the other New York. All of the Sears, Roebuck and Montgomery Ward and Miles Kimball and thousands of other mail-order catalogs are published in Chicago and the train schedules and telephone directories and the brochures and kits of industrial advertisers. In the way of great literature, however, there are only publishers Harriet Monroe, who founded *Poetry,* and Hugh Hefner, who founded *Playboy.* For her pains in discovering Ezra Pound, Miss Monroe also had the privilege of printing T. S. Eliot. For his pains in discovering the girl who is soft tonight and off your hands tomorrow, Hugh Hefner made $10 million.

It is the only city with fierce competition between both morning and evening newspapers. *Chicago Today* and the *News* compete for the A.M. circulation and the *Tribune* and the *Sun-Times* for the P.M. *Today* and the *Sun-Times* are liberal and the *News* and the *Tribune* conservative, to say the least. It is one of two cities in the country with a city news bureau. The City News Bureau in Chicago syndicates the Windy City doings for television stations and other newspapers throughout the country. In New York, the city news bureau goes by the name of the Little A.P.

The image of the hero and the bum animate two of the best books ever written about Chicago. The book about the bum is *Second City* (Knopf, 1952) by A. J. Liebling who conducted the "Wayward Press" column in the *New Yorker.* Liebling was antipathetic. He did not much respect the town. "The Midwestern friendliness I had been warned I would have to put up with was well dissipated by the airport personnel," he wrote. He called Chicago a "Second City," a diagnosis rather than a description. The disease was manifested by a desire to grow bigger than New York.

Despite his antipathy, Liebling was objective. "A thing that impressed me about Chicago from the hour I got there," he confided, "was the saloons. New York bars operated on the principle that you want a drink or you wouldn't be there. If you're civil and don't mind waiting, they will sell you one when they get around to it. Chicago bars assume nobody likes liquor and that to induce customers to purchase even a minute quantity, they have to provide a show."

The Courtesy Bar on Wells Street under the el not only offers its patrons cut-rate souvenirs of Chicago but can provide hard-boiled eggs for the hungry or a waffle iron for those who happen to have only now remembered the little woman's birthday. The bartender is not only alert and quick with a marvelous memory for names, but he minds his own business. He thinks nothing of serving you two double bourbons at 8:30 A.M. and wishing you a happy day at work. He keeps the faith that somehow you will turn up at 5:05 P.M. when the hard day in the shop is over.

The only writers Liebling found interesting in 1950 were the newspaper columnists Irving Kupcinet and Sidney J. Harris and the novelist Nelson Algren. The ranks have not swelled appreciably.

Liebling particularly admired *The Man with the Golden Arm,* but he left town before Algren had published *Chicago: City on the Make* (Doubleday, 1951). Algren is a native and memorialized his hometown in a fifty-page paean. He called Chicago an "October sort of city even in the spring."

"Yet once you've come to be part of this particular patch," he wrote, "you'll never love another. Like loving a woman with a broken nose, you may well find lovelier lovelies. But never a lovely so real."

GLEN COHEN AND EVENSTEIN

The city of Chicago has a population of 3,460,000. Cook County—and Cook County is Chicago and some surrounding suburbs—has 5,492,369. Metropolitan Chicago, which includes the suburbs of northern Lake County and western Du Page, makes the total population 7,546,000, the third largest in the country.

Of these, 1,159,000 are nonwhites.

Two hundred and sixty-five thousand are Jews. Once there were 300,000, but Chicago Jews, when they fade away, fade away to Los Angeles and the industrialized South.

The Jews are split fifty-fifty between the city and suburbs. For the most part, they live north of the Loop along the shore in the city, fanning west in the city's Forty-ninth and Fiftieth wards, wards so heavily populous with Jews that California Avenue is called Synagogue Row.

The Jews have spilled past the city limits into the northern suburban cities (the western ones belong to the WASP)—into Lincolnwood,

Skokie, Glencoe, Wilmette, and Evanston. Some, a few, have remained behind in Hyde Park, the South Side college area.

The move north has been under way since the end of World War II, so long that another generation has begun moving back to the city into the Lake Front apartments.

There have been Jews in Chicago since there was a Chicago—August 12, 1833, when its 350 citizens won their first charter, which granted them a town measuring one square mile. Aaron Friend and Isaac Harp advertised their wares daily in the *Chicago Democrat* in the eighteen-thirties.

By 1837, when Chicago incorporated itself as a city, winning a second charter, which increased its potential size, there were 20 Jews among its 4170 inhabitants. They were newly arrived immigrants from Bavaria and the Rhenish Palatinate. In 1845, the Jews organized a Burial Ground Society and founded their first temple, Anaha Ma'arave (Congregation of the People of the West).

German Jews in substantial numbers came to Chicago in the eighteen-forties. By 1860 some had become doctors and lawyers, many of them merchants, and some had become bankers.

In turn, these Jews were succeeded by shtetl Jews in the eighteen-nineties, the majority of whom became workers in the needle trades (Chicago was once a great clothing center). Others became stogie rollers and still others went into the burgeoning factories. According to a 1900 city census, there were over 2000 Jewish rag peddlers and almost 2000 Jewish fruit and scrap-iron peddlers.

Snobbery, the awareness of class distinction, which separated rich German from poor Russian, still persists in Chicago. It does not persist on the nursery-school level or in the Bar Association or among Jews in managerial positions, but it does persist on the millionaires' level.

There are nine Jewish country clubs in Chicago. Annually, the Jewish Federation sponsors Country Club Day, a fund-raising program which, among other events, includes intramural golf and tennis and handball competitions, capped by a dinner at which the various country club members make pledges. Seven of the nine country clubs participate in this gala. The two which do not are the country clubs of the German Jews. There are no schisms like Jewish schisms. Still Chicago sponsors three hundred Bonds for Israel dinners a year.

There are forty-seven institutes of higher education in the city itself, ranging from the University of Chicago, where a student must read one hundred great books to get out, to the Moody Bible Institute, where a student need read only one to get out. Nearby are North-western University and Lake Forest and Wheaton Colleges.

Jews are prominent in higher education. Edward Hirsch Levi is the president of the University of Chicago; Rolf Weil, of Roosevelt University; and Oscar Shabat, of Chicago City College.

The American Jewish Committee has sponsored several reports on the attitudes and questionings of Jewish college students. Not surprisingly, these reports discover an underlying pattern of disappointment among the young. It is hard, however, to determine what fosters this disappointment. It is even hard to conclude whether Jewish youth is capable of exploring the meaning of Jewish identity at all.

For example, I list below, in order of preference, Jewish writers to whom Jewish college students testified they most immediately relate:

> Philip Roth
> Elie Wiesel
> Chaim Potok
> Bernard Malamud
> Saul Bellow
> Leon Uris
> Isaac Bashevis Singer
> Martin Buber
> Erich Segal
> Norman Mailer
> Karl Marx
> Franz Kafka
> Sholem Aleichem
> Max Dimont
> Sigmund Freud
> Leo Rosten
> Abraham Heschel

Imagine! In that order. None of the students had gotten around to reading S. J. Perelman or Mike Gold or Nathanael West.

Most of us fumble trying to find out what youth wants because youth itself is fumbling. After compiling a reading list like this, the Jewish youth of Chicago still complain that their parents were Jews in the temple and goyim in the streets. On campuses throughout the country, Jewish youth complain that their parents made them forfeit a Jewish education.

But Eugene DuBow, the executive director of the Chicago American Jewish Committee, does not anticipate a widespread growth of Jewish education no matter how deprived youth feels. "There will be more," he said. "Certainly Jews can support more than six elementary schools in Chicago. Probably there needs to be more. But the Jewish parochial school will never replace the public school. There is a relationship between Jews and the public school that obtains with no other group. The public school worked for the Jews. Public schools didn't work for everyone else. And there is a difference between the parochial- and the public-school teacher. The first is always found wanting.

"But there is even another reason why the Jewish all-day school will not succeed at this time. And that is that the suburbs, which is where the Jews now live, are no longer stable. Within the suburb and between suburb and suburb there is always a fluid population movement."

John Rice, the executive director of the Federation, echoes DuBow. There is a limit, after all, to Jewish resources. The proponents of Jewish parochial education often intimate that its costs should be borne by the whole Jewish community, the Federation. We have seen, however, that the wisdom of the Federation's picking up the tab for the Jewish hospital is under debate. It would not seem likely it could offer more than minimal support for a parochial school system.

Mr. DuBow, who took an extraordinary length of time to fill me on these issues, entertained me with a luncheon in his office. We ate corned-beef sandwiches and cole slaw from a small round table which lacked a fourth leg. Every so often it tipped and we righted it like two Coast Guard officers trying to gulp their mess while the cutter weathered a squall.

But the sandwiches were so good they shouldn't happen to my enemy.

THE MAN ON FIVE AND THE JEWS ON TWO

Richard Daley is called "The Man on Five." His offices on the fifth floor of City Hall on LaSalle Street are hardly opulent. One wall is screened by a beige curtain and the other three are paneled in a light-colored wood. They are without adornment save for the seal of the city and a modest clock which can be reached by a ladder to move its hands forward when daylight saving time comes around. But when Hizzoner settles behind the great black desk he looks like General Patton settling in a tank to lead the relief column to Bastogne.

In the large red-carpeted anteroom, one wall is decorated with pictures of each of Chicago's mayors. Two well-dressed, self-effacing detectives who can plug you at forty yards try to look inconspicuous. There are also two cops sitting uncomfortably in front of typewriters, a telephone between them. What impresses the City Hall visitor is that there are always more people to handle the telephones than there are telephones to handle. Outside the City Hall press room, for example, there are three old-timers who are there supposedly to handle the calls for the reporters, who have been placing and receiving their own calls even before the city painted the press room the first time. Ray McCarthy of *Chicago Today* calls them "The Nairobi Trio." They are the faithful retainers from a forgotten administration.

The mayor's presence in City Hall is evidenced by his Cadillac smack beside City Hall's entrance. One cannot mistake the Daley Cadillac. Its license plate is 708-222, the number of votes he got when he won for the first time in 1955.

Daley also has offices across the street in the Shoreham Hotel. Democratic Party Headquarters are on the second floor. These digs, too, are businesslike and Spartan. The gloomy halls of the Shoreham, however, have been hallowed by the number of men who walked down them to Daley's office wanting to be President of the United States.

On the second floor of City Hall are the chambers where the City Council of Chicago convenes. The City Council consists of fifty aldermen, one from each of Chicago's fifty wards. The Council is a nonpartisan body and does not introduce legislation but passes on fiscal matters. Money is the heart and the brains of a city. Money makes a city.

Do not let "nonpartisan" deceive you. Mayor Daley controls an apparat, one wing of which is the City Council and the other the ward committeemen. In many wards, the only way to win election to the City Council is to earn the endorsement of the Democratic ward committeeman, of whom there are also fifty in Chicago.

The ward committeeman can garner the signatures by which a candidate's name is put on the ballot. The party will follow the ward committeeman's suggestion as to which nonpartisan it will endorse. The ward committeeman can muster the votes at a figurative snap of his fingers. There are 42,500 city jobs in Chicago and almost as many in Cook County. Everybody who has a job owes somebody a favor, usually the Daley apparat.

Ward committeemen are elected every four years by the registered members of the party. The committeemen wield great discretionary power. They are trusted lieutenants. Civic-minded and dutiful though they be, the chances are they will endorse for alderman that applicant who has rung the most doorbells for the party and has most convincingly argued his desire to participate in the great work the Honorable Richard J. Daley is about.

Though aldermen earn only $8000 a year and ward committeemen earn zilch, the door is always crowded.

Twelve percent of these *ipsos custodes* are Jews, seven of them aldermen and five of them ward committeemen, one of them, Seymour Simon, both.

By 1928, the Jewish vote in Chicago was solidly Democratic and remained as solidly Democratic as the old Solid South. A Jew, Colonel (because of World War II service in the judge advocate general's office) Jacob M. Arvey controlled the Democratic Party in Illinois from 1947 to 1959. He was responsible for the nomination and election of Adlai Stevenson to the governorship and Paul Douglas to the Senate in 1948 and for Stevenson's nomination as presidential candidate in 1952 and 1956. Arvey had been an alderman from the Twenty-fourth Ward since 1923 and later the United States Attorney General. He was the political boss in part because he was a Jew—the Jews were steady and it was their turn—and in part because he had an acuity for promoting individuals with exceptional political intelligence and because he was able to adapt to changing political conditions. He was a bulwark of Jewish organizational life, the key to success in Jewish wards. Even though the constituents couldn't care less about the B'nai B'rith or the Federation or UJA, they feel their representatives must. Organizational life, not piety, is what identifies the Jew.

But the voters in Chicago's Jewish wards these days are called the dancers. They are called dancers because the poll workers know that to split his ticket, a voter must move from one side of the machine to pull the levers on the other. Consequently, they watch feet and they watch Jewish feet dance voter after voter, bong after bong.

The seven Jews on the City Council are Paul Wigoda, an old-timer from the northernmost Forty-ninth Ward; Burton Natarus from the Forty-seventh; Christopher Cohen from the Forty-sixth; Leon M. Despres from the Fifth, the old Jewish neighborhood; William S. Singer from the Forty-third; and Jack Sperling, a Republican, from the Fiftieth.

Still dark-haired in his fifties, Paul Wigoda, a Daley Democrat, is noted as one of the mayor's best interpreters—one of Daley's weaknesses is an infelicity of expression. While the wards in Chicago are redistricted every ten years, the neighborhoods remain roughly the same. Wigoda has represented the Forty-ninth, one of whose borders is the lake, long enough to earn the seniority to ascend to Chicago's Traffic Commission as chairman with offices on the third floor.

In the thirties, the forties, and the early fifties, he said, the Forty-ninth was all Protestant. Now it is predominantly Jewish. While the constituents return him to office, Mr. Wigoda is worried about the political commitment of many to the New Left.

"Jews have never survived in a radical or revolutionary community. Never. Not in Russia, not in Argentina under Perón, not anyplace. But on the City Council we have a Jewish alderman who has allied himself with a black who signed the petition out of the Black Caucus in Gary. That alliance diminishes the Jewish voice in politics.

"The only time a Democrat lost in one of the sure Jewish wards," Wigoda went on, "was when he was Jewish and had no identity as a Jew. An Irish Catholic beat him. During the campaign, this Jewish candidate approached the rabbi and argued that it was important for him to serve on the temple's board of directors. The rabbi told him, 'I cannot put you on the board of directors because you are not a member of this congregation.'"

A lawyer, Wigoda is also a university lecturer on the role of Jews in politics. "Voters," he said, "cannot bear ambiguities, Jewish voters less than anyone."

Burton Natarus expressed a different though not necessarily contrary point of view. Short, neat, with a handsome embryonic face, Natarus is a quiet, almost diffident man, but he must do well by his clients because his law office is a plush one. He is in his first term and he is young. "I doubt seriously that my constituents know I'm a Jew," he said. "If they think about my origins, they probably think

I'm a Greek because of the name 'Natarus' [nay, tear us]. Someone among my ancestors must have been a notary because that's what the name means.

"There are Jews in the Forty-seventh, but there are also Filipinos and the airline stewardesses who fly out of O'Hare live there. There are rich people and poor people. The constituents on the Gold Coast want moorings for their boats and the constituents on Larrabee Street want jobs and food. I am the only alderman with a lot of nightclubs in his ward. The Forty-seventh is both business and residential and I get a lot of complaints about noise. It is a heterogeneous ward. The state representative is a black, Robert Thompson."

Natarus is the only alderman who publishes a newspaper, *42nd Ward Young Democrats*. Along with a detailed analysis of the fundamental needs of the ward—public safety, jobs, housing—is a photograph of Alderman Natarus and Hizzoner opening a new bicycle route. Hizzoner is on a two-seater, the man in front, the head of the League of American Wheelmen, pumping.

Christopher Cohen of the Forty-sixth Ward is also young, the son of Wilbur Cohen, a Kennedy cabinet appointee. Cohen keeps late office hours to meet with his constituents and has been known to give a reporter or two a ride home at night. One of the newsmen said, "He is the only alderman I would want as a neighbor."

Seymour Simon is another lawyer, a more than proficient lawyer. He represented the theater owners in a complex suit against the distributors and producers so successfully that after he won the case, the distributors and producers asked him to represent them in any future litigation. A man with a muscular, strong face, framed by gold-rimmed aviator eyeglasses, Mr. Simon sits beneath a huge canvas done by the Chicago artist Henry Boris in which logos spell out, "Self-satisfaction is the first step toward deviation."

The Fortieth Ward is over half Jewish with large Greek and Scandinavian neighborhoods. Mr. Simon was not always its alderman. Once he was the president of the Cook County Board of Commissioners, a powerful job in the city because it is through the president that county patronage is funneled. But Daley dumped him in 1971.

"I can tell you how but I am still not sure why," said Mr. Simon. "Maybe because I got into a bitter fight with Alderman Keane about rezoning land in the Fortieth for a garbage dump. Maybe because I gave jobs to Jews. Maybe Daley wanted someone else. But I was casually"—he stopped and repeated—"casually awaiting my renomination when Daley made a motion which carried, that the party appoint a slate-making subcommittee, an animal of which none of us had ever heard. An hour later I was called into his office and Daley said, 'Seymour, it is the opinion of this committee that you not be the nominee.' That is the way it's done. A man loses power like he loses a cuff link. He wakes up one morning and it isn't there."

Since his deposition, Mr. Simon has proved a vigorous critic of many municipal practices. On one occasion, he brought it to the City Council's attention that while the city parking lots were tax-exempt, there was no legal mandate to extend that exemption to the concessionaires who leased them or space thereon, as was indeed the city's practice. This suggestion generated neither passion among Daley's opponents nor reform among the establishment until on trying to reclaim his car from the Shoreham Hotel garage after the meeting, Simon learned it had been stolen.

"How can a thief steal a car from the Shoreham?" he asked.

"Didn't steal it from the Shoreham," answered the attendant. "When there's an overflow, we park the cars on the city lot. Stole it from the city lot."

It is a foregone conclusion that if a concessionaire cannot sanctify parked cars on the lot he certainly does not deserve an exemption.

Chubby, thirty-one-year-old William Singer is the Chicago boy who filed the challenge that resulted in the banishment of Richard Daley from the floor of the 1972 Democratic national convention. Singer, a native-born Chicagoan, a one-time aide to Senator Paul Douglas, a Bobby Kennedy worker in '68 who aligned himself with Senator McGovern after the assassination, filed his challenge on March 21, charging that the composition of Daley's delegation did not conform to the McGovern rules.

Anything but modest, Singer is probably truthful when he says he thought the challenge would lead to some give and take. But there's a lesson or two he might have to learn about politics—some men will lose rather than compromise.

Daley's expulsion hardly endeared Singer to the apparat. But then he had hardly endeared himself by winning an off-year election for alderman in 1969. He ran as an independent against the apparat candidate, Jim Gaughan, a shoo-in.

Midway through the campaign, in which Singer was getting nowhere, Eddie Barrett, that clever purveyor of voting machines whom we have met, publicly stated, for unfathomed reasons of his own,

"The followers of Singer remind me of the brigade of porcupines with long hair and long snouts."

The Forty-third Ward is a mixture of Mexicans, Puerto Ricans, Italians, a small number of blacks—and Jews. Singer capitalized upon the remark. He passed out campaign buttons with a snouty porcupine. The porcupine, especially the long-snouted variety, became the Singer symbol. He won by a narrow margin, thus instructing Ed Barrett in *his* last political lesson: Jews do not like jokes about their noses. In 1971, Singer won by 12,000 votes.

Singer says enmities among the Daley apparat die hard. "Do you know the rumor they are spreading about me?" he asked. "They say I have become a convert to Roman Catholicism."

"Why would they say a thing like that?"

"Because," answered Singer, returning the waves of passersby along LaSalle Street, "because Father Carl Sezak helped in my campaign." He shook his head at the villainy that stops at nothing.

There have been those who insist Billy Singer will run for mayor in '75. If he runs, there's always the chance he will win. But nobody will ever believe he is a convert, no matter how sibilant the whispers.

Republican Jack Sperling is a rangy, almost lanky man in his fifties who has represented the Fiftieth Ward for twenty-seven years. There are 44,000 residential dwellings in the Fiftieth, no hotels but several convalescent homes. Along with a Jewish population in excess of 60 percent live Germans and Greeks.

"You have to remember," said Sperling, "that for twenty years Nixon was the candidate. No matter what the office he ran for, I heard cruel things said about him and cruel things said about me for voting for him."

The cruelty doesn't seem to have left many scars. Sperling is a man of patent good humor. A Republican needs good humor to keep winning in a Democratic Jewish ward.

"Each election is different," said Sperling. "In the beginning, in the early fifties, only 15 percent of the ward was Jewish and I discounted their support. But in 1971 I went to them. I like to think I got Jewish votes because I'm charismatic, but it's not so. I got some Jewish votes because there are Jews who are Republicans and some because the Jews think if everything goes one way, it's no good. The Jews will vote for the voice crying in the wilderness."

Of the fifty aldermen, the best copy is always provided by Leon Despres. Despres was elected to the City Council as an independent in 1955, the year Daley became mayor. Despres has an artless dramatic flair.

Not long ago, the City Council deliberated on raising the elevated fare. Mr. Daley was for it. Several of the aldermen were not. The debate was long and tedious and unignited by metaphor. As the argument proceeded into the night, many of the Council members sent out for sandwiches and coffee or cakes and milk. Despres sent out for Triscuits, which he munched savagely as one by one the intransigents wilted before Daley's persuasive bellowing. The question was called. The fare raise passed.

Leon Despres rose in his place.

"You got something to say?" asked Hizzoner.

"Yes, I have something to say," answered Despres. "Mr. Mayor," said Despres, digging into the Triscuits and scattering them on the aisle, "the people have asked for bread." He stared at the Triscuits, then at the mayor. "And you have given them a stone." He has been called "the noblest alderman of them all."

Chicago is the city which gave the American vocabulary the word "clout." It has also bequeathed "Chinaman" to our political jargon. A Chinaman is the patron, the mandarin who dispenses jobs and favors to the deserving. The ward committeemen are the Chinamen of municipal politics. The five Jewish ward committeemen are Martin Tuchow of the Forty-eighth; Robert Cherry of the Forty-sixth; Seymour Simon; Bernard Neistein of the Twenty-ninth; and Marshall Korshak, the last the Chiang Kai-shek of the ward committeemen.

One of the ways a ward committeeman wins election is by inspiring the registered voters. The sure way to inspire a registered voter is to deliver the ward to the Democratic column.

"Redistricting," said Martin Tuchow, "had made a present of the Forty-eighth Ward to the Republicans. Bob O'Rourke, the Republican alderman, clapped his hands when the lines were drawn and said, 'Oh boy! We got a dynasty.' I personally recruited Marylou Hedlund to run against O'Rourke in the election. And Marylou Hedlund won. She ran on a platform that it is bad for Chicago to have too many dynasties."

Almost all of Tuchow's ward work is spent in trying to find jobs for his constituents. "It's a tough situation," he said. "The ward is filled with welfare people and welfare people float from one slum to the next."

The politician with the most charm is Marshall Korshak, now the city collector, who runs the office where citizens pay licensing fees, fines, and taxes. The wall of his office on the ground floor of City Hall boasts one photograph, that of Richard J. Daley, the only portrait I saw of him in any of the offices. Korshak has served as state representative, state senator, alderman, and as Cook County treasurer.

"I wouldn't want you to think I'm a hack," he said, chomping his cigar. "Goodness, do not think that. If things had worked out right, I'd have been governor. Probably senator. Nobody gets into this business to become city collector." Korshak is also known as Available Jones.

Tall, in his sixties, with a mane of silver hair, Korshak underneath has the soul of a poet. No politician in Chicago turns better phrases.

"In the beginning," he said, "all the Jews were Republicans. They were Republicans because of Abraham Lincoln. But they became Democrats because they were victims of oppression. The Democrats won the minorities because the Democrats enlarged upon the Bill of Rights."

Korshak pointed north. "Now they are not Democrats any longer. As a consequence they are living a political diaspora. When they were Democrats, they made the Board of Education cease and desist giving the test for teachers on Saturdays. That's the Jewish Sabbath," he added with a parenthetic wink.

"When they were Democrats, the Illinois State Legislature was empowered to invest surplus funds in Israeli bonds," said Korshak's companion, Bernard Neistein, another old-timer, the committeeman of the Twenty-ninth. There are no Jews in the Twenty-ninth. It is a black ward. Mr. Neistein did not petition for election. But neither did any black. So he won the post by a combination of acclamation and default. He, too, decried Jewish ingratitude.

"It's ugly," he said. "It is ugly because we should all remember the Republicans are not going to be in forever. When the Democrats are in, will they forgive us?"

"The Jew has become an independent voter," said Korshak, finger extended for emphasis. "Which is to say the Jew defects. The black does not defect." A second finger for added emphasis. "The trouble with the black is that he does not vote. I do not know which is worse."

"Both are bad," agreed Neistein.

I left the two Jewish Chinamen to their verbal ideograms. Politicians in Chicago are engaging because they do not labor under the misapprehension that the electorate thinks they are any better than they are.

Dignified Jack Sperling some time ago came into the City Hall press room to discuss an upcoming primary election for the members of the Republican delegation to the national convention. Also in the press room was Arnold Matankey, editor and publisher of the *Near North Side News*. Matankey had just informed the reporters that his newspaper was endorsing challenger Charles A. Banke for Sperling's seat.

Sperling, spying Matankey, asked how dared he write such an endorsement without providing an opportunity for him to answer.

"I called you four thousand times," Matankey said, giving no ground.

"You what?" asked the irritated Sperling. "You called me? When did you call me and what did you mean by that?"

"I mean," said Matankey, "that you are a liar."

Sperling, fifty-seven, the grandfather of six, weighing in at 178, landed a right.

Matankey, thirty-seven, weighing in at 200, proved he could take a punch because he came back with a hammerlock.

While the three other reporters scooped him, Ray McCarthy of *Chicago Today* separated the two politicians and reminded them they were in the press room.

Later in the day, the two men made up and apologized to the reporters for the distraction they occasioned. Henceforth, they promised, they would comport themselves in the press room as others comported themselves in the Century Club.

And Claude W. Holman, ward committeeman and alderman from the Fourth Ward, the president pro tem of the City Council, the black closest to Daley and the only alderman, in fact, disposed to poeticize about Daley with poetry as varied as that of Tennyson and Auden, was accused by another alderman of using municipal funds to pay his secretary.

"What do you want to know about my secretary?" asked the elderly Holman.

"Are you going to keep her on your staff?"

Holman looked about the chamber in stunned amazement at the absurdity of the question. "Of course, I'm going to keep her," he answered. "She's young. She's black. And she's beautiful. Who wouldn't keep her?"

Sun-Times reporter Harry Golden, Jr., found Marshall Korshak at the Civic Center awaiting the arrival of Daley to light the Christmas tree. Golden asked, "Marshall, I have heard a curious rumor. I have heard you will endorse Leon Despres for the City Council in the spring elections. Marshall, how do you explain such an unprecedented action?"

Korshak answered with what Golden described as an expressive Jewish shrug, shoulders rising like two Aetnas, hands slowly ascending, palms finally turning out to reveal empty innocence.

"The shrug," explains Golden, "means, 'I don't know,' which must be discounted since Korshak is the ward committeeman of the Fifth. Or it means, 'I know but Mayor Daley doesn't want anyone else to know.' "

The endorsement was an obvious move. First of all, there was no question that Despres was going to win. He was endorsed because he is the kind of opponent Mayor Daley cherishes. He is not a militant intent on storming City Hall with followers. Nor is Despres a politician who would sacrifice the interests of his constituents for personal ambition. He was endorsed by the Democrats because he clearly understands the issues and rationally debates them. "Thereby," remarked Golden, "helping other, less fortunate aldermen to understand them as well."

There are other Jews prominent in Chicago politics, the most newsworthy of them perhaps Richard C. Elrod, the sheriff of Cook County. A Northwestern alumnus in his thirties, Sheriff Elrod played Big Ten football. In October 1969, he was assistant corporation counsel for the city when the Students for a Democratic Society staged their Days of Rage protest in the Loop. Hundreds upon hundreds of hippies and radicals milled around the Picasso bearing placards and giving vent to agitated war cries.

Then they got out of hand. On Saturday, October 11, the SDS partisans began charging down the side streets, breaking windows, goading the police, busting barricades, fomenting riots.

Elrod and another corporation counsel, marshaled for emergency duty, were with six cops on Madison Street when a mob of Weathermen charged toward them. Elrod moved to help the police restrain them. One of the Weathermen slugged him with an iron pipe, paralyzing Elrod from the neck down.

Brian Flanagan, a twenty-four-year-old carpenter from New York, arrested on the scene, was tried in Chicago Criminal Court in 1970 on charges of aggravated assault in the attack on Elrod. Flanagan won acquittal when the prosecutor could not convince the jury that Flanagan was a member of the Weathermen or even a member of the SDS.

After the jury read their verdict, Flanagan held an impromptu press conference in which he declared, "I don't have to play these fucken games any more. I can get out of these clothes (a sport coat, gray flannels, blue button-down shirt, and tie). I sat in that fucken courtroom for a month. Law and order in Chicago is a farce. I want to get back into the streets where I can fight."

Elrod campaigned for his election from a wheelchair and after radical surgery repaired his spinal cord performs his duties on crutches.

Allen Hartman is the chairman of the Home Rule Commission, empowered by referendum to adopt a new constitution for the city. The Home Rule Commission has offered several detailed proposals by which it hopes to introduce substantive changes in municipal government which will affect housing, health, personnel administration, licensing, incurring debt, and raising revenue.

These recommendations are crucial to the city of Chicago and to cities everywhere, for they may pioneer in new ways for the city to support itself and prosper. Cities have been inhibited by state laws, the majority of them passed when cities were not megalopolises.

Hartman, the first assistant corporation counsel for Chicago, was drafted into the chairmanship primarily because he understood the provisions of the law and because he was brainy enough to resolve effectively many legal complexities.

A heavy-set man with jet-black hair and an easy manner, Hartman got into municipal law, he says, because he was a night-school graduate who didn't pass the bar examination until he was thirty-two. He grabbed at the first job that came his way.

To the suggestion that municipal law work must be tedious and protracted, Hartman bristled. "Why, it's the most exciting work in law. I wrote the cigarette tax ordinance one Sunday morning. I wrote an ordinance which gave the city the money, not the state. It is difficult to write a tax law in which the state does not share. My ordinance had to stand up in the courts, too. You cannot imagine the satisfaction I felt writing the cigarette tax."

Hartman's passion for his ordinance is exalted. He was Handel, describing how the clouds parted and the face of God shone through as he brought the Hallelujah Chorus to its crescendo. Up until now I had never realized people could have fun writing tax ordinances. One of the interesting things about traveling around the planet is finding out how others get their kicks.

One of Richard Daley's most resourceful advisors is Earl Bush, his press secretary, technically the director of the Public Relations Division of the mayor's office. Bush is assisted by Frank Sullivan, another former newspaperman, and Michael Nygoff, a noted writer of children's books.

Bush and Nygoff confessed that though they were Jews they were not particularly well informed about the Jewish community, although they said you could never tell about Sullivan. Sullivan guffawed. It was a hearty Irish laugh. The three of them looked as though they had a good time.

A short, wiry man, Bush was a friend and champion of Daley since the early fifties, and he entered the city administration in 1955 with Daley. His job is to write many of Daley's speeches, provide Hizzoner with background material on every conceivable subject, accommodate the press in gathering news, and not disseminate enthusiastically news adverse to the city.

"The job is harder than it used to be," Bush said. "While there are fewer newspapers, there is also a new breed of reporter. These fellows have never worked a beat but leaped upon us fully grown from their journalism courses. They often change facts or alter them to write their stories and I waste a lot of time setting editors straight. Mutual trust is tarnished coin."

Bush is more than Mr. Daley's intermediary. He is expected to contribute imaginative and innovative thinking to his job. In discussing Chicago's black-white problems, he said sensibly, "There is the growing problem of the 'underclass,' to which liberals have refused to address themselves. The underclass are the blacks on whom education, religion, and opportunity have had no effect. The underclass frighten whites but they terrorize and murder low-income blacks. They are creating ghost neighborhoods. The poor have no choice about where they live. But the underclass, through constant preying and murder, will drive out even the most abject of the poverty-stricken. Then nobody will move in and the underclass moves on. When Daley tries to work with this problem, he is working with the crux of the race problem. The number of people who do not realize this are legion. And so are the number of newspapers who have not informed their readership about it."

Most of the Jews like Richard J. Daley and Richard J. Daley likes them, and he is often sympathetic to their wants as Jews. After Munich, Daley brought a motion before the City Council condemning the terrorists and extending Chicago's sympathies to the victims.

He greets Jewish dignitaries and escorts visiting Israelis to City Hall. A strict Catholic—there is no quicker way out of Chicago politics than dallying with another woman—Daley is a traditional liberal in dealing with others. But the Jews he befriends and advances are not part of any Jewish movement nor are they in politics to protect Jewish interests, as indeed Jews once were. Most Jews in Chicago accurately grasp the fact that the rewards of political life are not worth the price. They also accurately grasp that Jews no longer need the extra break from political action.

LOS ANGELES: The Natives Were the Pioneers

LOS ANGELES IS THE WORLD IDEA

Los Angeles is one of two big American cities (the other is Dallas) that didn't need the river.

Both do have rivers. Dallas has a temperamental creek called the Trinity River. The Los Angeles River is underground. It provides some of the drinking water for the population of Greater Los Angeles, now in excess of 7 million. Angelenos also siphon drinking water from the melted snows of the Sierra Nevada. Waters from the diverted Colorado River irrigate the orange groves and avocado orchards. Sooner or later the city will be thirsty. If the politicians in Oregon and Washington remain obdurate about their rivers, the chances are that Los Angeles, like the Arab village in Kuwait or the kibbutz in the Negev, will slake its thirst with desalinated water.

Before it became subterranean, the river provided the city with its name. A Spanish exploring party which included a Franciscan monk, Juan Crespi, came across the narrow river which interrupted the broad desertlike plain on August 2, 1796, the feast day of Our Lady of the Angels. They named the river El Río de Nuestra Señora la Reina de los Angeles de Porciuncula (Porciuncula was the church in which St. Francis worshiped when he wasn't talking to the birds). These Spaniards founded a small inland settlement to complement the mountain mission, San Gabriel, and a nearby fort, called simply a "presidio." They named this settlement El Pueblo del Río de Nuestra Señora la Reina de los Angeles. The first forty-four settlers from Sonora, Mexico, included Spaniards, Indians, mulattos, blacks, a mestizo, and a tailor, none of whom could read or write. In recapitulating the history of this pueblo, the *Los Angeles Times* soap-opera-ed, "Can eleven illiterate families with twenty-two children find happiness in a heathen wilderness?"

Since then, the population has always expanded west, away from the desert and toward the sea, into the valley to the north and onto the plain to the south. By the time Angelenos wanted to open up the eastern hinterland, they did not need a navigable waterway; they already had the bulldozer. When they needed a harbor, they already had the dredge and dug one of the greatest man-made harbors in the world.

California became a Mexican province in 1822 when Mexico won independence from Spain. The Mexicans lifted the ban on foreign trade, which made San Francisco with its natural port the important city. The Mexicans encouraged settlers in the south by passing out land grants to deserving aristocrats, friends of the administration, soldiers honorably discharged, and foreigners with ready cash.

Southern California became the domain of cattlemen who titled themselves rancheros. The rancheros were not cowboys. They left the work to the Indians and the peons and brought the siesta and fiesta to peaks unrivaled by any of history's noted indolents.

President James Polk declared California part of our "manifest destiny" in 1845. Two years later, Mexico surrendered California. Beef was still bringing good prices. The parties were better than ever. The naps were longer.

But then San Francisco became El Dorado. One of the foreigners with land patents from Mexico was a Swiss immigrant named John Sutter, who was managing his very own barony in the Sacramento Valley when gold was discovered near his sawmill in 1848. The Gold Rush effectively made northern California an organic part of the United States. It also made a pauper out of Sutter, who died in Pennsylvania, a pensioner, waiting for the Congress to reimburse him for lands and livestock expropriated by the adventurous, the improvident, and the lawless. It also put an end to the ranchero shindig in the south.

For along with the adventurous, the improvident, and the lawless, behind the prospectors and the sourdoughs, came the speculators and the promoters, the canny and the legalistic. They needed nothing more than a knowledge of the United States law respecting title, which was anything but imprecise. The vague boundaries established by the Mexicans, the overlapping grants, the administrative inaccuracies, forced almost all of the rancheros into the courts—where they lost.

The range economy of Southern California went bust in 1857.

Competition from Texas and Missouri ranchers, nearer the markets, herding beef more cheaply ranged, helped end it. The Civil War did the rest. San Francisco was Union, Los Angeles Confederate. In addition, drought blistered Southern California for three years until 1862, when floods dumped corrals and drowned ranch hands into the Pacific. Smallpox was epidemic in 1863, abating only after it had killed off the Indian and peon population and devastated the white.

The first land boom was over. But as often as greed and natural disaster have ended one land boom in California, ambition and innovation have inspired another.

The landowners turned to vinting and to citrus. The transcontinental railroad was joined at Promontory, Utah, in 1869. By 1876, Los Angeles was linked to the rest of the country by the competing Southern Pacific and Santa Fe Railroads. The quest for health brought thousands of Americans to Southern California. The arthritic and the asthmatic, the tubercular and the exhausted, inundated the land, transported from other, more demanding, more savage climates for fares as low as ten dollars. Farmers and the children of farmers left bone-wearying land and fierce weather to seek year-round sunshine and an easier life under the palms.

The hotels, boardinghouses, resorts, convalescent homes, and hospitals materialized as magically as popcorn stands and shooting galleries materialize along a boardwalk. The number of Jews coming west for their health, for example, made hospitals, sanitariums, and old-age homes the priority of Jewish philanthropy for many years. Eternal life was a prospect to the American Midwest long before the Los Angeles City Council knew what it had. In 1902, the city fathers forced the Kaspare Cohn Hospital, now the Cedars of Lebanon, outside the city limits because its doctors were treating tuberculosis, a disease prohibited by ordinance.

In their *History of the Jews of Los Angeles* (Jewish Publication Society, 1970) Max Vorspan and Lloyd P. Gartner quote an Eastern newspaperman on the city in 1886: ". . . the thoroughfares are crowded with tourists, healthy and sick, rich and poor, and I suppose good and bad. The whole city is a hotel: every house, with few exceptions, no matter how wealthy the occupants, has rooms to rent and rents them at astonishing figures."

What the rush for health did for Southern California was to make it an organic part of the United States, too. It created a personality for the city. Not every writer can celebrate Los Angeles' élan with the enthusiasm of that Eastern journalist. "Scattered among these masquerades," wrote Nathanael West fifty years later in *The Day of the Locust,* "were people of a different type. Their clothing was somber and badly cut, bought from mail order houses. While the others moved rapidly, darting into stores and cocktail bars, they loitered on the corners or stood with their backs to shop windows and stared at everyone who passed. When their stare was returned, their eyes filled with hatred. At this time Tod knew very little about them except they had come to California to die."

This immigration made Los Angeles a city *sui generis,* a city in which the newcomer is always in the majority, where the difference between the old and the new is at best fifteen years, where the establishment is buried under the avalanche of the arriviste and the febrile. It is a city which enjoys an eternal land boom. Into the nineteen-seventies, construction and finance were the city's biggest business. Twenty percent of the home builders in Los Angeles, incidentally, are Jews, controlling 40 percent of the market, though there are few Jews in industrial or commerical building. The Jewish builder has replaced the film magnate as the pioneer among the millionaires.

The housing developments that march down valleys and up mountains are rapidly become passé. The architects and the planners now build "environments," cities within cities, marinas which accommodate 35,000 pleasure craft, urban renewal projects in the core, and campus communities, five of them alone around and in Los Angeles.

It remains the greenest of cities. The weather makes it a year-round hothouse. While the city has apartments and condominiums, it has never been the cliff-dweller's paradise. It is a city of homes and the homes have front and back yards. What amazed many Americans when they saw the photographs of the rioters in the Watts area was that Watts was not the tenement-jammed slum: Watts is filled with homes and bungalows, admittedly run-down homes and bungalows, no place to spend a summer season.

The growth of American cities has followed a Hegelian progression starting in the East and ending in the West. Boston, New York, Philadelphia, and Charleston grew because they were natural port cities. Cincinnati, St. Louis, and Chicago because the railraods made them great terminals (Chicago was linked by rail with New York by 1850). Plastic, restlessly growing Los Angeles became the Idea made absolute because of the car and the airplane. The airplane ended

L.A.'s quasi isolation from the Eastern centers of commerce and perhaps, more importantly, from the reaches of the Pacific.

The car transformed Los Angeles into the World Soul City because it made it integral, the whole accessible to all of the parts.

It is a subsidized World Soul City. Distances in Los Angeles are vast. The only way to proceed from one point in town to another is by freeway, unless a traveler wants to start at dawn and end at sunset in the same bus. Dozens of six- and eight-lane freeways, all of them built with federal funds, convey traffic. The chief complaint against this freeway system is that it does not convey traffic freely enough. The traffic jams are monumental, inducing a tedium that can only be described as Sartre-esque. The complaint against the cars is that they produce the smog in the land the Indians named "The Valley Where the Smoke Never Rises."

"Freeways," writes Christopher Rand in *Los Angeles: The Ultimate City* (Oxford University Press, 1967), "can't begin to obscure the mountains, and to the plain they can only add an overlay pattern that is either inconspicuous or positively helpful. The L.A. freeways are also pleasantly landscaped, and their design at crucial points is enjoyable. The city's main downtown freeway exchange, which is on four levels if one counts ramps, is like an exquisite watchworks when observed in action, and the newest interchange out toward the ocean—an unusually widespreading one designed, incidentally, by a woman engineer—is a delightfully soaring yet delicate work of concrete sculpture. These things add distinction to the city, rather than subtracting from it, and L.A.'s freeway system as a whole is perhaps the best thing of its kind ever built."

The 354-page *Los Angeles Popular Street Atlas* is as much a necessity for the homeowner as the telephone directory. To go from the American Jewish Committee offices at 590 North Vermont Avenue to editor Herb Brin's Jewish Heritage at 2130 Vermont is no walking, taxiing, or busing matter. There is probably a good five, maybe seven miles between the two offices. Taxis do not want to venture to the Heritage because it is on the outskirts of Watts. Moreover, taxis do not cruise in Los Angeles; they are summoned, when summoned at all, by telephone. Surface transportation is nonexistent. To arrive at 590 North Vermont means you will exit from one freeway, to get to the Heritage use another, and to get home use still a third. The encyclopedic *Atlas* is the only help the motorist has.

Los Angeles was not part of the American industrial complex until World War II. To millions of Americans, Los Angeles was for many years Hollywood and Beverly Hills with the Rose Bowl somewhere in between. There are still those who refer to Los Angeles as the Coast, forgetting that inland Ventura County grows more lemons than any other place in the world, that San Bernardino County produces more eggs, and that Long Beach pumps more oil.

Los Angeles was always a citadel of antiunionism. As soon as it had won its first strike in New York, the Amalgamated Clothing Workers began warning cutters, furriers, spongers, and shipping clerks not to venture west. There was not enough industry to support them, and what industry there was did not pay union wages. While the legitimate theater was unionized by the Equity strike of 1919, there was no agitation in the movies for union contracts until 1937. Not until the sixties did Cesar Chavez begin to win rights for migrant workers in the citrus groves and vineyards.

Los Angeles became the industrial giant it is with the sudden growth of the aviation industry occasioned by World War II and later by the technology that made the aerospace industry possible. Donald Douglas set up in L.A. in 1922, joined later by Lockheed, North American, and Ryan and Consolidated, which is in San Diego. One of the reasons they settled there was to assemble airplanes out of doors. These firms had built the commercial airliners the country needed by the end of the thirties, when World War II suddenly produced a demand for aircraft without limits.

With the end of the war, thousands of war workers packed up and left. But a new immigration began, 16,000 people a month, an influx that would almost double the size of the area in ten years from 2,285,000 in 1940 to 4,151,687 in 1950. By 1950, almost 800,000 veterans who had passed through on their way to the Pacific war or had trained in California camps had returned to live in Los Angeles, more than in any other city. The city had 2,615,495 jobs in 1960. Bank deposits, which totaled $3.2 billion in 1947, soared to almost $10 billion in 1960.

Now the city from which Jewish garment workers were warned away is close to New York in the manufacture of ready-made clothing. "California attire," the studied casualness of dress, has spawned a needlework industry which numbers 2500 garment-producing units. California designs are but another harbinger of the Los Angelization of the world. Nothing, as the ole romantic Georg Wilhelm Friedrich reminds us is as popular as a World Idea whose time has come.

IT IS ALSO TOTAL NUDITY

Roy Rogers, the singing star of Western movies, announced in October 1972 that he was relocating his Roy Rogers Museum from Apple Valley to Victorville. The museum will be the focal point of this new development and will be called "Roy Rogers Western World." A major portion of this new museum will be a 40,000-square-foot building, in early-Western motif, which will house the complete history of Roy Rogers, Dale Evans, and their children.

In the same week, Mayor Sam Yorty announced his latest program for senior citizens: a beauty pageant featuring swimsuit competition for women sixty and up. Yorty boasted that the pageant directors had no difficulty in recruiting the contestants, only in recruiting the judges.

Walter Dickson, who is not a bathing beauty, escapes boredom by making windmills out of pie pans, bicycle wheels, and plastic oleomargarine containers. Now seventy-five, Dickson took up windmilling to keep his mind clear so he could determine what to do with his life. His yard in Palms is so choked with a variety of looping, whirling, and spinning creations that tourists often stop, thinking they have come across a public park.

Superior Court Judge Thomas C. Yager ordered Mrs. Gerald Paul Glickman, Gerald Paul's second wife, to pay $8,852.50 in alimony arrears to Mrs. Claire Glickman, Gerald Paul's first wife. The second Mrs. Gerald Paul and Gerald Paul had facilitated their marriage by persuading the first Mrs. Gerald Paul to consent to a crisp and speedy divorce. They signed a joint agreement to pay the first Mrs. Gerald Paul alimony and child support. Gerald Paul now lives with his mother and in the court's view is an "uncollectible." Gerald Paul has helped to set legal precedent. Personally, I think a rabbi ought to talk to that boy.

A Big Dipper cleans Long Beach Harbor. The $100,000 steel-hulled catamaran is the first boat ever designed and built exclusively for harbor housecleaning. Each month it scoops up 180 cubic yards of trash and debris left by Long Beach bathers. One hundred and eighty cubic yards is forty tons. Just imagine waiting for a freight train with forty boxcars to pass.

Los Angeles was the first city with pornographic radio. Housewives telephone disc jockey Bill Balance to describe how they put it over on the old man.

"Lissen," says one of the anonymous callers, "I've been married to a telephone repairman for eighteen months."

"And he does a lot of night work?"

"Yes, and I've come to—know this other man."

"And how long has this been going on?"

"Eighteen months, nineteen months."

"You knew him before you were married?"

"Oh, we've had a long relationship."

"Then what's your problem?"

"Actually, I don't have a problem. I just wanted to call in and tell you how much I enjoy the program."

Spanish-language radio enjoys growing popularity. One of the prime movers in this effort is Danny Villaneuva, the former place-kicker for the Los Angeles Rams. A young Chicano actor happily announced he had a job doing two commercials. Then he added, "By golly, one day I learrrn Ingles, then bingo!"

In California, Goodyear and Firestone Rubber advertise their snow tires, which they call "rain tires," and urge motorists to change tires whenever it rains, which is, on the average, four times a year. Prestone advertises its antifreeze for reasons best known to advertising-agency councils. The theory is that television viewers in Los Angeles like to look at pictures of winter.

The balmy weather has galvanized the homo- and heterosexual communities of Venice Beach into a year-round civil-rights fight. Both communities have vowed to bathe nude. The cops send the naked ladies to the Sheriff's Valley Services and the naked men to West Los Angeles Municipal Court.

The rap is indecent exposure if the prosecutor proves lewd intent. But the courts bargain. The court informs defendants that anyone convicted of indecent exposure must register as a sex offender forever and ever, which, the judge informs them, is a stigma. However, to save the county time and money, the judge intimates that he will accept a guilty plea of disturbing the peace, which is not a stigma.

Nudists complain that this is a devious way of suppressing legal undress. To combat this, flamboyant Eugene Callan, a Los Angeleno noted for his advocacy of international nudity, has founded Beachfront, U.S.A. "We will reopen the beaches," vows Callan, "and we will celebrate the two hundredth anniversary of the United States by the thousands on the beaches in the nude."

What makes this maelstroming teapot tempest interesting is that the visitor can pass restaurant after restaurant along Century Boulevard advertising, "Our Sizzling New York Cut—$3.85. Fresh Seafood Platter, drawn butter—$3.60 plus TOTAL NUDITY."

The Los Angeles sophisticate is the man who knows where to dine without a naked waitress shelling his clams. In one instance, I lunched at Monte's, the House of Steaks, with actors Dan Tobin, Andy Duggan, and Jack Weston and writer James Lee. Our service was rendered by ladies modestly cosseted as English barmaids.

"We don't call this the House of Steaks," Duggan confided. "We call it the House of Blue Veins because the bodices of the waitresses are cut so low."

"How does one find such a decorous place?" I asked.

"Simple," said Weston. "Just follow a middle-aged lady up from San Diego."

ALONG THE SAN ANDREAS FAULT

In the last census, the city of Los Angeles counted 2,829,828. Los Angeles County numbered 7,102,897. Among this population were 500,000 Jews. Seven percent of the area, therefore, are Jews, and this 7 percent constitutes between 8 and 9 percent of the Jews in the country. After New York and Tel Aviv, Los Angeles is the third largest Jewish city in the world.

This many Jews creates not only a geographic but a psychological diaspora. The more Jews there are, the more unlikely it is they will gravitate around a single sun. It was front-page news when Henry Dreyfuss and his wife, Doris, committed suicide by carbon monoxide in the garage of their South Pasadena home. Dreyfuss was a world-famous industrial designer who had produced, among other inventions, the dial, pushbutton, and Princess telephones; the 20th Century Limited passenger train; and the two-hundred-foot perisphere at the 1939 New York World's Fair. Neither in the news stories nor in the obituaries did anyone mention that Henry Dreyfuss was a Jew—

probably because neither he nor his wife was a member of a congregation nor an officer in a Jewish organization nor a substantial contributor to a Jewish charity.

Others who avoided network Judaism were the movie Jews. They lived at a total remove from the Jewish community, founding their own enclaves in Hollywood and Beverly Hills, and, as has been charitably suggested, thought of their stay in Southern California as an extended business trip rather than a permanent move. This is not true of their descendants, many of whom are committed to Jewish causes, philanthropy, and culture. These descendants are always identified by their ancestry. No matter which of the Firesteins, for example, is a president or board member of a Federation drive or hospital, he is described as a member of the Max Factor family; the location of the Jewish Community Building of the Federation-Council is always referred to as occupying the site of the Pantages estate. It is as though all the Jews have become spiritualists determined to make the Goldwyns and the Schencks and the L. B. Mayers *ex post facto* community balabatim.

It is always harder to raise money from many Jews than it is from few Jews. The Federation, therefore, must invent new, adventurous ways to meet its quota. One of the ways is to invite six or eight men to a private dinner party to meet Prime Minister Golda Meir, who has flown directly from Jerusalem for the occasion. The cost to the guests is $1 million a plate, although sometimes wives eat for free.

The movement of Jews in Los Angeles has been north from the original settlement on Temple Street, Boyle Heights, and Central Avenue in the Wilshire-Fairfax district. Jews moved north to Beverly Hills, to the Van Nuys-Sherman Oaks district, on to the northern boundaries of Resada-Encino and into the North Valley district, now almost 20 percent Jewish. An earlier affluent group moved due west to the Westwood-Brentwood district which has a present Jewish density of roughly 15 percent.

If the map of the city of Los Angeles looks like anything, it looks like the map of Texas with the Jews moving from Abilene to Amarillo and into Oklahoma.

Disregarding safety, the Jews are following the contour of the San Andreas Fault, keeping to the east. The Jews in San Francisco also follow the contour of the fault, only they keep to the west. The fault, a long crack which runs north and south, produces earthquakes when one side chafes the other. It is not inconceivable that the movement of the fault will one day somersault all the Los Angeles Jews into San Francisco and all the San Francisco Jews into Los Angeles. The chances are that the Jews will not, in this exodus, take their synagogues and temples with them.

The premier Jewish families of Los Angeles were the Cohns, Newmarks, and Hellmans, all sooner or later made one by interintermarriage. Harris Newmark, who came to Los Angeles in 1853, died in 1916, the recognized patriarch of the Jewish community. He dealt in hides and wool and started one of the first successful grocery chains. His posthumous diary, *Sixty Years in Southern California* published in 1916, has proved an invaluable source for state archivists and historians. Kaspare Cohn, Newmark's nephew, improved on the hide cellers, but he also pioneered in financing the city's utilities. He acquired realty and was one of Southern California's largest landowners. Cohn and Newmark financed these ventures from banks they established by keeping the Basque shepherds' money on deposit.

Isaias Wolf Hellman directly changed the city's destiny. He had come to Los Angeles from Bavaria in 1859 with his brother Herman and run a general store, in whose safe he stored prospectors' gold dust. He found this not the safest system for the gold or himself. He started the multibillion-dollar Farmers and Merchants Bank by offering to buy the gold dust from the prospectors at current rates and then promised to hold this money on deposit, letting the miner withdraw it when and as he chose. The Farmers and Merchants has weathered every depression and bust and, excepting the state, is the largest property owner in California.

Hellman made banking a commercially sound venture in California, the first to do so. But he was notorious for his acuity. His brother Herman, a similar success in the wholesale grocery business, once found Isaias's acuity so heartless he withdrew all his deposits and closed all his accounts in the Farmers and Merchants Bank and transferred them to the Merchants National Bank.

Isaias Hellman, his Catholic partner, John Downey, and the Protestant philanthropist D. W. Childs donated the three hundred acres to the Methodists for the founding of what is now the University of Southern California, a school famous for never having suffered from a shortage of fullbacks.

There are some other notables among early Jews, one of them Joseph Newmark, a brother of Harris, who introduced the first Oriental to California in 1854 when he arrived in Los Angeles with a Chinese manservant.

There was also Henry Edelman, the ne'er-do-well son of Rabbi Abraham, the first spiritual father of Congregation B'nai B'rith. Early in his career Henry won appointment as deputy county clerk for the Superior Court. Shortly thereafter, he was arrested and tried but acquitted of fraud in the payment of jury fees and expenses. Subsequently, Henry opened a saloon. Subsequently, Henry was again arrested, this time charged with operating a slot machine, the first of the one-armed bandits. Henry insisted he knew the law. Henry was right. He became the first Edelman to be twice acquitted.

Last but not least of these notables is Wolf Cohn, the first Jew to be scalped by the Indians. Wolf was a peddler plying his trade between Salt Lake City and Los Angeles when the Kiowas went berserk over some not so fancied injustice. Wolf Cohn is buried in the Home of Eternity Cemetery in San Bernardino, the oldest Hebrew cemetery in the West.

The society in which the Cohns, Newmarks, and Hellmans moved was an open one for them and for other Jewish merchants and businessmen. Hellman represented not Jewish banking interests but Hellman banking interests. The Jews were assimilated as citizens, sought for membership in social clubs, for elective and appointive office, and as partners in a variety of commercial enterprises. There was a line over which Jews would not step. They did not encourage mixed marriages nor would they convert, although the Jewish Concordia Club of Los Angeles always had the merriest Christmas party. John Newmark Levi, in an oral deposition published in *Western States Jewish Quarterly* (January 1972) describes the way Jews lived between 1910 and 1920:

Family life was much more important in the old days. We saw a lot more of the family then, than we do now. We all lived in close proximity. For example, when we lived on Lake Street, great-grandfather Harris [Newmark] lived on Westlake, two blocks from us. My great aunt, Mrs. Jacob Loew, lived on Alvarado. My great uncle, Maurice H. Newmark, lived on Beacon Street. My great aunts, Clara Kingsbaker (the widow of Moses) and Rosa Jacoby (the widow of Morris), also lived on Lake Street. They were sisters of Jacob Loew, my father's uncle.

Another one of the family, Louis S. Nordlinger, a double cousin and a cousin of my wife as well, lived on Ninth Street around Union. It seems that the whole family lived within walking distance, perhaps no more than six or seven blocks. Most of the kids we went to public school or Sunday school with, lived within an area of probably ten or twelve square blocks.

This period of grace ended in the nineteen-twenties with the rise of anti-Semitism fostered by the xenophobic Ku Klux Klan and by the superstitions and prejudice of the marginal workingman. Its effect on Los Angeles Jewry was different because the Los Angeles Jewish community was qualitatively different from all other Jewish communities in America.

A wave of immigrants did not provide Los Angeles with its Jewish settlement. In 1912, the German Jewish community worried about an influx of immigrants which might descend on the city via the newly opened Panama Canal, but these worries proved groundless. There were never many peddlers in Los Angeles. The distances were considerable which discouraged the pushcart and the 2000 immigrants who did come in 1900 were aided and financed by the Industrial Removal Office in New York City. The Jewish settling force in Los Angeles was instead the sons of immigrants.

. . . The nature of Gentile immigration [write Vorspan and Gartner] to Los Angeles from other parts of the country affected the destinies of Los Angeles Jewry and impressed upon it a character unparalleled among the urban Jewish communities of the United States. For the masses who populated the great cities of the East and Middle West were mostly, like the Jews, European arrivals—Poles, Germans, Irish, Italians, Slovaks, and many others. As did the Jews, they spoke their own languages, formed distinct neighborhoods, maintained cultural and social ties with each other and the old country, and tended to practice distinctive trades. . . . The massive immigration to Los Angeles was not of Europeans but mainly of rural and small town people out of the Middle and Central West. These were regions marked by stormy agrarian protests against new economic forces from the 1870's until the end of the nineteenth century, and their emigrants functioned in their southern California home as a force for the preservation of the ways of life and thought of an earlier America. At a time when other large cities were becoming heavily Catholic, Los Angeles became strongly evangelical Protestant with Fundamentalist tendencies. A new social and religious tone, moralistic and puritanical, began to pervade the city, and its overtones were not hospitable to Jews.

In 1933, thirteen Jews formed the Los Angeles Jewish Aeronautical Association because flying clubs were all Gentile. Flying a private plane is a more popular hobby on the Coast than raising horses and dogs is in the East. Out of the JAA came several navigators, pilots, and bombardiers in World War II and Sam Lewis, now a senior pilot for El Al Airlines.

The Old World discipline which has influenced and governed religious practice in the United States is sometimes felt not at all in Los Angeles. The quaking table and materializing ectoplasm are not a vogue but an institution. Jeane Dixon foretells the future with the surety with which Norman Vincent Peale elsewhere lauds the Christian ethic. Evangelists from Billy Sunday through Aimee Semple McPherson to Billy Graham have found in Southern California the fertile acres where the desire for salvation renews itself as often as wheat in Kansas—and is more easily reaped. The town booster from Des Moines becomes the perfervid religious zealot in Los Angeles. The exotic and the arcane, black magic and astrology, are flourishing commercial enterprises.

Not half of the city's Protestant churches are affiliated with a national denomination. For many years, Jews supported a variety of "profit temples" in which a free-lance rhetorician styled himself "rabbi" and occupied a pulpit. The profit temple was often the actual property of the profiteering rabbi as English public schools were often the property of the headmaster.

Newly ordained rabbis from seminaries in the East and Midwest regarded Los Angeles as remote and bizarre and shunned pulpits there. Congregations were never large enough to attract them. Membership in the synagogue and temple was sparse because the Jews were always newly arrived, never sure that Los Angeles was home, and therefore loath to join a congregation. They were no different from Midwesterners, who were equally unsure about their commitment and felt more secure by renewing memories of past places at an Iowa Reunion Picnic or at a Missouri Friendship Club.

The effects of transplantation are nowhere as patent as in the architecture of the Jewish house of worship. Artist Marvin Rubin, in a by-lined feature for *West* magazine, published weekly by the *Los Angeles Times,* observes: "Jews have established unique traditions in religion, language, law, science, literature, music, commerce, theater, and even cuisine. However, there is not a trace of an architectural tradition. They have had to constantly move, and the least developed of the arts has been the least portable—architecture. Every congregation in this community has been on its own, minus guidance, with the resulting mishmosh of styles," and Rubin forwards several illustrations of Los Angeles temples. The Wilshire Boulevard Temple, which resembles St. Bartholomew's in New York, he terms "Eppis-Copalian"; another is "El Rancho Reform" because it copies the ranch-style house. "Haimishe Gothic," "Shtik Shtucco," and "B'nai Broadway" are three more classifications. And those temples which incorporate the Spanish adobe style Rubin designates "Mission Meshuggeneh."

"A Yiddish-speaking grandparent is a rarity in Los Angeles," Jack Goldowitz, the director of the North Valley Jewish Community Center, told me. "It's as though when you come here, you shuck old ways, including old grandparents and old languages."

Goldowitz, who affects a Priapian beard and is a champion handball player, surviving a ruptured Achilles tendon to come back last year stronger than ever, has lived in California for the past decade.

"You can buy kosher burritos in lots of places, but there is only one kosher restaurant in the Fairfax area. You cannot find that eastern Jewish milieu because the Jewish devotion here isn't as ingrained."

There is a Jewish amateur theater group in the North Valley, Goldowitz told me, which has successfully staged productions for years. These people belonged either to the Reform temple, Ahaval Shalom, or to the Conservative, Ramat Zion. Temple membership meant nothing in theatrical productions until Ramat Zion built a new synagogue with a raked-seat auditorium, a perfect showcase for these would-be actors.

At that point the rabbis from Ahaval Shalom forbade their congregants to perform on Ramat Zion's stage. They didn't want their people entering the new synagogue because it was newer and bigger and looked more affluent, and the rabbis knew their congregants would find this attraction irresistible. They would join Ramat Zion at Ahaval Shalom's expense.

BELOW THE LINE

There are 10,000 Jews in Los Angeles on welfare. Another 8000 should be on welfare: they are either spending the last of their savings or living off their children or subsisting on Wheaties.

Many of these Jews are elderly. In a study initiated by the American Jewish Committee under the directorship of Neil Sandberg, researchers learned that elderly Jews eligible for public assistance from the Los Angeles County Department of Public Services did not even apply for it. They had their pride or they did not know their rights or some of them were unaware of the existence of welfare or some were physically unable to get to a welfare office.

But 30 percent of these poor were not elderly. They were Jews receiving aid to children. They were divorcees or widows or widowers with families they were unable to feed.

Half of the job-seeking Jewish poor in Los Angeles have less than eleven years of schooling. One in five has less than an eighth-grade education.

There are proportionately as many Jewish poor in Miami as there are in Los Angeles. The plight of these people is doubly poignant, as Ann Wolf, a social welfare consultant from UCLA points out in her pamphlet "The Invisible Poor" (American Jewish Committee). "The warmth of the climate drew the old and retired to these cities in the hope of a comfortable and secure old age. These cities did not turn out to be the land where the streets are paved with gold, and this second disappointment is the one that cannot be corrected. There is almost no time left."

Ms. Wolf notes first that the source of Jewish population growth in the United States was not a natural growth, as was true for the rest of America, but derived from the heavy migration of Eastern European Jews between 1890 and 1924. The poor are the remnants of this vast immigration, survivors of the immigrant cohort. They find themselves, she notes, the last holdouts in areas which have ceased being Jewish, locked into neighborhoods that no longer offer them the support and security they need.

Ms. Wolf estimates that there may be as many as 700,000 Jewish poor in the United States suffering the problems suffered by all the poor, but afflicted as well with the problems peculiar to Jews, problems in intergroup relations, problems of a Jewish identity which exists in a society whose image of the Jew is not always accurate, an image the Jewish community insists on perpetuating.

There was a time when Los Angeles did not have Jewish poor. Its geography precluded the exploited immigrant. And the Jews were not so numerous that the philanthropies could not somehow make provision or lend aid to the unfortunate.

The pattern of poverty in Los Angeles is an American pattern. The poor are part of the "below-the-line" costs of this society, an actuarial term borrowed from the movie industry. "Above-the-line" costs in the production of a film include the salaries paid the stars, the directors, and the writers, and the money paid for acquisition of the property. Below-the-line costs are those that must be paid the grips and the stagehands, the rental of the cameras, and the studio space, the money paid the recording engineers and the film cutters and the light men—the costs that the public doesn't see or realize but that are a component part of the film-making process.

The people who fall into or are gripped by poverty are the below-the-line workers—not the lawyers or the real estate agents or the schoolteachers, but the factory workers and the service personnel and the unskilled. People above the line are making more money than they ever made. Below-the-line costs, however, are what determine the "hard ticket," what we used to call "advanced prices" for movie admission. Welfare is the hard ticket for mid-nineteen-seventies society.

ABOVE THE LINE

There are a variety of reasons why Jews got into the motion-picture business.

Carl Laemmle, a shoe-store manager, went into films because he noticed on his first visit to a movie how small an inventory a theater owner had to carry—just the film and the projector, and when the movie was over, the customers left the inventory behind. Laemmle started Universal Pictures and eventually stocked the heaviest inventory any entrepreneur ever carried when he built Universal City, the first of the mammoth studios.

Lewis Z. Zeleznik was a bankrupted jeweler who found work in a booking agency and started to trade in movie stocks. When his speculations proved profitable, he changed his name to Selznick and formed World Pictures. One of his sons, Myron, was the first successful actors' agent and another, David O., went on to produce *A Star Is Born* and *Gone With the Wind*.

Samuel Goldfish was a super glove salesman who thought Congress had ruined him when it lowered the tariff on imports in 1912. He persuaded his brother-in-law, Jesse Lasky, and a vaudeville writer, Cecil B. de Mille, to join him in a movie venture. The three rented a barn in Hollywood at Selma and Vine, where they filmed *The Squaw Man*.

Other Jews, like Sam and Jack Warner, got into the business because they owned Nickelodeons and were starved for pictures they intuitively understood their audience wanted. A powerful trust, the Motion Pictures Patent Company, insisted that producers turn out only one- instead of six-reel films. The Jews went out to California not only for the sunshine but because it was at a far remove from the trust's New York offices.

Whatever the reasons, for many years there was a Jewish contingent producing most American movies. The film historian Norman Zierold suggests that Jews were attracted to the movies because they came "from a babble of language backgrounds and saw pictures on a screen which everyone could understand." Vorspan and Gartner, on the other hand, suggest that Jews knew the business instinctively: "Both in clothing and in motion pictures, Jewish entrepreneurs, starting from a mass distribution base, created mass production industries for garments and entertainment. With daring and finesse, they organized innumerable individual skills (of sewing and photography) for the vast market of voiceless consumers."

But the day of the Jewish film mogul is over. The studios have sold off their land for housing and commercial developments and auctioned off the props, costumes, curios, and Jews. Movies are filmed abroad and those still made in Hollywood are made for television.

Still there are many Jews in "the business," the euphemism for mass entertainment. They are the writers, the producers, the agents, the casting directors, the lawyers, and sometimes the directors and the actors.

They have never been the technicians, the camera or lighting men, the scene designers, or the film cutters, professions filled now by the children and grandchildren of the pioneer movie technicians, a craft as notorious for its nepotism as the plumbing or electrical trades.

Nor has there ever been a contingent of Jewish actors, though to be sure Jews have become actors, some of them stars, some of them even quite good actors.

George Bernard Shaw said the only three geniuses ever produced by the movies were David Wark Griffith, Walt Disney, and Charlie Chaplin. What kind of a Jew Charlie Chaplin is or for that matter what kind of a Jew Douglas Fairbanks was is fortunately a question I cannot answer. The public knew them as stars before they knew them as Jews, and I suspect most stars and for that matter most artists insist on a relationship with their public and with the image the public has of them before they insist on anything else.

"The Titans of Hollywood were the heads of the studios," Dave Harmon told me, "and the majority of the Titans were Jewish—I omit Walt Disney because he was never in competition with them. The Titans ruled in a Golden Age they thought would never end. But it ended."

Harmon is a Jew from Buffalo who came to Hollywood as a movie writer in 1954 at the crucial moment the movies had begun to lose some of their appeal in the public imagination. But Harmon survived the change, doing well enough as a movie and television writer to own the house Linda Darnell built at 901 North Amalfi Avenue in Pacific Palisades. It is white with an exotic hedge guarding a walk that leads to a columned portico above which hangs a balcony. Jammed bookshelves reach to the ceiling on two walls of the living room, which is uncluttered by furniture. In one corner is a well-lighted bar which could adequately serve the guests of a small hotel.

Harmon has an enviable reputation professionally and a reputation as well as an authority on the history of the movies. He has researched the movies as others research the battles of the Civil War or the sinking of the *Titanic*. He has learned from his own experience and added to it from conversations with old-timers and close friends who were part of the Hollywood establishment in the thirties and the forties.

"When I came out here," he went on, "Hollywood was by no means dead. There were one hundred and five writers at MGM ready to turn out anything from Westerns to passion plays. Surprisingly, a large number of these writers were Jews, filled with passion and compassion and, for their contribution, poorly paid. They worked out of a creative impulse, but that is not how the Titans made films. The Titans came out here for one reason and for one reason only—

to manufacture a product for the theaters they owned. They made movies to fill theaters. They considered every production in terms of what the public would buy. They made and sold pictures the way their contemporaries on Thirty-fourth Street made and sold dresses. Because the Titans owned both the studios and the theaters, they made some exceptions. They often produced a great picture with meaning which lost money because these loss leaders helped their image.

"The Titans were very Jewish and never denied it and very daring but not necessarily smart. They were men of vision but it turned out to be tunnel vision. They realized the world was attuned to the comings and goings of the movie colony. Within that colony, these men wielded enormous power. But they overestimated that power. Even at its peak, the movie industry never had more than thirty or forty thousand employees. The citrus industry employs more than that in Los Angeles County on any given Thursday.

"Granted the orange supplied vitamins but the movies supplied a greater need in the lives of the populace. These men controlled what went into each and every movie. The Titans played down their Jewishness. They did not condone anti-Semitism, what they wanted was merely non-Jewish. They built a WASP dream world for a polyglot audience. The Titans kept a low profile and invested their films with a Puritan ethic. A married couple, for example, always occupied twin beds. Sex was not for the silver screen. Times have changed. The Titans never did. Their personal ethics were a different story, but since I can only quote rumors and hearsay, I'd prefer to skip it.

"To put things in proper perspective," Harmon said, "it is important to remember these bold, daring, powerful men were also filled with fear. A phone call, a frown, a look their way from the Catholic Church or the Legion of Decency and they reshot pictures, recut others, and buried still more forever in their vaults. The Divine Right of Titans had its limits.

"Blumberg, Cohn, Zukor, the Warners ruled empires, but The Man was Louis B. Mayer of MGM. When he called the tune, people danced or else they found another way to make a living. The amazing thing is they never changed their names but they made everyone else change theirs. The Titans were in pictures to make money and to draw profits from a domestic and foreign market. Many of them were comparatively new Americans, and anti-Semitism was a Damoclean sword about which they worried. Boy, were they Americans! They were extremely patriotic Americans, and the image they wanted everyone to see was an image of blue eyes and blond hair. Jews were behind, but not on, film.

"For a few decades they had no problem raising money. They controlled the production, distribution, and exhibition of the films so there was no chance of losing money. The banks for a sure return at a reasonable rate of interest were more than willing to finance them.

"Some of the Titans financed their own pictures, but mostly the banks were behind the production costs. In 1948, the government made the Titans divorce themselves from the exhibition of films, forcing them to sell off their theaters. At that point, the Jews began to lose power and the Gentiles to gain it. The Gentiles supplied the bulk of the financing and when the Jews could not guarantee the return, Gentiles demanded not only a higher interest rate but more control of what went into the film.

"Even so, the key to becoming rich in pictures hasn't changed," said Harmon, holding up a finger for emphasis. "The Titans were geniuses in a number of respects, one of which was bookkeeping. As an example: a studio head called his counterpart in New York to complain that a star wanted a million dollars plus 10 percent of the profits.

" 'Is she worth a million?' asked the man in New York.

" 'Yeah,' said the man in Hollywood, 'she's worth a million.'

" 'Schmuck, sign her. Who's keeping the books, her or us?'

"You see," Harmon continued, "unless a picture is a runaway success, a *Gone With the Wind* or *The Sound of Music,* there are never any profits. The secret is in what the producers write against the cost of the picture. Each studio has a different secret and it guards that secret more zealously than the government guards Fort Knox.

"The Jewish Titans gave some of their power to Gentile censors and some of it to Gentile bankers, but they surrendered all of it when television came along. Their tunnel vision cost them the store. They regarded television as an enemy. They tried to isolate it, sweep it under the rug. They forbade their contract players from appearing on it. For a time they hoarded their old films. They did everything except look at the fact and the fact was there for all to see: people adored television.

"If the Titans had any vision, they would have owned it. When it began, television was always done live. As it grew, it needed more and more product. A movie had 16,000 play dates and television one. There was no way for television to realize profits unless it went to film. The scope of it, the thirst for it, the economics of it, demanded film. And who knew how to produce films? The Hollywood Titans. And what did they do? They passed.

"The networks came out to Hollywood in the early fifties, they approached these Jews who had started with nothing and built empires and the Jews turned their business proposition down. The Titans forced the networks to go into production and to hire others to turn out film. The first television studio in this town was so small that it is now a mini-mart, but Lucille Ball and Desi Arnaz eventually owned a studio all their own. What has happened to the other giant studios? Well, Universal is still going strong, but Columbia has moved in with Warners, Paramount is rapidly shrinking, and the giant, MGM —you can shoot deer in what is left of it.

"The Jews in New York controlled the money in the old days and the Jews in Hollywood controlled the production. But at that, nothing much has changed except the names—Paley of CBS, Sarnoff of NBC, and Goldenson of ABC. But in Hollywood, the changes are stupendous. Gulf and Western are Paramount and Kinney Enterprises are Warners and the list grows longer and the Jewish Titans fade quickly."

Alex Segal's home on Spoleto Drive is atop a mountain at the foot of which surges the Pacific. Across the valley, Segal can point out a castle which belongs to Walter Matthau. Expensive houses ascend the mountain one behind the other like Sherpa supply bearers behind English mountain climbers on Everest. Space is at a premium in Los Angeles, so houses are close together no matter what their price. But the lots are as trim as postage stamps. Everything grows luxuriantly in California and must be trimmed daily. Matthau's house looks like a castle because there are no houses around it.

All have swimming pools. The private swimming pool is neither an affectation nor an ostentatious accessory in Southern California. The Spanish-style ranch house has few and narrow windows in front, but glass doors and glass walls face the patio in the rear. The house opens in upon itself and the pool, sometimes no bigger than a bathtub, becomes the hearth, which in the land of no snow or sleet is as it should be.

Segal's pool was as long but no wider than a single cinder track for the ten-yard dash. Other pools are often shaped like a kidney or a heart and there is one like a four-leaf clover.

Segal is burly with big brown eyes and hair jet-black though he is in his fifties. One could call him intense were it not for his wit, which constantly interrupts his pursuit of grave causes. Once a famous Broadway and television director, Segal is now the head of the Drama Department of the University of Southern California.

Segal is a devoted sports enthusiast. His analytic mind could probably have gotten him a job as the editor of *Sports Illustrated* or writing a column in the *Daily News* had he not made a good thing out of the theater.

Fall Sundays on Spoleto Drive are reserved for the professional football games, which begin at 10 A.M. because of the time differential. On CBS and NBC the football doubleheaders proceed until roughly 4:30, at which instant one of the local stations beams a tape of yesterday's Southern Cal game. Resolutely Segal refuses to read the Sunday papers lest news of Saturday's score disturb his expectancy.

On the Sunday to which he generously invited me to share this ritual, he apologized for the thoughtlessness of his daughter, who had recently set up her own apartment and usurped one of the two color sets in his den, which meant we could not watch two games at once.

When I suggested that two games at once might prove distracting for the uninitiated, Segal barked, "You are wrong. Watching two games at once teaches you that what goes on doesn't go on down there on the field or on the sidelines or on the bench. No, sir, it goes on in the electronosphere, where the mesons and ions have their own master-plan game. If you watch two games at once you will soon realize the two quarterbacks are passing at the same time, the teams are penalized for offsides simultaneously, and the commercials on each of the networks come on like the Dolly sisters." He pointed to the electronosphere, which was in the area directly forward of his leonine head, as though a halo had slipped toward his nose.

During these festivities, Segal's wife, Ruth, reverently entered the room only to serve coffee, then martinis, then double-decker hamburgers, and finally, in the gloaming, as the Trojans for the second time that weekend swept to inevitable victory, beer.

"She is certainly considerate," I remarked.

"She knows I work hard during the week," Segal answered confidently, unaware that there are other areas in the country where watching five football games on Sunday will fill a little woman with as much hysteria and craziness as if hubby were reading a newspaper.

Alex Segal is a graduate of Carnegie Tech Drama School who taught at Montana University in Missoula in 1944–45. Dissatisfied with academia, or at least with the state of the theater in Montana, Alex and Ruth came to Los Angeles in 1945 to work in the movies. On the day they arrived, a general strike by the craft unions closed all the studios.

"We didn't have the money for train fare to New York," Segal said, "so we shared one of those car rides where everyone chips in for the gas and oil and the men take turns driving. There were seven of us in the flivver, including a sailor with a cast in his eye who kept fondling a loaded Luger he'd won in a crap game.

"We were so broke in New York, we had to live with friends, never a comfortable arrangement. Ruth worked in *Harvey* and *Detective Story* and other plays to support us while I made the rounds with no luck. By no luck, I mean people wouldn't show me the water fountain.

"Then I met a professor from Carnegie Tech who got me a job as a carpenter in a television studio in Philadelphia for forty dollars a week. A year later, I was making a thousand a week directing Richard Boone and Paul Newman and James Dean in early television."

Unlike many men in their fifties, Segal acquired a reputation early as a painstaking and innovative director. When an ABC vice-president once interrupted his concentration in the monitoring booth, Segal knocked out his front teeth. He has directed such plays as *One Flew over the Cuckoo's Nest, All the Way Home,* and *We Take the Town,* and such movies as *Death of a Salesman.*

He has much to say about the inability of many actors to comprehend that a play must also have meaning. The best actors he has ever worked with, he says, are Frederic March and Robert Preston.

During the week, Segal invited me to dinner. There was little talk of the future destiny of the Los Angeles Rams. The movie writer Norman Lessing was there. Last June, Norman sequestered Bobby Fischer while the master tried to decide whether or not and how and when to go to Reykjavik. There was serious talk with Norman about the knight-to-rook-four move and unfortunately I forgot to ask Segal if chess takes place in the electronosphere, too.

A dinner party in Los Angeles breaks up early, as early as 10:30 P.M., because of the long distances people travel to and fro. Los Angeles has always had an early work day. Brokers, for example, often are in their offices at 7 A.M. when the New York exchanges start trading. The movie folk always went to work early, first to take advantage of the daylight and later because makeup and costuming took so much time.

Jack Klugman's home on North Fairing Road in Los Angeles is near the crest of a mountain so steep that the Klugmans ought nightly to fall to their knees and thank God the driveway can never ice over. It is high enough in the mountains so that the chapparal blows across the lawn. Klugman's swimming pool could offer Mark Spitz a tiring workout, and from his living room at night one can take in the panoramic lights of Los Angeles in all their chaotic disarray. Artur Rubinstein could hide six pianos in the living room, but the Klugmans also subscribe to the happy notion that the less furniture, the better, the greatest innovation in interior decoration since the invention of wall paper.

Klugman plays Oscar Madison, the sloppy roommate in television's *The Odd Couple.* A skillful actor, one who insists that "rehearsals is where it's at," Klugman has essayed a wide range of character roles for two decades. He was one of the jurors in *Twelve Angry Men,* Jack Lemmon's AA sponsor in *Days of Wine and Roses,* the father in *Goodbye, Columbus.* He had a lot to say about directors, by the way, the best of whom he said were Larry Peerce and Robert Mulligan.

Though he has starred in *The Odd Couple* for three years Klugman is newly moved to the Coast. He brought his family from Westport, Connecticut, to Los Angeles in the spring of 1972 mostly, he confides, because he couldn't bear the coast-to-coast commuting with his laundry.

"But what the hell is out here?" he asked, surveying patio and grounds. "Sunshine and ease, that's what's out here, a sameness. See, it's cloudy today. That means 144 extra accidents on the freeways. The natives believe the cloud is an evil incubus drawing the oil out of the asphalt, making the cars into aquaplanes skimming and crunching into each other.

"But the money is tremendous," he said. "It's enough money to force me into an attendant life-style. And when the producers sell the show for syndication, I get a share, and that's what we call 'saving money,'" and Klugman held out his hand as though supporting a pumpkin of greenbacks.

"My wife had to be taught how to spend money," he said, putting the pumpkin back. "You do an awful lot of odd jobs in this business and you have to live within real tight budgets because sometimes there aren't any odd jobs. She was always careful about the money. She figured it was mine because I earned it. Now I have to convince her that one of the reasons you make money is so you can call a cab for a kid when you're too busy to schlep him to a piano lesson."

Klugman's wife is Brett Sommers, herself an actress, a willowy woman with a secure and hearty laugh. Whether she is a good cook I cannot say, because Klugman made the lasagna that evening. Klugman bakes a lasagna that could put Mamma Leone out of business. He serves it with a pork hock and sausages and offers a table wine, which he pours from bottles with corks instead of screw-on tops.

"What do I know from being Jewish?" Klugman apologized. "I left Carnegie Tech and I thought about my name: Klugman. Should I change it? What will 'Klugman' do for me in the theater? I decided to leave it alone. Jack Klugman was the one person with me all the time. Sometimes my name cost me jobs. A casting director would ask for an Irish cop and my agent would say, 'You're in luck, I got Jack Klugman for you.' One of the reasons I have worked in this business is that I speak perfectly but the director would say, 'Let me think about it.' And what he meant was that Jack Klugman can do an Irish cop but the name 'Klugman' does not sound like an Irish cop's.

"But let me tell you about something Jewish," he said suddenly, his face lighting up. "I have two sons, Adam, who is eight, and David, six. They go to Camp Greylock in the summer. Last year Adam telephoned his mother and he said, 'Mom, there's only two kids in camp who aren't Jewish.' Brett asks, 'Who are they?' And Adam says, 'Danny Malloy, and my brother.'"

The marriage between Jew and Gentile is so endemic among theater folk that 100 percent true-blue Christian men are often thought Jewish because they have married *shicksas*.

The two Jews I met in the business who did belong to a temple were Stuart Robinson and Bernie Weintraub. They were nominal temple members "for the sake of the children."

Weintraub and Robinson are agents, representing actors, writers, and "hyphenates." Hyphenates are writer-producers. Writers become producers because in the taping process of a TV show there are so many changes needed in the script that it is a necessity that the producer make them.

Robinson looks not at all like an agent. He is professorial and deliberate. He went to UCLA to become a physical therapist. After a short stint in a veterans' hospital, Robinson noticed that the psychiatrists were always available for ping-pong games but rarely for consultation. Through Ingo Preminger, the brother of the famous Otto, Robinson got a job in a literary agency and met Bernie Weintraub, and they set up shop together.

Weintraub, who started in the mail room of the William Morris Agency, is the salesman, restless, aggressive, quick. He deals with subjects in the clipped, elliptical New York manner.

They are a good team. Most agents are neither businesslike nor literary. There are agents who have trouble recalling their clients' names; there are other agents who try to expedite acceptance by sending all the scripts out at once in a mail sack; and there is an agent who, in the process of describing his accomplished clients, once boasted to me that he represented Ben Lucien Burman. When I returned a blank stare, this agent gaudily informed me, "Ben Lucien Burman wrote *Steamboat 'Round the Bend*. He's the American Mark Twain."

Robinson and Weintraub are not typical. More agents fail on their own these days than succeed. For every two that do make a go of it, there are forty selling used cars.

Weintraub and Robinson have offices on Melrose Place which are approached through a mews and then up two open staircases. These two agents hold forth in a big room with ceiling-high windows bathing the rattan rug in sunlight.

Success depends upon the quality of services they offer their clients —advice, help, friendship, brains. But the important promise they make a writer or an actor or hyphenate is that they will be *there* when he needs them. One of their most prolific and successful clients joined them when he had to make a decision on an extremely complicated project over the weekend and found that his former agent was sunning himself in the inaccessible Bahamas.

Paramount among their clients' interests is the contract, which will assure a man or woman a fair share of whatever bounties may result from his or her original work. No one except writers and agents knows the lengths to which publishers and producers will go to cadge or cheat. The producers have convinced the public of their devotion to art and the publishers of their gentility. But they will break a contract if it suits them. A healthy circumspection of the craven and the corrupt is the hallmark of the good agent. I give Weintraub and Robinson high marks. Robinson and Weintraub work hard, ever on the alert for chicanery. They represent the writers who helped bring *Maude* to CBS, the men who created *Anna and the King of Siam,* and those who create the *Bob Newhart Show.*

An easy informality attends these energies. You do not wait in the anteroom of Hollywood agents while they roll bandages for the Red Cross as you do in New York. As a matter of fact, on entering, Robinson and Weintraub introduced me to Aaron Kozak, an accountant who keeps the books for many actors, writers, producers, playwrights, and the romantic like. Kozak, a jolly, impish man, travels all over the world keeping up with his clients. If you happen to have a kid who's good at arithmetic, this is the kind of job toward which you ought to point him.

I was introduced to these above-the-liners through the offices of James Lee, a playwright as well as movie and television writer, who, as Bernie Weintraub put it, "is so goyischer he's cute."

But the truth is that everyone doesn't need to be Jewish in this business. Lee's *succès d'estime,* later transformed into a hugely popular movie, was the off-Broadway play *Career,* produced in 1957. The play dealt with the fortunes and misfortunes of a young man from Michigan determined to become a star on Broadway. Sam Lawson, the hero, succeeds, but it takes him some twenty-odd years before he sees his name in lights, by which time everything from the willingness to love to the ability to respond to friendship has been beaten out of him. He is left with his success and the realization that he has fulfilled the image he set for himself at a terrible cost.

In a basic sense, *Career* is an operatic treatment of the personal history of so many of the men who have struggled through to success in the business. What it takes to succeed with the public, I am convinced, is the ability to envision the grim effects of failure. This is not a Jewish or an Irish or an Italian attribute; it is American. We understand so little about failure that we fear it more than we do cancer, which we are sure, at least, is a virus.

Hollywood and television and the stage were made to order for Jews, because there are few of them who would cavil with the notion that success is survival.

ST. LOUIS: City of Private Places

Some of the best private art collections, the best in that they are the most varied and the most valuable, are housed in St. Louis. One of the reasons these treasures are here, of course, is that there is a great deal of money in St. Louis. Morton May, the chairman of the May's Department Store chain, lives here, and Joseph Pulitzer and Etta Steinberg and the Joseph Hellmans and the Richard Weils. Another reason is that one among these collectors has exquisite discrimination and taste and has imparted these values to friends.

There is also an active artists' colony in the city, from whom, however, the rich do not buy, principally, I suppose, because money wants to travel. Howard Jones, who teaches at Washington University, is a St. Louisian with an international reputation. He has successfully experimented with electronic sculpture, sculpture in light and sound. Another St. Louisian with an international reputation is sculptor Ernest Trova. Arthur Osber, an artist of wide national reputation, who has painted in Chicago, New York, and Rome, now lives in St. Louis and is a professor of painting at Washington University.

There are many other painters and sculptors in the city. I choose to write about three of them who are nominally Jews. I do not mean to identify them as leaders of the St. Louis arts contingent nor as members of an elite but simply as artists of a first-rate reputation.

A reputation is far more important to a painter than it is to a writer, an actor, or a musician. One good book can secure a writer's reputation forever and a juicy part can produce a star. But a painter or a sculptor cannot establish a reputation with one canvas or one statue: it often takes decades of work to win a reputation and more decades to widen it.

Lee Wallas, who has just reached her sixties, has achieved a widespread reputation. She is the widow of Seymour Wallas, a St. Louis businessman, the first St. Louis businessman, in fact, to insist on integrating his factory as early as the nineteen-forties, not easy in St. Louis, which is virtually a Southern town.

"Which didn't help him," said Lee, "when the workers went out on strike. They put nails under his tires, too."

While not reckless of the proprieties, Lee Wallas is very much her own woman. She has an obvious love of order and arrangement, and a dedication to work; in short, a woman who knows her own mind.

Born in St. Louis in 1911, Lee Wallas studied with André Lhote and Fernand Léger in Paris. She sailed to France at eighteen, despite her parents' objections, and stayed for four years. She made a bare living painting restaurant signs and teaching English at Berlitz at night. The Nazi war threat and the French laws prohibiting foreigners from employment forced her reluctant return to St. Louis.

When her children were grown and she was almost fifty, she enrolled at Washington University and earned both her bachelor of fine arts and master of fine arts degrees.

Mrs. Wallas shows her work at the Oeschlaeger Gallery in Chicago and the Gallery in Fort Lauderdale. The prestige of a gallery often enhances an artist's reputation; in fact, the gallery's prestige is often crucial to the future of a painter. Curiously, St. Louis has only one gallery, the Greenberg Gallery, which deals solely with canvases and sculpture, although there are many in Kansas City and Chicago.

A reputation also is gained by a painter from the judgment of fellow painters who bestow prizes, awards, and medals for meaningful and innovative work. Lee Wallas has won many of these, one, she confessed, because she is sure the judges did not know Lee was a woman's name.

When she appeared at the museum to collect her award, the surprise and consternation on the museum director's face was a dead give-away. Since his letter announcing the award began "Dear sir" she was well prepared for his embarrassment.

Perhaps one of her most prestigious awards was the Medal of Honor of the National Association of Women Artists for her painting "The Window." The painting is composed of a double horizontal bank of six shoji windows, five of them closed. At the sixth a small Japanese face disconsolately looks out.

In 1942, Lee and Seymour Wallas took into their family a Japanese boy from one of the concentration camps in Colorado. They raised

Ichiro Mori, now a successful architect, along with their own two younger children, Charles and Eugenie. The Wallases called Ichiro "Itchy."

"The Window" sums up a wealth of personal history. When Charlie Wallas was a senior in medical school he was working day and night on a research project hoping to win an award important to his career. One night, completely exhausted and discouraged, he called Lee to say he was giving up the project. She said, "I'll make a bargain with you. Win the award—I know you can—and I'll give you any one of my paintings you choose." He said, "Even 'The Window'?" He won the award, became a doctor and, of course, owns "The Window."

One might describe Lee Wallas's work as a rendering of the esthetic of everyday life. These are mood paintings. Often single figures in a room or on a landscape offer psychological studies of the human condition. Recently, Mrs. Wallas has been involved intensely with the exploration of gestalt through painting, and her work reveals her interest in existential philosophy. Among her numerous awards are two consecutive annual purchase prizes of the Springfield Art Museum. Her painting "Threshold" hung in the Missouri State Pavilion of the New York World's Fair—the only woman painter included in the Missouri Exhibit. Her work is also represented in numerous private collections including that of Winthrop Rockefeller.

Lee Wallas lives in the center of St. Louis on Pershing Place. Pershing Place is a self-contained residential neighborhood, three blocks long with gates at both ends. Though it is in the center of the city, it is lined with trees and so sequestered from commerce and traffic that the children leave their tricycles on the sidewalk and their wagons on the broad front lawns at night. It is a cul-de-sac, one of many in St. Louis which is often called the City of Private Places.

Her home at 4534 Pershing Place is a contemporary two-story brick house not ten years old. Every building in St. Louis is brick. There isn't a clapboard or shingled house or church in St. Louis because it is against the law to employ any other building material than brick or stone. In fact, when Lee Wallas built her studio in her backyard, a glass-fronted A-frame in cedar, she had a protracted and complex argument with the Building Commission which she finally won.

There were only a few paintings in the studio. When I commented on the absence of other canvases, Lee Wallas said, "You will find there are empty hooks in my house. Empty hooks are good news. Empty hooks mean paintings sold."

Artist Joan Rosen, who formerly shared a studio with Lee Wallas, now works in a large third-floor studio in her imposing brick house in Clayton, in which Vincent Price, the movie star and art impresario for Sears, Roebuck, grew up. The Rosen house reproduces authentically a Williamsburg interior even to the subtle Oriental motif which stems from the Far East trade of the seventeen-hundreds.

In the entrance hall hangs one of the Rosen paintings, a large non-representational canvas which, like all her recent work, reflects an interest in Oriental philosophy. Mrs. Rosen is a student of the *I Ching* and practices Transcendental Meditation. Here the resemblance ends. Joan Rosen is blond and blue-eyed and avoids rice. The mother of two children, Andrew and Cindy, now in college, she is relaxed and amusing. Likely to work all night and sleep all day, but with what may seem to be disorganized and unscheduled methods, she is still prolific.

Her first artistic effort was a canary, which she painted in the first grade. She remembered telling her parents she was going to become an artist.

"You cannot become an artist," they told her, "because you would have to live in a garret and give up too many nice things."

But the vision of a garret on the Left Bank with a northern skylight compelled her, though she has never found it. But, she says, she's painted in some interesting garrets and studios. One of them, over a printing plant, had been the former home of an Alcoholics Anonymous chapter. She moved from it when too many callers interrupted her working hours asking, "Where the hell's the meeting?"

The best she has managed was a studio on Euclid and McPherson streets, in the heart of the gallery area in St. Louis. Every Sunday she took the Gallery Walk along with hundreds of patrons. The Gallery Walk was a popular pastime because the galleries served champagne and were the only places in St. Louis where one could get a drink on Sunday.

Her paintings are nonobjective studies which even to the untrained eye reveal vigor and audacity. Mrs. Rosen studied at the State University of Iowa and at Washington University, where she received her B.F.A. and M.F.A. degrees. She is a recipient of the National Watercolor U.S.A. Purchase Award and the Newcastle Award of the National Association of Women Artists, and her paintings hang in the permanent collections of Winthrop Rockefeller, the Honorable James Symington, the congressman-son of the senator, the Springfield

Art Museum, among many others. She was the first woman to be invited to show in the Missouri State Council of the Arts traveling exhibit and is listed in *The International Who's Who of Women.*

Rodney Winfield looks like an Indian, lean, hard aquiline features, and black hair. He affects a headband to keep his shoulder-length hair out of his eyes when he tours St. Louis in his 1953 MG runabout. He wore a crescent-shaped silver necklace, carved cherubim occupying a flat plane about six inches wide. But the necklace was far from affectation. The design was worked in silver repoussé, hammered silver, and was one of ten Winfield was working. He wore the necklace to get the feel of it. Winfield did not think any other American artist or sculptor was working in silver repoussé, although he knew of two Europeans.

A noted liturgical sculptor, Rodney Winfield had not long before executed the silver repoussé on a three-paneled wooden screen in St. Louis's Ethical Society Building on Clayton Road, which is a cross between a pagoda and a Mayan temple. The society had commissioned Winfield to design twelve medallions about one inch in diameter, which were mounted on light wooden panels of the screen in the meeting room. The medallions celebrate the society's founders and patrons.

Although he has been working in it for more than two decades, Winfield says silver repoussé is still in many ways an experimental medium. His liturgical art ranges from minute mosaics for an Episcopal church to colossal sculpture for a Jewish temple.

Winfield, in his mid-forties, has lived in St. Louis for twenty years. A young man, newly married, employed as a timekeeper in a dreary New Jersey factory, he came to the city when his father, a social-work supervisor, accepted a post in St. Louis. Winfield Sr. advised his son there might be a job designing church windows for Emil Frye, one of the leading American artisans in stained glass.

Winfield remembers that his first commission was for a small Louisiana parish church, all of whose windows had been knocked out by a hailstorm. The stained-glass window was to portray St. Theresa of Avila, and Frye suggested that its pictorial content depict St. Theresa and her brother making mudpies which were not mudpies but convents and monasteries.

"The mudpies wouldn't come," said Winfield. "So I went to a library and read St. Theresa and the commentaries about her. Then I went to Frye and told him St. Theresa had nothing to do with mudpies, she was one of the profound mystics in Catholic theology. And Frye said, 'No kidding?' "

Winfield since has never attempted a diptych descent from the cross, a Talmudic ark, or a design for a Baptist nave without becoming theologically expert. Immodestly he states that he is probably as theologically well versed as any seminarian. He is presently working on a stained-glass window for the Washington Cathedral in the nation's capital which will celebrate man's entry into space. It is of radical design. The windows in the Washington Cathedral consist of a large center panel with two smaller transepts on either side. Traditionally each of the surfaces contains complementary though separate pictorial representations. In this instance, however, Winfield will place a continuum, an unending curve, which will traverse both transepts and the center pane uniting all three.

Perhaps his steel and bronze sculpture in Temple Israel in Ladue, an affluent suburb of St. Louis, is one of his most controversial and impressive achievements. It rears thirty feet on the altar rising by wrought and sculpted sheets of steel, ten by five feet, which on their surfaces propose all of the Hebraic symbols, from the burning bush to the Ten Commandments. A thirty-foot I beam supports the colossus in the rear. Steel chairs with walnut seats complement the figure, becoming part of the sculpture itself.

What derricks and winches moved the structure into the temple, I wondered?

"I built it in here," Winfield said. "I wrought each of the sheets in a workshop about twelve by ten feet and hung it as soon as I had finished. The sculpture went up sheet by sheet. I had never sculpted before I won this commission. All I had going for me was that once I had learned how to work with paper. So I treated each steel sheet as a piece of paper."

The colossal sculpture in the reception foyer of the Wohl Shoe Company is also Winfield's. A polished-aluminum frame supports a field of layered leathers, the shapes of which are the various patterns that go into shoes. What pleases the shoe-company executives is that visiting businessmen and cobblers always stop to count and pick out the different patterns.

We visited last Shaare Zedek, an Orthodox synagogue in University City, another of the suburbs. Winfield had designed the stained-glass windows in the sanctuary and the chapel.

"I should have had much more recognition for these windows," he said, "because nothing like them has been tried before. But the building is a crummy building."

He was right. Shaare Zedek was made of glazed concrete blocks, its regular windows like portholes, so that it most resembled an elementary school put to sea.

In the sanctuary, the stained glass stretches vertically across the rear of the altar. The glass is baffled in strips of blue and green. As the visitor walks across the back of the sanctuary, the windows ripple, creating the effect of venetian blinds opening or closing, admitting a different hue with every step.

In the chapel, Winfield's stained-glass composition is even more innovative. With the use of white and black, rare colors for stained glass, Winfield has created negative and positive light. Again the windows are baffled, but they are divided into three tiers of three panes each, each tier set as it were on a table.

"But you see what's happened," said Winfield with a sigh. "They've let those trees in front of the window grow so full that the light is obscured. The effect is lost."

As we returned our borrowed yarmulkas to a locker in the hall, a stout, bearded cantor not yet thirty, wearing a striped shirt and checkered tie, greeted us.

After introducing himself and explaining the purpose of his visit, Winfield asked the cantor, "I wonder if I could ask you a favor. Could you have those evergreens in front of the chapel trimmed? The windows need more light to be effective."

"I'll tell you what those windows need," said the cantor dogmatically. "They need to be opened. It can get hot in that chapel in the summer."

As we crossed the street to his car, Winfield said, "They are very sweet people, but as you can see, they are not totally with it."

"All of which proves what?" asked the intrepid Lee Wallas. "That Jews are interested in the arts?"

"Well," I said uncomfortably, "you will admit that you and Rodney and Joan knew the names of the quick-witted rabbis and who of the Jewish lawyers are preeminent."

"Rodney and Joan and I are Jews. But Rodney has been married to a Christian Scientist for over twenty years and has grown children that are neither Christian Scientists nor Jews. Seymour Wallas dressed up as Santa Claus every Christmas until our little girl noticed that Santa had the same blood blister on his thumb as Daddy. And Joan's

Oriental themes hardly resemble Chagall's. And I don't think you know anything more about Jews than we do. Seymour Wallas went to temple with you one Rosh Hashanah and said you moved from your seat five times so that everyone would be sure to notice you were there because you only go once a year."

I allowed as I changed my seat as often as it pleased me. "Place is important to Jews," I explained. "We do not know God's name and the Hebrew word for God is the same as the word for 'place.' In fact, God is often called 'the Place.' "

"Knowing God's nickname doesn't exactly make you an expert on Jews," she said, still unsatisfied.

GOD LIVES ON THE CORNER

Like Chicago and Cook County, St. Louis and St. Louis County are two different entities occupying the same place. The county, of course, stretches past the metropolis in a crescent in which there are ninety-eight separate incorporated cities. The most populous of these Missouri suburbs running from north to south are Ferguson, University City, Clayton, and Webster Grove.

Six hundred and twenty-two thousand live in St. Louis and almost four times that many in the county, 2,331,371. Jews put their population casually at 60,000. The *American Jewish Year Book* put the population at 57,500 and casually the man in the street adds 2500 just to round off the figure. But Bernard Edelstein, the executive vice-chairman for Federation Development and Endowment Funds humorously explained, "The 'seven' was a misprint. It was really 'four.' We love exaggeration."

Nevertheless, St. Louis is a singular Jewish community. It and Cincinnati were the only two cities of the pre-Civil War West which had a Jewish community by the eighteen-forties. One must realize that by 1776, there were not 3000 Jews among 4 million Americans, and by 1848 there were only 75,000 among more than 23 million. But there were enough Jews in St. Louis to found Achduth Israel, or the United Hebrew Congregation, in 1841, a year after this community had established a Hebrew cemetery.

Jews came to St. Louis because it was a German city. Germans had begun immigrating to the American Midwest after the Napoleonic Wars and German Jews immigrated with them. By 1871, the Jews in St. Louis were numerous and affluent enough to found the United Hebrew Relief Association which offered aid and succor to the refugees from the Great Chicago Fire. These Jews came from Germany, Austria, Bohemia, Hungary, France, and England. The first rabbi of Temple Shaare Emeth, Solomon Sonnenschien, raised large sums of money from his congregation for *der Faderland* during the Franco-Prussian War. It was a Reform Jewish community because it was in Germany and Austria that Reform Judaism was born.

The shtetl Jews who began arriving in the eighteen-eighties, superstitionally Orthodox in their beliefs and desperately poor in their situation became a source of embarrassment to these Jewish burghers. At one point, Jewish leaders in St. Louis importuned the Immigrant Aid Society in New York to cease sending Russian Jews west, the greenhorns had exhausted and drained the local philanthropies and it didn't seem as if the community could absorb any more schnorrers (beggars).

Despite the inundation of Russian Jews, St. Louis remained a Reform community. Today it is perhaps the strongest Jewish Reform city in the world.* St. Louis Jews boast about this and boast as well that the Jews in St. Louis were Zionists long before the Jews in Cleveland. In fact, St. Louis Jews supported organized Zionism before there was a Zion. In 1900, the Jews of St. Louis sponsored a kibbutz, Poriah, in the Jezreel Valley near the Sea of Galilee not far from Deganya, the first kibbutz; and the Mogen David flew at the St. Louis World's Fair in 1904.

Bernard Edelstein and David Rabinovitz, the executive director of the Federation, the first broad-faced and urgent, the second soft-voiced and retiring, explained that social differences did predominate in St. Louis for many years. "But these differences have been erased. First of all, St. Louis itself is a revolving door community. McDonald-Douglas is here, Monsanto, Anheuser-Busch, Chrysler, Tiffany Industries, and the May's chain bring people in all the time and send them out."

Rabinovitz pointed out, "There's a large third-generation segment among Jews, and a fourth generation, too. And the boys and girls who go away to college come back to St. Louis as men and women. They may not go into the store or for that matter become part of their father's medical practice, but they come back. The younger Jews

---

* There are only five Reform rabbis in all of Israel, and of them only one has a congregation.

refuse to perpetuate social differences because social differences produce inefficiency."

"When this younger generation came into the Federation after World War II, they found some social consideration always inhibited the elders," said Edelstein. "So they took the Federation away from them. They depersonalized it. What they didn't do, the Six-day War did."

"And as they depersonalized the Federation," said Rabinovitz, "at the same time they are trying to deinstitutionalize the shul. They think the shuls are too big, too crowded, too faceless."

Reform Judaism had a profound influence on the city. A Reform temple was the first of any religious denomination in St. Louis to leave for the suburbs. The Reform rabbi is not only American-born and American-educated, but probably the son of an American-born and American-educated father, himself perhaps a rabbi. Consequently, the Reform rabbi is an assimilationist.

A Conservative rabbi told me, "Ethnicity is a word without cogency in this city." He went on to say that the Jews had voted for Humphrey in 1968 and if they voted for Nixon in 1972 it was because many, many of them were annoyed at Senator McGovern's dumping Senator Thomas Eagleton, who, after all, was a Missourian, like Harry Truman and Senator Symington.

In a communitywide Federation meeting held in a Reform temple because of its ample auditorium, many of the Orthodox who attended did not wear their yarmulkas, an omission about which their rabbi is still wagging an accusatory finger.

But Reform Judaism is not all pervasive. Indeed not. There are three Conservative and seven Orthodox congregations in the area besides five Reform. Conservative B'nai Amoona, which has a congregation of over 1000 families, is one of the pivotal congregations in the city. Its rabbi, Bernard Lipnick, who has the precision of mind and the bearing of a retired general in business, said, "The Reform test popularity and the Orthodox test authority. By default, the Conservatives have inherited a vast middle ground. Without any effort or concern on our part, membership keeps growing." Incidental to our purpose but worthy of reporting was Rabbi Lipnick's opinion as to whither the Jewish vote. He thought the constant concern of politicians and national magazines about whether the Jews would vote for Nixon or McGovern amusing, but he also ventured, "Americans, I think, have become aware of alienation and they think Jews know more about it than anyone else."

St. Louis is also a city where there has been a remarkable growth of the "unstructured synagogue." Jews dissatisfied with the size, impersonality, and denominational characteristics of the local synagogue have increasingly formed small nuclei with fellow sympathizers to worship God and discuss Judaism in each other's homes. The anti-synagogue, or the test-tube temple, makes Judaism immediate and personal. Rabbis scoff. One said of the unstructured Jews that they were modern Essenes traipsing around the Negev when the Western Wall was in Jerusalem.

In reaction to the Reform influence, perhaps St. Louis is the only city with a Vaad Hoier (Committee of One). The Orthodox Jews in St. Louis, in fact, have had a Vaad Hoier for fifty years. Presently, the Vaad Hoier is Rabbi Milton Eichenstein. His voice on religious matters is the voice of all the Orthodox. The Vaad Hoier does not issue bulls or edicts. Rather he determines policy as the representative of the Orthodox.

When the Federation voted to fund the salary of a hospital chaplain, the board consulted the rabbis as to which candidate they should hire. The board could have had seven votes from the seven Orthodox synagogues, but they had only one vote from the Vaad Hoier and it was for the hiring of a Reform rabbi.

Rabbi Milton Polin of Orthodox Tpheris Israel was the only man in St. Louis to recognize the flag of Chicago in my lapel, a gift, by the way, from the boys in the City Hall press room. Polin introduced himself as a Chicago boy and said not at all ruefully that the Litvak style prevailed among the Orthodox in Chicago but the Hassidic prevailed in St. Louis. More ruefully, however, he confided that, Vaad Hoier or no, the balabatim control the synagogues although the rabbis control the kashruth and marriage and divorce.

Polin's synagogue is housed in a reconverted Roman Catholic church, one of the sturdiest Catholic churches I have ever visited, made of stone, brick and oak. But Congregation Tpheris Israel is about to move west from the Mississippi to Missouri River, to small, suburban Chesterfield.

"In St. Louis," said Rabbi Polin, "a Jewish neighborhood is good for two generations. One generation builds it up by moving in and the next tears it down by moving out. By and large, the Jews in

St. Louis are fanning out. It does not seem to me that in the coming decade there will be an Orthodox Jewish neighborhood."

The largest Jewish congregation in Missouri is Reform Temple Shaare Emeth. Its rabbi is Jeffrey Stiffman who doesn't look old enough to get married, let alone perform a wedding ceremony. Stiffman suggested that his youth may well be a reflection of the Jewish community as it enters the seventies. The neighborhoods, the temples and synagogues, the charities and philanthropies were for many years dominated by the elders. St. Louis had a Germanic coloration and the Germans love the paterfamilias.

"Congregations expect different attitudes from their rabbis. In worship, the congregation here likes experimentation but not radical innovation. When they are dissatisfied with some of the prayers in the prayer book, they expect me to improvise. They want change, but they are tentative about what kind of change."

As for the movement of Jews westward, Stiffman said there was a growing realization among many Jews that they had sold the city short. "If you look at the symphony there's no lack of Jews among either the musicians or the audience. People have also discovered that the problems they thought they fled in the city pursue them into the country."

Shaare Emeth is a huge temple. Stiffman has argued persuasively with his Board that it should stay put. If it moves, it will splinter the congregation and a move may be precipitous for Stiffman feels that there are many Jews who will return to the city.

B'nai Amoona, Tpheris Israel, and Shaare Emeth constitute a triangle on the corner of Trinity and Delmar in University City, the largest contiguous suburb of St. Louis. On this corner are also a Masonic shrine, a Greek Orthodox church, and a Methodist church. It is said that God lives on the corner of Trinity and Delmar. But it was not His presence the folks sought when they made this corner virtually a religious circuit court. The trolley tracks which led out of St. Louis ended here and Trinity and Delmar was therefore the most accessible suburban corner for spiritual spas as the middle class began leaving the city twenty-five years ago.

University City has a large Jewish population. It is administered by a Jewish mayor, Nathan Kaufman. It is also a "tipping" neighborhood, one not yet predominantly black but which may not remain predominantly white. Multitract development has brought many blacks from the city and it is also more profitable to sell a private home to a black on an FHA loan than to a white. The black will pay more. It is a beautiful suburb, its streets lined with trees shading substantial brick homes. The rabbis say some of their congregants stay put to maintain the city's integrated population and others leave to escape it, using as their rationale the complaint that the schools are deteriorating.

University City represents the American dilemma played out in slow motion. The dilemma is uncomplicated by busing or housing or employment opportunities. A neighborhood needs families, houses, and schools. The crucial problem of the black community is family unity. The lack of it has its effect on schools and houses.

University City also has the most interesting history of all American suburbs because it was not only the first suburb whose architecture was French Renaissance, it was the first planned suburb. It was the creation of Edgar G. Lewis, the optimistic and canny publisher of *Woman's National Daily Magazine,* who saw his chance to make a fortune in 1904, the year St. Louis entertained the world at the Louisiana Purchase Exposition.

The Fair Grounds occupied the two-by-one-mile tract which is now Forest Park on the western edge of the city. Near it, Lewis bought eighty acres of cow pasture on Delmar Road, where he pitched an ever-expanding tent city which included not only a resident doctor but a hospital and a nursery, a barbershop, and several hostels where a night's lodging for visitors to the fair cost fifty cents. His restaurants served a hot meal for twenty-five cents and a five-course dinner for fifty cents.

Soon a racetrack girdled the eighty acres.

Why not transform these grounds into a city? he thought.

Promptly, Lewis commissioned George Zolnay, a Hungarian sculptor who had designed buildings for the fair to help him lay out University City, so-called because its streets were named after famous universities—Yale, Syracuse, Princeton, Cambridge, etc.

Zolnay designed and Lewis built first a six-story octagonal tower adorned with cupids for his publishing enterprises. A winding staircase of Italian marble and bronze led to a domed white roof which contained a great searchlight, nightly illuminating the Fair Grounds. It was in its time the most powerful searchlight in the world and it cleaved the heavens until 1930 when the Civil Aeronautics Board requested that it be shut off because it distracted airline pilots. The domed octagon is University City's present town hall.

Zolnay also designed the two concrete pylons on top of which rampant lions guard the entry to University City on Trinity and Delmar. He planned as well two replicas of the Parthenon to stand west and south of the octagon and he built a replica of a windowless Egyptian temple and planned a replica of the Taj Mahal.

Lewis, in the meantime, sold lots to the unwary. Some moved in. They made Edgar Lewis mayor in 1906.

But in 1911, the Legislature banned racing in Missouri and Lewis was without ready cash. Then the federal government began investigating his mail-order banking methods which they concluded were questionable. Thousands of investors had lost $7 million in University City. All they had for their money were the angry lions atop the pylons and the elegant though eclectic placidity of the temples.

Lewis headed west and Zolnay headed east. Zolnay landed the commission to design another Parthenon in Nashville, Tennessee, and Lewis landed in California, where he was imprisoned in 1928 for perpetrating a similar suburban scheme. He was paroled in 1931 and again imprisoned in 1935. He died an obscure bankrupt in Atascadero, California, in 1950.

University City somehow survived. All of which goes to prove that not every pioneer wins the West.

WHY DOES A HEARSE HORSE SNICKER?

The most eminent lawyer to practice in St. Louis was Louis Dembitz Brandeis, Associate Justice of the United States Supreme Court from 1916 until 1939.*

The first Jew to serve on the Supreme Court, Brandeis weathered a bitter and protracted fight in the Senate over his appointment. Brandeis was the Ralph Nader of his day, a noted "people's lawyer" who had defended the public interest in Massachusetts against the utilities and served as well as counsel for the people in proceedings which determined the constitutionality of wages and hours laws in California, Oregon, Illinois, and Ohio. Woodrow Wilson sent Brandeis's name up in the days when the Court was still called the "Bulwark of Privilege."

Brandeis had practiced law in Boston for thirty-seven years before

* Charles Evans Whittaker, who was also an Associate Justice, is still a member of the Missouri Bar, but he practices in Kansas City.

this appointment but he had first been admitted to the bar in St. Louis in 1878, a year after he was graduated from the Harvard Law School. Though born and raised in Louisville, Kentucky, Brandeis came to St. Louis because his sister, Fanny, to whom he was close, had married a St. Louis attorney, Charles Nagel. Nagel found Brandeis his first job with James Taussig's law firm at a salary of fifty dollars a month with the chance to develop an independent practice. A second reason for St. Louis was that Brandeis's Harvard roommate and close friend, Walter Bond Douglas, came from the city and had returned to it in his own law office.

Perhaps Brandeis came, too, because in the eighteen-seventies, St. Louis, which faced both east and west was America's fastest growing city. In 1878, there were 300,000 people in the city and 33,000 in the county.

Brandeis tried his first case in St. Louis in 1879 and wrote his brother, Alfred, "I occupied the floor for only three minutes to make a motion. I noticed that my voice trembled somewhat."

He left St. Louis suddenly in 1879 to accept an appointment as clerk to Chief Justice Harold Gray of the Supreme Judicial Court of Massachusetts and to set up as well a law partnership with his classmate, Sam Warren, of Boston.

The short St. Louis career of Louis Brandeis has been carefully and accurately traced by Burton C. Bernard, a Jew with law offices both in St. Louis and across the Mississippi River in Illinois. Burton inspired the proceedings in 1966 which commemorated the fiftieth anniversary of Brandeis's elevation to the High Court. A committee of the bar installed the bronze bust of Brandeis by Eleanor Platt from her model done in 1942 (the original of which is in the Supreme Court Building in Washington), in the hallway of the Old St. Louis Courthouse, a red-granite landmark from whose steps slaves were once auctioned.

Brandeis was one of the first American Zionists who helped convince American Jewry that "to be good Americans, we must be better Jews, and to be better Jews we must become Zionists."

He also did yeoman service for the reputation of thousands of Jewish lawyers who came after him. When his former law clerks planned a birthday party in his honor, he remarked that a far more appropriate tribute would be a personal message describing the public service each of them had performed.

Brandeis would admire the students in law schools today. Jerome
Sidel, another St. Louis lawyer, told me that the students are more
and more politically motivated. They are young men and women interested in social law, controlling pollution, dealing with the poor, protecting consumer rights. There are many more women in law school
now than in his day which was the post-World War II era.

"Many of the women," said Sidel, "are interested in the rights of
juveniles, for which there wasn't even a class offered in my time.

"There's a great need for public lawyers, particularly here in St.
Louis. We, too, have our undefended poor and the Ozarks are not
far from here. There are already public-law firms dealing solely with
social problems, but they often need support from foundation and
government grants. If there is a central problem with producing a
generation of Brandeises it is how is a Brandeis going to accommodate
life on $10,000 a year while his colleagues accommodate life on ap-
preciably more."

Sidel himself presides over a firm which has a large commercial-
law clientele. "I have formed strong attachments with many clients
and from these attachments come still more clients," he said. "But
public law may be an opportunity for many young lawyers because
the market is saturated today. Every ten or fifteen years there comes
a point when there are simply too many lawyers. Hard times winnow
out a lot of them and then there is a point where there are too few
lawyers."

Harry Soffer put himself through Washington University Law
School at night in the years when the tuition was $100 a month.
A cherubic man in his seventies, Soffer said there were one or two
respects in which he could compare himself to Brandeis. "I still charge
some of my clients the same fees I charged them in the nineteen-
thirties," he said. "I remember the first Jewish Federation drive, when
some of these fellows contributed $7.50. Now they contribute
$100,000, but they are still under the impression that a room down-
town should cost a single fellow six dollars a week."

He, too, is devoted to the public cause. "I am a Republican,"
he said. He is, as a matter of fact, one of the Republican members
of the St. Louis Board of Elections. Since the St. Louis Board of
Elections operates on an annual budget of $1 million, which does
not include the cost of poll workers or polling places, and since it
employs eighty-four full-time civil-service workers, only in the broad-
est sense could Soffer's devotion be called Brandeisian.

The question why so many Jews become lawyers had an easy answer for Soffer. "We are the aristocrats of learning," he said, "and
we live in the cities where commerce thrives and courts sit. If you
want to know why so few Jews are Brandeises," he concluded, "I
can only answer I have met very few Lincolns among Republicans
lately."

ARCH AND THE RIVER

St. Louis is the only American city in this century to have built
a lasting monument for the centuries.

The Arch—the Jefferson National Expansion Memorial—commem-
orates the Louisiana Purchase, which made St. Louis the jumping-
off point for the great western movement, past the Missouri, over
the Great Divide, across the plains and deserts to the Pacific.

Mayor Bernard F. Dickman and philanthropist and civic booster
Luther Ely Smith conceived the memorial in 1933. They spent the
next ten years convincing citizens that cities do not live by bread
alone. After the war, St. Louis sponsored a national competition for
a meaningful design.

The prize, awarded in 1948, was $50,000, won by the then young
and later world-famous architect, Eero Saarinen, appropriately
enough an immigrant, who was born in Kirkkonummi, Finland, in
1910.

Saarinen saw the concern of the memorial as a landmark of the
present. Monuments which best expressed their time were simple
shapes, pyramids, obelisks, domes. None of these seemed right for
the site which was a levee, a man-made abutment into the fierce cur-
rents of the Mississippi. But a great arch, framing the Old Courthouse,
did seem right.

He wrote: "We believed that to stand the test of time the arch had
to be the purest expression of the forces within. This arch is not a true
parabola, as is often stated. Instead it is a catenary curve—the curve
of a hanging chain—a curve in which the forces of thrust are con-
tinuously kept within the center of the legs of the arch. The mathe-
matical precision seemed to enhance the timelessness of the form,
but at the same time its dynamic quality seemed to link it to our own."

Having awarded its prize, St. Louis from budget to budget saved
up the money with which to build the Arch. The Arch itself cost

$32 million and the landscaping in the park in which the Arch is contained cost another $8 million. The Arch has been described as a triumph not only over problems of design, engineering, and construction but over financial and organizational perils. One can imagine how many times in that fifteen years the Board of Education wanted that money or an antismut campaign could have used it or councilmen wanted to appropriate it for a raise they needed.

The Arch presents itself as a continuous swerve of stainless steel but indeed it is made up of hundreds of twelve-foot triangular sections, the steel shell sheathing concrete. The steel, manufactured by the Pittsburgh and Des Moines Steel Company in Warren, Pennsylvania, has a double skin, and after each section was welded in place it was filled with concrete. Two hundred and fifty-two tension bars, thin steel rods, created the stress when hydraulic jacks tightened them as the concrete hardened.

Each leg is anchored by 12,000 tons of concrete in a massive triangular formation, 90 feet long on each side. These two legs are sunk 45 feet into bedrock. They are 630 feet apart, the exact height to which the Arch soars and swoops. Only the Eiffel Tower in Paris is taller (by 324 feet).

The work began in 1959. "Creeping cranes" daily jacked up the steel scaffolding on both ends of which workmen assembled the Arch. During this process, St. Louisians realized the immensity and magnitude of the Arch's engineering perfection, for it was obvious as the Arch climbed that if one of the legs were ¼ inch off at the base, the curve would not meet precisely. But as jacks held apart the two curves at the apex and workmen inserted the last section, behold! The joining was exact, imperceptible.

The Arch runs north and south, parallel with the river. From the 64-foot observation deck one sees St. Louis below, a miniature toy town of brick. A central truth about this country is that men crossed rivers to find impenetrable jungles, which they transformed into toy towns within a working lifetime. Right here, Lewis and Clark might have crossed over from Illinois to start the expedition to find a land route to the Pacific.

The city was named for the Crusader King of France. The most important man to live within it, however, was a shiftless and illiterate slave named Dred Scott. Scott's master, Henry Blow, made rich from Missouri lead mines, a Southerner who opposed slavery, argued before the Supreme Court of the United States that Dred, who had lived in Wisconsin and Illinois, free states, became free on his return to Missouri, a slave state.

In a five-to-four decision in 1857, the Supreme Court said Dred Scott was not a citizen of Missouri and therefore not entitled to sue in federal courts.

That decision helped provoke a Civil War, not that the impending struggle worried Scott, who lived out the rest of his life as the porter in the old Barnum Hotel near the riverfront.

Facing east, you see the Mississippi, made muddy from the waters of the Missouri which empty into it just north of the city. The current is multiveined, strong and thick as muscles. Two paddleboats are secured on the dock, the Robert E. Lee and the Becky Thatcher, restaurants serving *haute cuisine,* their specialty, Mississippi catfish.

Two hundred years ago this river was infested by pirates: the Mississippi was, in fact, one of the last pirate refuges in the world (the other, the Barbary Coast in north Africa). The Mississippi at St. Louis is as wide as the sea, wider than any other river in a land of wide rivers.

What rivers in this world compare to the Mississippi? Only two, the Nile and the Amazon, are longer. Only three, the Nile, the Volga, and the Yangtze, are the same life-bearing arteries. The Nile and the Yangtze inspired religions. The Volga divides European from Asian Russia. But none of these have inspired the literature—and the hope—that the Mississippi inspired, if that literature were only the history of Lincoln's trip by flatboat to New Orleans, *The Memoirs of W. T. Sherman,* and Mark Twain's *Huckleberry Finn.*

EPILOGUE

Plus ça change . . .

Of course.

If you wanted to find the American Jewish community in 1900, a New York cop would tell you to get off at the Houston Street stop on the Third Avenue El. You couldn't miss it. The streets would be jammed with pushcarts and the tenements jammed with Jews. There would be as many coffee shops as there were pushcarts and inside there would be old men sipping tea and debating Talmudic law or socialism.

That is how Hutchens Hapgood found the ghetto in 1901, when he went into it to write a series for the *Atlantic Monthly,* which became the classic *Spirit of the Ghetto,* the best book on Jews ever written by a Christian.

"East Canal Street and the Bowery," wrote Hapgood, "have interested me more than Broadway and Fifth Avenue." He went on to describe these streets teeming with peddlers and ragpickers, sweatshop workers and scholars, and "shrewd-faced little boys with melancholy eyes," in whose soul, if we could penetrate it, we would see "a mixture of almost unprecedented hope and excitement on the one hand, and of doubt, confusion, and self-distrust on the other."

The Third Avenue Elevated is gone lo! these seventeen years, and the Jews on east Canal and the Bowery longer than that. The shrewd-faced little boy is an old man puttering around a Florida golf course in a caddy car with a striped umbrella.

It is no longer a short trip downtown to find the Jewish community, but that community is just as easy to find. If you asked a haver at the Somerville havurah where the Jewish community was, sooner or later you would find your way to the offices of the Jewish Federation on Euclid Avenue in Cleveland; if you talked to young campers at Greylock, sooner or later you would find that Tpheris Israel, B'nai Amoona, and Shaare Emeth were on the corner of Trinity and Delmar in University City.

If the passage of years has done anything, it has made it easier to find the Cleveland Federation and Rabbis Lipnick, Polin, and Stiffman. Jews never tire of cataloguing the agencies of the Jewish network. David Ben-Gurion, Israel's first prime minister, told me that when the Turks banished him from Palestine before World War I, he came to New York City and there sought a militant Zionist the Turks had banished earlier. Ben-Gurion went to every Jewish organization, verein, meeting hall, and union headquarters for over a year, never finding a trace. When he finally met his man, it was wholly by accident. They lived in the same tenement on Mott Street. It would be no trouble to locate a long-lost Zionist before lunch today. There are fourteen *national* Zionist organizations in America.

As for the *plus c'est la même chose,* I started hawking newspapers in 1911 from the corner of Delancey and Norwalk streets from 4 P.M. to 6 P.M. every afternoon. I sold the *Journal, World, Mail, Telegram, Sun, Globe,* and *Post.* Once a week I sold a Chinese newspaper, *Mong Gee,* a profitable sideline. *Mong Gee* cost a nickel and I kept three cents. I also hawked several Yiddish-language newspapers, among them the famous *Jewish Daily Forward.* The *Forward* was a better profit-maker than *Mong Gee.* The *Forward* published several editions and newsboys learned how to exploit each. I started shouting "Extra!" as soon as a new bundle hit at my feet. The gambit paid off handsomely during World War I. The East Side Jews were overwhelmingly pro-German. All of them had emigrated fleeing Russian pogroms. Most had felt the cruelty of tsarist oppression.

So no matter what the skirmish, I shouted, "Russians Retreat Again!" I shouted it even when the Russians advanced. If, however, the *Forward* reported a clear-cut Russian victory, I shouted instead, "Extra! Emperor Franz Josef dying!" Franz Josef was the old reliable. The Jews adored him. And he was, fortunately for newsboys, very, very old.

Of all the papers I sold in 1911, only the *New York Post* and the *Forward* still publish. On the occasion of the *Forward*'s seventieth birthday in 1967, *Life* magazine asked me to celebrate the event with an editorial. It is hard to believe that a Yiddish-language newspaper has outlived *Life,* but indeed that is the fact. There are, to be exact, still thirteen weekly and monthly Yiddish-language periodicals in New York as well as two Hebrew-language journals out of 108 Jewish publications.

At the turn of the century, there were not only Jews but thriving Jewish communities in the ten cities I visited in 1972. These communities have grown and moved out to the suburbs, where they have the same degree of unanimity and common purpose now that they did then—which is the belief that Jews ought to live together. In the enclave, however, Jews are riven by the same causes and events which rend Americans no matter where they live.

The singular change among Jewish communities is that they are no longer intent on maintaining unanimity, which was, at best, a façade. And which they could not maintain.

Jews used to keep two histories: one as members of the Chosen People and one as members of the Diaspora. These histories often contradicted each other. One example will do.

In the late eighteen-nineties, the American Jewish Historical Society determined to publish a Jewish Encyclopedia. One of the prime movers in this effort was Leon Huhner, curator of the society, a noted lawyer, historian, and poet whose patriotic verses enjoyed wide circulation during World War I. What motivated Huhner and the society was the realization that American nativism was beginning to take root. The "100 percent" American was raising his voice demanding that the gates be closed to foreign immigration. Past those gates, in New York harbor, dozens of converted passenger ships lay daily at anchor while they awaited their turn at the piers to disgorge thousands of Russian Jews. The Encyclopedia would describe how the ignoble immigrant becomes the ennobled patriot and thus still the voices.

Huhner chose for his part in the venture a survey of the Jews of Colonial Charleston, South Carolina.* The Jews were Charleston's merchants and exporters, wrote Huhner, and the Revolutionary War was cruel to their enterprise. They abandoned their establishments either to enlist in the Colonial militia or to leave the city lest their presence lend the occupying British aid and comfort.

Huhner described how the patriot Francis Salvador, an officer in a Charleston company, rode to quell a hostile Indian raid encouraged by the British, was wounded in ambush and scalped; how his death was avenged many times over by the famous "Jewish Company" from

* Originally Charles Town until its incorporation in 1783.

Charleston commanded by Captain Richard Lushington; how another Jew from Charleston, Major Robert Moses, was personally commended by Washington for valor; how the line officers of one South Carolina regiment were all Jews; how General Christopher Gadsden, captured by the British after the fall of Charleston, recounted in his diary the rigors of imprisonment in St. Augustine, where, to preserve his sanity and morale, he learned Hebrew from Jews who were his fellow prisoners.

The entry which appeared when the Encyclopedia was published in 1903 should have put the nativist away forever and ever—except that it wasn't true and would have made no difference to the nativist if it were. Huhner was spinning myths and the myths were blown away by Rabbi Barnett Elzas of Temple Beth Elohim in Charleston.

Elzas, who was crusty if nothing else, was born in Eydkuhnen, Germany, in 1867 but grew up in Leeds, England, where his father was master of a Hebrew school. He had come to Charleston in 1893 where he studied not only medicine and pharmacy but also history. He is the only historian to write a complete history of the Jewish residency in one state—*Jews of South Carolina from the Earliest Times to the Present Day,* which was published by Lippincott in 1905, for which Elzas used only primary sources. He had at hand every magazine and newspaper published in the state including the *South Carolina Gazette.* He studied the probate records, the mesne conveyances, the tombstones of the Hebrew cemetery, and traced even those Jews who at one time or another had letters waiting for them at the post office. Barnett Elzas knew by name every Jew who had ever lived in Colonial Charleston—all sixty-eight of them.

In his ill-tempered review of Huhner's entry, Elzas noted that while there was a Captain Lushington, there was no "Jewish Company." "There was no company organized in Charleston in 1779," he wrote. "The Militia Act of 1778 prohibited the formation of new companies after that date. The Lushington Company was formed in 1738 and during the years 1778 to 1780 contained a number of Jews, who were by no means a majority. The most careful investigation fails to reveal that there were sixty male Jews between the ages of sixteen and sixty, which was Lushington's complement.

"Christopher Gadsden studied Hebrew while a prisoner at St. Augustine. This is not romantic enough. Mr. Huhner volunteers the further information that his teachers were fellow prisoners who more than likely were Jews. Unfortunately, the list of prisoners at St. Augustine is readily available and there is not a Jew among them. It is worthy of note, however, that long before the Revolution, Hebrew had been part of the curriculum in the schools of Charleston."

And so on. Elzas even produced a list of Tory property amerced by the passage of South Carolina's Confiscation Act of 1783, on which several Jewish names appear. It is obvious that the Jews of Charleston were not of one mind about the Revolutionary War—they were of sixty-eight minds.

"It is absurd," concluded Elzas, "to impute patriotism to an entire group as it is to an entire population. An entire population never fights. Some are physically unable to fight, others are not interested in fighting, and some have families and cannot afford to fight. Is not the tale unfolded glorious enough? The fact that the Jews of South Carolina furnished as many men as their neighbors?"

This was not popular opinion in the nineteen-hundreds. To wit: the Encyclopedia perpetuated Huhner's entry through another edition.

Jews of the immigrant years and probably because of the immigrant years felt they had to be of one mind on issues. They took pains to celebrate their unanimity as Americans.

History had convinced them they were exiles, eternal proscripts in the Diaspora. They must endure the centuries as aliens, awaiting reunification in the Homeland in an unforeseeable future when they could pick up again and continue another history all their own.

But the Jews of the English-speaking world, certainly of the American Jewish community, have come to realize that the Diaspora need not be temporary—they long that it be eternal. They are not exiles within it, but citizens. The duty and the privilege of the citizen is to express his conscience whether it accords with the conscience of all or is isolate.

The Jews of the Lower East Side feared anti-Semitism. The Jews of Shaker Heights and West Hartford and Evanston fear it, too. But they have learned something the immigrant Jew of seventy years ago could not have known. While there has always been anti-Semitism in America—and there still is—it has never been respectable. In Europe, anti-Semitism is a profession. There have been Jews in America for over three hundred years. Millions of Jews have lived in America for almost a full century. Assimilation has proceeded so easily for most Jews that now they are hard pressed to revive the characteristics which differentiated them from others for so long. Which is to say of the American Jewish community that it becomes Jewish existentially. But with the exception of the black man, every other American has to convert to become what he is, too.